BLACK LEGACY PRESS™
WWW.BLACKLEGACYPRESS.ORG

SLAVE NARRATIVES

VOLUME III
FLORIDA NARRATIVES

By
United States.
Work Projects Administration

Copyright © 2024 by BLACKLEGACYPRESS.ORG

All rights reserved. No part of this publication may be reproduced or transmitted in any form or by any means electronic or mechanical, including information storage and retrieval systems without permission in writing from the publisher, except for student research using the appropriate citations.

ISBN: 978-1-63652-195-4

SLAVE NARRATIVES

A Folk History of Slavery in the United States.
From Interviews with Former Slaves

**UNITED STATES.
WORK PROJECTS ADMINISTRATION**

TYPEWRITTEN RECORDS PREPARED
BY
THE FEDERAL WRITERS' PROJECT
1936-1938
ASSEMBLED BY
THE LIBRARY OF CONGRESS PROJECT
WORK PROJECTS ADMINISTRATION
FOR THE DISTRICT OF COLUMBIA
SPONSORED BY THE LIBRARY OF
CONGRESS

WASHINGTON 1941

VOLUME III
FLORIDA NARRATIVES

**Prepared by
The Federal Writers' Project of
The Works Progress Administration
For the State of Florida**

TABLE OF CONTENTS

JOSEPHINE ANDERSON 1
SAMUEL SIMEON ANDREWS 9
BILL AUSTIN 19
FRANK BERRY 25
MARY MINUS BIDDIE 29
REV. ELI BOYD 37
RIVANA BOYNTON 39
MATILDA BROOKS 49
TITUS I. BYNES 53
PATIENCE CAMPBELL 59
FLORIDA CLAYTON 63
"FATHER" CHARLES COATES 65
IRENE COATES 73
NEIL COKER 79
YOUNG WINSTON DAVIS 83
DOUGLAS DORSEY 89
AMBROSE DOUGLASS 95
FOLK STUFF, FLORIDA 99
FLORIDA FOLKLORE 105
WILLIS DUKES 111
SAM AND LOUISA EVERETT 115
DUNCAN GAINES 121

CLAYBORN GANTLING	127
ARNOLD GRAGSTON	133
HARRIETT GRESHAM	143
BOLDEN HALL	151
REBECCA HOOKS	157
REV. SQUIRES JACKSON	163
"PROPHET" JOHN HENRY KEMP	169
CINDY KINSEY	175
RANDALL LEE	179
EDWARD LYCURGAS	191
AMANDA MCCRAY	199
HENRY MAXWELL	205
CHRISTINE MITCHELL	207
LINDSEY MOORE	209
MACK MULLEN	213
LOUIS NAPOLEON	219
MARGRETT NICKERSON	225
DOUGLAS PARISH	233
GEORGE PRETTY	239
ANNA SCOTT	253
WILLIAM SHERMAN	261
SAMUEL SMALLS	273
SALENA TASWELL	275
DAVE TAYLOR	287
ACIE THOMAS	307
SHACK THOMAS	315

LUKE TOWNS	323
WILLIS WILLIAMS	327
CLAUDE AUGUSTA WILSON	337
CHARLEY ROBERTS	345

United States. Work Projects Administration

JOSEPHINE ANDERSON

FOLK STUFF, FLORIDA
Jules A. Frost
Tampa, Florida
October 20, 1937

HANTS

"I kaint tell nothin bout slavery times cept what I heared folks talk about. I was too young to remember much but I recleck seein my granma milk de cows an do de washin. Granpa was old, an dey let him do light work, mosly fish an hunt.

"I doan member nothin bout my daddy. He died when I was a baby. My stepfather was Stephen Anderson, an my mammy's name was Dorcas. He come fum Vajinny, but my mammy was borned an raised in Wilmington. My name was Josephine Anderson fore I married Willie Jones. I had two half-brothers youngern me, John Henry an Ed, an a half-sister, Elsie. De boys had to mind de calves an sheeps, an Elsie nursed de missus' baby. I done de cookin, mosly, an helped my mammy spin.

"I was ony five year old when dey brung me to Sanderson, in Baker County, Florida. My stepfather went to work for a turpentine man, makin barrels, an he work at dat job till he drop dead in de camp. I reckon he musta had heart disease.

"I doan recleck ever seein my mammy wear shoes. Even in de winter she go barefoot, an I reckon cold didn't hurt her feet no moran her hands an face. We all wore dresses made o' homespun. De thread was spun an de cloth wove right in our own home. My mamy an granmamy an me done it in spare time.

"My weddin dress was blue—blue for true. I thought it was de prettiest dress I ever see. We was married in de court-house, an dat be a mighty happy day for me. Mos folks dem days got married by layin a broom on de floor an jumpin over it. Dat seals de marriage, an at de same time brings em good luck.

"Ya see brooms keeps hants away. When mean folks dies, de old debbil sometimes doan want em down dere in da bad place, so he makes witches out of em, an sends em back. One thing bout witches, dey gotta count everthing fore dey can git acrosst it. You put a broom acrosst your door at night an old witches gotta count ever straw in dat broom fore she can come in.

"Some folks can jes nachly see hants bettern others. Teeny, my gal can. I reckon das cause she been borned wid a veil—you know, a caul, sumpum what be over some babies' faces when dey is borned. Folks borned wid a caul can see sperrits, an tell whas gonna happen fore it comes true.

"Use to worry Teeny right smart, seein sperrits day an night. My husban say he gonna cure her, so he taken a grain o' corn an put it in a bottle in Teeny's bedroom over night. Den he planted it in de yard, an driv plenty sticks roun da place. When it was growin good, he put leaf-mold roun de stalk, an watch it ever day, an tell us don't nobody touch de stalk. It raise three big ears o' corn, an when dey was good roastin size he pick em off an cook em an tell Teeny eat ever grain offn all three cobs. He watch her while she done it, an she ain never been worried wid hants no more. She sees em jes the same, but dey doan bother her none.

"Fust time I ever knowed a hant to come into our quarters was when I was jes big nough to go out to parties. De game what we use to play was spin de plate. Ever time I think on dat game it gives me de shivers. One time there was a strange young man come to a party where I was. Said he name Richard Green, an he been takin keer o' horses for a rich man what was gonna buy a plantation in dat county. He look kinda slick an dressed-up—diffunt from de rest. All de gals begin to cast sheep's eyes at him, an hope he gonna choose dem when day start playin games.

"Pretty soon dey begin to play spin de plate an it come my turn fust thing. I spin it an call out 'Mister Green!' He jumps to de middle o' de ring to grab de plate an 'Bang'—bout four guns go off all at oncet, an Mister Green fall to de floor plum dead shot through de head.

"Fore we knowed who done it, de sheriff an some more men jump down from de loft, where dey bean hidin an tell us quit hollerin an doan be scairt. Dis man be a bad deeper—you know, one o' them outlaws what kills folks. He some kinda foreigner, an jes tryin make blieve he a niggah, so's they don't find him.

"Wall we didn't feel like playin no more games, an f'ever after dat you coundn't git no niggahs to pass dat house alone atter dark. Dey say da place was hant-ed, an if you look through de winder any dark night you could see a man in dere spinnin de plate.

"I sho didn't never look in, cause I done seen more hants aready dan I ever wants to see agin. One night I was goin to my granny's house. It was jes comin dark, an when I got to de crick an start across on de footlog, dere on de other end o' dat log was a man wid his haid cut off an layin plum over on his shoulder. He look at me, kinda pitiful, an don't say a word—but I closely never waited to see what he gonna talk about. I pure flew back home. I was so scairt I couldn't tell de folks what done happened till I set down an get my breath.

"Nother time, not so long ago, when I live down in Gary, I be walkin down de railroad track soon in de mornin an fore I knowed it, dere was a white man walkin long side o' me. I jes thought it were somebody, but I wadn't sho, so I turn off at de fust street to git way from dere. De nex mawnin I be boin[TR: goin?] to work at de same time. It were kinda foggy an dark, so I never seen nobody till I mighty nigh run into dis same man, an dere he goes, bout half a step ahead o' me, his two hands restin on his be-hind.

"I was so close up to him I could see him plain as I see you. He had fingernails dat long, all cleaned an polished. He was tull, an had on a derby hat, an stylish black clothes. When I walk slow he slow down, an when I stop, he stop, never oncet lookin roun. My feets make a noise on de cinders tween de rails, but he doan make a mite o' noise. Dat was de fust thing got me scairt, but I figger I better find out for sho ifen he be a sperrit; so I say, gook an loud: 'Lookee here, Mister, I jez an old colored woman, an I knows my place, an I wisht you wouldn't walk wid me counta what folks might say.'

"He never looked roun no moren if I wan't there, an I cut my eyes roun to see if there is somebody I can holler to for help. When I looked back he was gone; gone, like dat, without makin a sound. Den I knowed he be a hant, an de nex day when I tell somebody bout it dey say he be de genman what got killed at de crossin a spell back, an other folks has seen him jus like I did. Dey say dey can hear babies cryin at de trestle right near dere, an ain't nobody yit ever found em.

"Dat ain de ony hant I ever seen. One day I go out to de smokehouse to git a mess o' taters. It was after sundown, but still purty light. When I gits dere de door be unlocked an a big man standin half inside. 'What you doin stealin our taters!' I hollers at him, an pow! He gone, jes like dat. Did I git back to dat house! We mighty glad to eat grits an cornbread dat night.

"When we livin at Titusville, I see my old mammy comin up de road jus as plain as day. I stan on de porch, fixin to run an meet her, when all of a sudden she be gone. I begin to cry an tell de folks I ain't gonna see my mammy agin. An sho nuff, I never did. She die at Sanderson, back in West Florida, fore I got to see her.

"Does I blieve in witches? S-a-a-y, I knows more bout em den to jes 'blieve'—I been rid by em. Right here in dis house. You ain never been rid by a witch? Well, you mighty lucky. Dey come in de night, ginnerly soon after you drop off to sleep. Dey put a bridle on your head, an a bit in your mouth, an a saddle on your back. Den dey take off their skin an hang it up on de wall. Den dey git on you an some nights dey like to ride you to death. You try to holler but you kaint, counta the iron bit in your mouth, an you feel like somebody holdin you down. Den dey ride you back home an into your bed. When you hit de bed you jump an grab de kivers, an de witch be gone, like dat. But you know you been rid mighty hard, cause you all wet wid sweat, an you feel plum tired out.

"Some folks say you jus been dreamin, counta de blood stop circulatin in yaur back. Shucks! Dey ain never been rid by a witch, or dey ain sayin dat.

"Old witch docter, he want ten dollers for a piece of string, what he say some kinda charm words over. Tells me to make a image o' dat old witch outa dough, an tie dat string roun its neck; den when I bake it in de oven, it swell up an de magic string shet off her breath. I didn't have no ten dollar, so he say ifen I git up five dollar he make me a hand—you know, what collored folks cals a jack. Dat be a charm what will keep de witches away. I knows how to make em, but day doan do no good thout de magic words, an I doan know dem. You take a little pinch o' dried snake skin an some graveyard dirt, an some red pepper an a lock o' your hair wrapped roun some black rooster feathers. Den you spit whiskey on em an wrap em in red flannel an sew if into a ball bout dat big. Den you hang it under your right armpit, an ever week you give it a drink o' whiskey, to keep it strong an powful.

"Dat keep de witches fum ridin you; but nary one o' dese charms work wid dis old witch. I got a purty good idee who she is, an she got a charm powfuller dan both of dem. But she kaint git acrosst flaxseed, not till she count ever seed. You doan blieve dat? Huh! I reckon I knows—I done tried it out. I gits me a lil bag o' pure fresh flaxseed, an I sprinkle it all roun de bed; den I put some on top of da mattress, an under de sheet. Den I goes to bed an sleeps like a baby, an dat old witch doan bother me no more.

"Ony oncet. Soon's I wake up, I light me a lamp an look on de floor an dere, side o' my bed was my dress, layin right over dat flaxseed, so's she could walk over on de dress, big as life. I snatch up de dress an throw it an de bed; den I go to sleep, an I ain never been bothered no more.

"Some folks reads de Bible backwards to keep witches fum ridin em, but dat doan do me no good, cause I kaint read. But flaxseed work so good I doan be studyin night-ridin witches no more."

SAMUEL SIMEON ANDREWS

American Guide, (Negro Writers' Unit)
Rachel A. Austin, Field Worker
John A. Simms, Editor
Jacksonville, Florida
October 27, 1936

For almost 30 years Edward Waters College, an African Methodist Episcopal School, located on the north side of Kings Road in the western section of Jacksonville, has employed as watchman, Samuel Simeon Andrews (affectionately called "Parson"), a former slave of A.J. Lane of Georgia, Lewis Ripley of Beaufort, South Carolina, Ed Tillman of Dallas, Texas, and John Troy of Union Springs, Alabama.

"Parson" was born November 18, 1850 in Macon, Georgia, at a place called Tatum Square, where slaves were held, housed and sold. "Speculators" (persons who traveled from place to place with slaves for sale) had housed 84 slaves there—many of whom were pregnant women. Besides "Parson," two other slave-children, Ed Jones who now lives in Sparta, Georgia, and George Bailey were born in Tatum Square that night. The morning after their births, a woman was sent from the nearby A.J. Lane plantation to take care of the three mothers; this nurse proved to be "Parson's" grandmother. His mother told him afterwards that the meeting of mother and daughter was very jubilant, but silent and pathetic, because neither could with safety show her pleasure in finding the other. At the auction which was held a few days later, his mother, Rachel, and her two sons, Solomon Augustus and her infant who was later to be known as "Parson," were purchased by A.J. Lane who had previously bought "Parson's" father, Willis, from a man named Dolphus of Albany, Georgia; thus were husband and wife re-united. They were taken to Lane's plantation three miles out of Sparta, Georgia, in Hancock County. Mr. Lane owned 85 slaves and was known to be very kind and considerate.

"Parson" lived on the Lane plantation until he was eight years old, when he was sold to Lewis Ripley of Beaufort, South Carolina, with whom he lived for two years; he was then sold to Ed Tillman of Dallas, Texas; he stayed on the Tillman plantation for about a year and until he was purchased by John Troy of Union Springs, Alabama—the richest slave-holder in Union Springs, Alabama; he remained with him until Emancipation. He recalls that during one of these sales about $800.00 was paid for him.

He describes A.J. Lane as being a kind slave-holder who fed his slaves well and whipped them but little. All of his other masters, he states, were nice to children, but lashed and whipped the grown-ups.

Mr. Lane's family was comprised of his wife, Fannie (who also was very kind to the slaves) five children, Harriett Ann, Jennie, Jeff, Frankie and Mae Roxie, a brother (whose name he does not recall) who owned a few slaves but was kind to those that he did own. Although very young during slavery, "Parson" remembers many plantation activities and customs, among which are the following: That the master's children and those of the slaves on the plantation played together; the farm crops consisted of corn, cotton, peas, wheat and oats; that the food for the slaves was cooked in pots which were hung over a fire; that the iron ovens used by the slaves had tops for baking; how during the Civil War, wheat, corn and dried potatoes were parched and used as substitutes for coffee; that his mother was given a peck of flour every two weeks; that a mixture of salt and sand was dug from the earthern floor of the smokehouse and water poured over it to get the salt drippings for seasoning; that most medicine consisted of boiled roots; when thread and cloth were dyed with the dye obtained from maple bark; when shoes were made on a wooden last and soles and uppers fastened together with maple pegs; when the white preachers preached "obey your masters"; that the first buggy that he saw was owned by his master, A.J. Lane; it had a seat at the rear with rest which was usually occupied by a man who was called the "waiter"; there was no top to the seat and the "waiter" was exposed to the weather. He recalls when wooden slats and tightened ropes were used for bed springs; also the patience of "Aunt Letha" an old woman slave who took care of the children in the neighborhood while their parents worked, and how they enjoyed watching "Uncle Umphrey" tan cow and pig hides.

"Parson" describes himself as being very frisky as a boy and states that he did but very little work and got but very few whippings. Twice he ran away to escape being whipped and hid in asparagus beds in Sparta,

Georgia until nightfall; when he returned the master would not whip him because he was apprehensive that he might run away again and be stolen by poorer whites and thus cause trouble. The richer whites, he relates, were afraid of the poorer whites; if the latter were made angry they would round up the owners' sheep and turn them loose into their cotton fields and the sheep would eat the cotton, row by row.

He compares the relationship between the rich and poor whites during slavery with that of the white and Negro people of today.

With a face full of frowns, "Parson" tells of a white man persuading his mother to let him tie her to show that he was master, promising not to whip her, and she believed him. When he had placed her in a buck (hands tied on a stick so that the stick would turn her in any direction) he whipped her until the blood ran down her back.

With changed expression he told of an incident during the Civil War: Slaves, he explained had to have passes to go from one plantation to another and if one were found without a pass the "patrollers" would pick him up, return him to his master and receive pay for their service. The "patrollers" were guards for runaway slaves. One night they came to Aunt Rhoda's house where a crowd of slaves had gathered and were going to return them to their masters; Uncle Umphrey the tanner, quickly spaded up some hot ashes and pitched it on them; all of the slaves escaped unharmed, while all of the "patrollers" were badly injured; no one ever told on Uncle Umphrey and when Aunt Rhoda was questioned by her master she stated that she knew nothing about it but told them that the "patrollers" had brought another "nigger" with them; her master took it for granted that she spoke the truth since none of the other Negroes were hurt. He remembers seeing this but does not remember how he, as a little boy, was prevented from telling about it.

Asked about his remembrance or knowledge of the slaves' belief in magic and spells he said: "I remember this and can just see the dogs running around now. My mother's brother, "Uncle Dick" and "Uncle July" swore they would not work longer for masters; so they ran away and lived in the woods. In winter they would put cotton seed in the fields to rot for fertilizer and lay in it for warmth. They would kill hogs and slip the meat to some slave to cook for food. When their owners looked for them, "Bob Amos" who raised "nigger hounds" (hounds raised solely to track Negro slaves) was summoned and the dogs located them and surrounded them in their hide-out; one went one way and one the other and escaped in the swamps; they would run until they came to a fence—each kept some "graveyard dust and a few lightwood splinters" with which they smoked their feet and jumped the fence and the dogs turned back and could track no further. Thus, they stayed in the woods until freedom, when they came out and worked for pay. Now, you know "Uncle Dick" just died a few years ago in Sparta, Georgia."

When the Civil War came he remembers hearing one night "Sherman is coming." It was said that Wheeler's Cavalry of the Confederates was always "running and fighting." Lane had moved the family to Macon, Georgia, and they lived on a place called "Dunlap's Hill." That night four preachers were preaching "Fellow soldiers, the enemy is just here to Bolden's Brook, sixteen miles away and you may be carried into judgment; prepare to meet your God." While they were preaching, bombs began to fly because Wheeler's Cavalry was only six miles away instead of 16 miles; women screamed and children ran. Wheeler kept wagons ahead of him so that when one was crippled the other would replace it. He says he imagines he hears the voice of Sherman now, saying: "Tell Wheeler to go on to South Carolina; we will mow it down with grape shot and plow it in with bombshell."

Emancipation came and with it great rejoicing. He recalls that Republicans were called "Radicals" just after the close of the Civil War.

Mr. Lane was able to save all of his meat, silver, and other valuables during the war by having a cave dug in the hog pasture; the hogs trampled over it daily.

"Parson" states that among the papers in his trunk he has a piece of money called "shin plasters" which was used during the Civil War.

The slaves were not allowed to attend schools of any kind; and school facilities immediately following Emancipation were very poor; when the first teacher, Miss Smith, a Yankee, came to Sparta, Georgia and began teaching Sunday School, all of the children were given testaments or catechisms which their parents were afraid for them to keep lest their masters whip them, but the teacher called on the parents and explained to them that they were as free as their former masters.

"Parson" states that when he was born, his master named him "Monk." His grandfather, Willis Andrews, who was a free man of Pittsburg, Pennsylvania, purchased the freedom of his wife Lizzie, but was never able to purchase their four children; his father, also named Willis, died a slave, was driven in an ox-cart to a hole that had been dug, put in it and covered up; his mother nor children could stop work to attend the funeral, but after the Emancipation, he and a brother returned, found "Uncle Bob" who helped bury him and located his grave. Soon after he had been given his freedom, "Parson" walked from Union Springs, Alabama where his last master had taken him—back to Macon, Georgia, and rejoined his mother, Rachel, his brothers, Samuel Augustus, San Francisco, Simon Peter, Lewis, Carter, Powell Wendell and sisters, Lizzie and Ann; they all dropped the name of their master, Lane, and took the name of their grandfather, Andrews.

"Parson" possesses an almost uncanny memory and attributes it to his inability to write things down and therefore being entirely dependent upon his memory. He had passed 30 years of age and had two children who could read and write before he could. His connection with Edward Waters College has given him a decided advantage for education and there are few things that he cannot discuss intelligently. He has come in contact with thousands of students and all of the ministers connected with the African Methodist Episcopal Church in the State of Florida and has attended all of the State and General Conferences of this Church for the past half century. He has lived to be 85 years of age and says he will live until he is 106. This he will do because he claims: "Your life is in your hand" and tells these narratives as proof:

"In 1886 when the present Atlantic Coast Line Railroad was called the S.F.W. and I was coming from Savannah to Florida, some tramps intent upon robbery had removed spikes from the bridge and just as the alarm was given and the train about to be thrown from the track, I raised the window and jumped to safety. I then walked back two miles to report it. More than 70 were killed who might have been saved had they jumped as I did. As a result, the S.F. and W. gave me a free pass for life with which I rode all over the United States and once into Canada." He proudly displays this pass and states that he would like to travel over the United States again but that the school keeps him too close.

"I had been very sick but took no medicine; my wife went out to visit Sister Nancy—shortly afterwards I heard what sounded like walking, and in my imagination saw death entering, push the door open and draw back to leap on me; I jumped through the window, my shirt hung, but I pulled it out. Mr. Hodges, a Baptist preacher was hoeing in his garden next door, looked at me and laughed. A woman yelled 'there goes Reverend Andrews, and death is on him.' I said 'no he isn't on me but he's down there.' Pretty soon news came that Reverend Hodges had dropped dead. Death had come for someone and would not leave without them. I was weak and he tried me first. Reverend Hodges wasn't looking, so he slipped up on him."

"Parson" came to Umatilla, Florida, in 1882 from Georgia with a Mr. Rogers brought him and six other men, their wives and children, to work on the railroad; he was made the section "boss" which job he held until a white man threatened to "dock" him because he was wearing a stiff shirt and "setting over a white man" when he should have a shovel. This was the opinion of a man in the vicinity, but another white friend, named Javis warned him and advised him not to leave Umatilla, but persuaded him to work for him cutting cord wood; although "Parson" had never seen wood corded, he accepted the job and was soon given a pass to Macon, Georgia, to get other men; he brought 13 men back and soon became their "boss" and bought a house and decided to do a little hunting. When he left this job he did some hotel work, cooked and served as train porter. In 1892 he was ordained to preach and has preached and pastored regularly from that time up to two years ago.

He is of medium size and build and partially bald-headed; what little hair he has is very grey; he has keen eyes; his eyesight is very good; he has never had to wear glasses. He is as supple as one half his age; it is readily demonstrated as he runs, jumps and yells while attending the games of his favorite pastimes, baseball and football. Wherever the Edward Waters College football team goes, there "Parson" wants to go also. Whenever the crowd at a game hears the scream "Come on boys," everyone knows it is "Parson" Andrews.

"Parson" has had two wives, both of whom are dead, and is the father of eight children: Willis (deceased) Johnny, Sebron Reece of Martin, Tennessee, Annie Lee, of Macon, Georgia, Hattie of Jacksonville, Ella (deceased) Mary Lou Rivers of Macon, Georgia, and Augustus somewhere-at-sea.

"Parson" does not believe in taking medicine, but makes a liniment with which he rubs himself. He attributes his long life to his sense of "having quitting sense" and not allowing death to catch him unawares. He asserts that if he reaches the bedside of a kindred in time, he will keep him from dying by telling him: "Come on now, don't be crazy and die."

He states that he enjoyed his slavery life and since that time life has been very sweet. He knows and remembers most of the incidents connected with members of the several Conferences of the African Methodist Episcopal Church in Florida and can tell you in what minutes you may find any of the important happenings of the past 30 or 40 years.

REFERENCE
1. Personal interview with Samuel Simeon Andrews in the dormitory of Edward Waters college Kings Road, Jacksonville, Florida

BILL AUSTIN

American Guide, (Negro Writers' Unit)
Martin Richardson, Field Worker
Greenwood, Florida
March 18, 1937

Bill Austin—he says his name is NOT Williams—is an ex-slave who gained his freedom because his mistress found it more advantageous to free him than to watch him.

Austin lives near Greenwood, Jackson County, Florida, on a small farm that he and his children operate. He says that he does not know his age, does not remember ever having heard it. But he must be pretty old, he says, "''cause I was a right smart size when Mistuh Smith went off to fight." He thinks he may be over a hundred—and he looks it—but he is not sure.

Austin was born between Greene and Hancock Counties, on the Oconee River, in Georgia. He uses the names of the counties interchangeably; he cannot be definite as to just which one was his birthplace. "The line between 'em was right there by us," he says.

His father was Jack; for want of a surname of his own he took that of his father and called himself Jack Smith. During a temporary shortage of funds on his master's part, Jack and Bill's mother was sold to a planter in the northern part of the state. It was not until long after his emancipation that Bill ever saw either of them again.

Bill's father Jack was regarded as a fairly good carpenter, mason and bricklayer; at times his master would let him do small jobs of repairing of building for neighboring planters. These jobs sometimes netted him hams, bits of cornmeal, cloth for dresses for his wife and children, and other small gifts; these he either used for his small family or bartered with the other slaves. Sometimes he sold them to the slaves for money; cash was not altogether unknown among the slaves on the Smith place.

Austin gives an interesting description of his master, Thomas Smith. He says that "sumptimes he was real rich and all of us had a good time. The wuk wasn't hard then, cause if we had big crops he would borrow some he'p from the other white folks. He used to give us meat every day, and plenty of other things. One time he bought all of us shoes, and on Sunday night would let us go to wherever the preacher was holdin' meeting. He used to give my papa money sumptimes, too.

"But they used to whisper that he would gamble a lot. We used to see a whole lot of men come up to the house sumptimes and stay up most of the night. Sumptimes they would stay three or four days. And once in a while after one of these big doings Mistuh Smith would look worried, and we wouldn't get no meat and vary little of anything else for a long time. He would be crabby and beat us for any little thing. He used to tell my papa that he wouldn't have a d— — cent until he made some crops."

A few years before he left to enter the war the slave owner came into possession of a store near his plantation. This store was in Greensboro. Either because the business paid or because of another of his economic 'bad spells', ownership of his plantation passed to a man named Kimball and most of the slaves, with the exception of Bill Austin and one or two women—either transferred with the plantation or sold. Bill was kept to do errands and general work around the store.

Bill learned much about the operation of the store, with the result that when Mr. Smith left with the Southern Army he left his wife and Bill to continue its operation. By this time there used to be frequent stories whispered among the slaves in the neighborhood—and who came with their masters into the country store—of how this or that slave ran away, and with the white man-power of the section engaged in war, remained at large for long periods or escaped altogether.

These stories always interested Austin, with the result that one morning he was absent when Mrs. Smith opened the store. He remained away 'eight or nine days, I guess', before a friend of the Smiths found him near Macon and threatened that he would 'half kill him' if he didn't return immediately.

Either the threat—or the fact that in Macon there were no readily available foodstuffs to be eaten all day as in the store—caused Austin to return. He was roundly berated by his mistress, but finally forgiven by the worried woman who needed his help around the store more than she needed the contrite promises and effusive declarations that he would 'behave alright for the rest of his life.'

And he did behave; for several whole months. But by this tine he was 'a great big boy', and he had caught sight of a young woman who took his fancy on his trip to Macon. She was free herself; her father had bought her freedom with that of her mother a few years before, and did odd jobs for the white people in the city for a livelihood. Bill had thoughts of going back to Macon, marrying her, and bringing her back 'to work for Missus with me.' He asked permission to go, and was refused on the grounds that his help was too badly needed at the store. Shortly afterward he had again disappeared.

'Missus', however, knew too much of his plans by this time, and it was no difficult task to have him apprehended in Macon. Bill may not have had such great objections to the apprehension, either, he says, because by this time he had learned that the young woman in Macon had no slightest intention to give up her freedom to join him at Greensboro.

A relative of Mrs. Smith gave Austin a sound beating on his return; for a time it had the desired effect, and he stayed at the store and gave no further trouble. Mrs. Smith, however, thought of a surer plan of keeping him in Greensboro; she called him and told him he might have his freedom. Bill never attempted to again leave the place—although he did not receive a cent for his work—until his master had died, the store passed into the hands of one of Mr. Smith's sons, and the emancipation of all the slaves was a matter of eight or ten years' history!

When he finally left Greene and Hancock Counties—about fifty-five years ago, Austin settled in Jackson County. He married and began the raising of a family. At present he has nineteen living children, more grandchildren than he can accurately tell, and is living with his third wife, a woman in her thirties.

BIBLIOGRAPHY
1. Henry Harvey, old resident of Jackson County; Greenwood-Malone Road, about 2-1/2 miles N.W. of Greenwood, Florida

2. Interview with subject, near Greenwood, Florida, (Rural Route 2, Sneads)

United States. Work Projects Administration

FRANK BERRY

American Guide, (Negro Writers' Unit)
Pearl Randolph, Field Worker
John A. Simms, Editor
Jacksonville, Florida
August 18, 1936

Frank Berry, living at 1614 west Twenty-Second street, Jacksonville, Florida, claims to be a grandson of Osceola, last fighting chief of the Seminole tribe. Born in 1858 of a mother who was part of the human chattel belonging to one of the Hearnses of Alachua County in Florida, he served variously during his life as a State and Federal Government contractor, United States Marshal (1881), Registration Inspector (1879).

Being only eight years of age when the Emancipation Proclamation was issued, he remembers little of his life as a slave. The master was kind in an impersonal way but made no provision for his freedmen as did many other Southerners—usually in the form of land grants—although he gave them their freedom as soon as the proclamation was issued. Berry learned from his elders that their master was a noted duelist and owned several fine pistols some of which have very bloody histories.

It was during the hectic days that followed the Civil War that Berry served in the afore-mentioned offices. He held his marshalship under a Judge King of Jacksonville, Florida. As State and Federal Government Contractor he built many public structures, a few of which are still in use, among them the jetties at Mayport, Florida which he helped to build and a jail at High Springs, Florida.

It was during the war between the Indians and settlers that Berry's grandmother, serving as a nurse at Tampa Bay was captured by the Indians and carried away to become the squaw of their chief; she was later re-captured by her owners. This was a common procedure, according to Berry's statements. Indians often captured slaves, particularly the women, or aided in their escape and almost always intermarried with them. The red men were credited with inciting many uprisings and wholesale escapes among the slaves.

Country frolics (dances) were quite often attended by Indians, whose main reason for going was to obtain whiskey, for which they had a very strong fondness. Berry describes an intoxicated Indian as a "tornado mad man" and recalls a hair raising incident that ended in tragedy for the offender.

A group of Indians were attending one of these frolics at Fort Myers and everything went well until one of the number became intoxicated, terrorizing the Negroes with bullying, and fighting anyone with whom he could "pick" a quarrel. "Big Charlie" an uncle of the narrator was present and when the red man challenged him to a fight made a quick end of him by breaking his neck at one blow.

For two years he was hounded by revengeful Indians, who had an uncanny way of ferreting out his whereabouts no matter where he went. Often he sighted them while working in the fields and would be forced to flee to some other place. This continued with many hairbreadth escapes, until he was forced to move several states away.

Berry recalls the old days of black aristocracy when Negroes held high political offices in the state of Florida, when Negro tradesmen and professionals competed successfully and unmolested with the whites. Many fortunes were made by men who are now little more than beggars. To this group belongs the man who in spite of reduced circumstances manages still to make one think of top hats and state affairs. Although small of stature and almost disabled by rheumatism, he has the fiery dignity and straight back that we associate with men who have ruled others. At the same time he might also be characterized as a sweet old person, with all the tender reminiscences of the old days and the and childish prejudices against all things new. As might be expected, he lives in the past and always is delighted whenever he is asked to tell about the only life that he has ever really lived. Together with his aged wife he lives with his children and is known to local relief agencies who supplement the very small income he now derives from what is left of what was at one time a considerable fortune.

REFERENCE
Personal interview with subject, Frank Berry, 1614 West Twenty-Second Street, Jacksonville, Florida

United States. Work Projects Administration

MARY MINUS BIDDIE

FLORIDA FOLKLORE
SLAVE CUSTOMS AND ANECDOTES

Mary Minus Biddie, age one hundred five was born in Pensacola, Florida, 1833, and raised in Columbia County. She is married, and has several children. For her age she is exceptionally active, being able to wash and do her house work. With optimism she looks forward to many more years of life. Her health is excellent.

Having spent thirty-two years of her life as a slave she relates vividly some of her experiences.

Her master Lancaster Jamison was a very kind man and never mistreated his slaves. He was a man of mediocre means, and instead of having a large plantation as was usual in those days, he ran a boarding house, the revenue therefrom furnishing him substance for a livelihood. He had a small farm from which fresh produce was obtained to supply the needs of his lodgers. Mary's family were his only slaves. The family consisted of her mother, father, brother and a sister. The children called the old master "Fa" and their father "Pappy." The master never resented this appellation, and took it in good humor. Many travelers stopped at his boarding house; Mary's mother did the cooking, her father "tended" the farm, and Mary, her brother and sister, did chores about the place. There was a large one-room house built in the yard in which the family lived. Her father had a separate garden in which he raised his produce, also a smokehouse where the family meats were kept. Meats were smoked in order to preserve them.

During the day Mary's father was kept so busy attending his master's farm that there was no time for him to attend to a little farm that he was allowed to have. He overcame this handicap, however, by setting up huge scaffolds in the field which he burned and from the flames that this fire emitted he could see well enough to do what was necessary to his farm.

The master's first wife was a very kind woman; at her death Mary's master moved from Pensacola to Columbia County.

Mary was very active with the plow, she could handle it with the agility of a man. This prowess gained her the title of "plow girl."

COOKING
Stoves were unknown and cooking was done in a fireplace that was built of clay, a large iron rod was built in across the opening of the fireplace on which were hung pots that had special handles that fitted about the rod holding them in place over the blazing fire as the food cooking was done in a moveable oven which was placed in the fireplace over hot coals or corn cobs. Potatoes were roasted in ashes. Oft' times Mary's father would sit in front of the fireplace until a late hour in the night and on arising in the morning the children would find in a corner a number of roasted pota-

toes which their father had thoughtfully roasted and which the children readily consumed.

LIGHTING SYSTEM
Matches were unknown; a flint rock and a file provided the fire. This occured by striking a file against a flint rock which threw off sparks that fell into a wad of dry cotton used for the purpose. This cotton, as a rule, readily caught fire. This was fire and all the fire needed to start any blaze.

WEAVING
The white folk wove the cloth on regular looms which were made into dresses for the slaves. For various colors of cloth the thread was dyed. The dye was made by digging up red shank and wild indigo roots which were boiled. The substance obtained being some of the best dye to be found.

BEVERAGES & FOOD
Bread was made from flour and wheat. The meat used was pork, beef, mutton and goat. For preservation it was smoked and kept in the smokehouse. Coffee was used as a beverage and when this ran out as oft' times happened, parched peanuts were used for the purpose.

Mary and family arose before daybreak and prepared breakfast for the master and his family, after which they ate in the same dining room. When this was over the dishes were washed by Mary, her brother and sister. The children then played about until meals were served again.

WASHING and SOAP
Washing was done in home-made wooden tubs, and boiling in iron pots similar to those of today. Soap was made from fat and lye.

AMUSEMENTS
The only amusement to be had was a big candy pulling, or hog killing and chicken cooking. The slaves from the surrounding plantations were allowed to come together on these occasions. A big time was had.

CHURCH
The slaves went to the "white folks" church on Sundays. They were seated in the rear of the church. The white minister would arise and exhort the slaves to 'mind your masters, you owe them your respect.' An old Christian slave who perceived things differently could sometimes be heard to mumble, "Yeah, wese jest as good as deys is only deys white and we's black, huh." She dare not let the whites hear this. At times meetin's were held in a slave cabin where some "inspired" slave led the services.

In the course of years Mr. Jamison married again. His second wife was a veritable terror. She was always ready and anxious to whip a slave for the least misdemeanor. The master told Mary and her mother that before he would take the chance of them running away on account of her meanness he would leave her. As soon as he would leave the house this was a signal for his wife to start on a slave. One day, with a kettle of hot water in her hand, she chased Mary, who ran to another plantation and hid there until the good master returned. She then poured out her troubles to him.

He was very indignant and remonstrated with his wife for being so cruel. She met her fate in later years; her son-in-law becoming angry at some of her doings in regard to him shot her, which resulted in her death. Instead of mourning, everybody seemed to rejoice, for the menace to well being had been removed. Twice a year Mary's father and master went to Cedar Keys, Florida to get salt. Ocean water was obtained and boiled, salt resulting. They always returned with about three barrels of salt.

The greatest event in the life of a slave was about to occur, and the most sorrowful in the life of a master, FREEDOM was at hand. A Negro was seen coming in the distance, mounted upon a mule, approaching Mr. Jamison who stood upon the porch. He told him of the liberation of the slaves. Mr. Jamison had never before been heard to curse, but this was one day that he let go a torrent of words that are unworthy to appear in print. He then broke down and cried like a slave who was being lashed by his cruel master. He called Mary's mother and father, Phyliss and Sandy, "I ain't got no more to do with you, you are free," he said, "if you want to stay with me you may and I'll give you one-third of what you raise." They decided to stay. When the crop was harvested the master did not do as he had promised. He gave them nothing. Mary slipped away, mounted the old mule "Mustang" and galloped away at a mules snail speed to Newnansville where she related what had happened to a Union captain. He gave her a letter to give to Mr. Jamison. In it he reminded him that if he didn't give Mary's family what he had promised he would be put in jail. Without hesitation the old master complied with these pungent orders.

After this incident Mary and her family left the good old boss to seek a new abode in other parts. This was the first time that the master had in any way displayed any kind of unfairness toward them, perhaps it was the reaction to having to liberate them.

MARRIAGE

There was no marriage during slavery according to civil or religious custom among the slaves. If a slave saw a woman whom he desired he told his master. If the woman in question belonged on another plantation, the master would consult her master: "one of my boys wants to marry one of your gals," he would say. As a rule it was agreeable that they should live together as man and wife. This was encouraged for it increased the slave population by new borns, hence, being an asset to the masters. The two slaves thus joined were allowed to see one another at intervals upon special permission from the master. He must have a pass to leave the plantation. Any slave caught without one while off the plantation was subject to be caught by the "paderollers" (a low class of white who roved the country to molest a slave at the least opportunity. Some of them were hired by the masters to guard against slaves running away or to apprehend them in the event that they did) who would beat them unmercifully, and send them back to the plantation from whence they came.

As a result of this form of matrimony at emancipation there were no slaves lawfully married. Orders were given that if they preferred to live together as man and wife they must marry according to law. They were given nine months to decide this question, after which if they continued to live together they were arrested for adultery. A Mr. Fryer, Justice of the Peace at Gainesville, was assigned to deal with the situation around the plantation where Mary and her family lived. A big supper was given, it was early, about twenty-five slave couples attended. There was gaiety and laughter. A barrel of lemonade was served. A big time was had by all, then those couples who desired to remain together were joined in wedlock according to civil custom. The party broke up in the early hours of the morning.

Mary Biddie, cognizant of the progress that science and invention has made in the intervening years from Emancipation and the present time, could not help but remark of the vast improvement of the lighting system of today and that of slavery. There were no lamps or kerosene. The first thread that shearer spun was for a wick to be used in a candle, the only means of light. Beef tallow was used to make the candle; this was placed in a candle mould while hot. The wick was then placed in the center of the tallow as it rest in the mould; this was allowed to cool. When this chemical process occured there was a regular sized candle to be used for lighting.

Mary now past the century mark, her lean bronze body resting in a rocker, her head wrapped in a white 'kerchief, and puffing slowly on her clay pipe, expressed herself in regard to presidents: "Roosevelt has don' mo' than any other president, why you know ever since freedom they been talkin' 'bout dis pension, talkin' 'bout it tha's all, but you see Mr. Roosevelt he don' com' an' gived it tu us. What? I'll say he's a good rightus man, an' um sho' go' vot' fo' him."

Residing in her little cabin in Eatonville, Florida, she is able to smile because she has some means of security, the Old Age Pension.

REV. ELI BOYD

DADE COUNTY, FLORIDA, FOLKLORE
Ex-Slaves

Reverend Eli Boyd was born May 29, 1864, four miles from Somerville, South Carolina on John Murray's plantation. It was a large plantation with perhaps one hundred slaves and their families. As he was only a tiny baby when freedom came, he had no "recomembrance" of the real slavery days, but he lived on the same plantation for many years until his father and mother died in 1888.

"I worked on the plantation just like they did in the real slavery days, only I received a small wage. I picked cotton and thinned rice. I always did just what they told me to do and didn't ever get into any trouble, except once and that was my own fault.

"You see it was this way. They gave me a bucket of thick clabber to take to the hogs. I was hungry and took the bucket and sat down behind the barn and ate every bit of it. I didn't know it would make me sick, but was I sick? I swelled up so that I all but bust. They had to doctor on me. They took soot out of the chimney and mixed it with salt and made me take that. I guess they saved my life, for I was awful sick.

"I never learned to read until I was 26 years old. That was after I left the plantation. I was staying at a place washing dishes for Goodyear's at Sapville, Georgia, six miles from Waycross. I found a Webster's spelling book that had been thrown away, and I learned to read from that.

"I wasn't converted until I went to work in a turpentine still and five years later I was called to preach. I am one of thirteen children and none of us has ever been arrested. We were taught right.

"I kept on preaching until I came to Miami. I have been assistant pastor at Bethel African Methodist Church for the past ten years.

"I belong to a class of Negroes called Geechees. My grandfather was brought directly from Africa to Port Royal, South Carolina. My grandmother used to hold up her hand and look at it and sing out of her hand. She'd make them up as she would look at her hand. She sang in Geechee and also made rhymes and songs in English."

RIVANA BOYNTON

FEDERAL WRITERS' PROJECT
American Guide, (Negro Writers' Unit)
Cora Taylor
Frances H. Miner, Editor
Miami, Florida

[TR: also reported as Riviana.] |

1. Where, and about when, were you born?

Some time in 1850 on John and Mollie Hoover's plantation between Savannah and Charleston near the Georgia line.

2. If you were born on a plantation or farm, what sort of farming section was it in?

They raised rice, corn wheat, and lots of cotton, raised everything they et—vegetables, taters and all that.

3. How did you pass the time as a child? What sort of chores did you do and what did you play?

I had to thin cotton in the fields and mind the flies at the table. I chased them with a fly bush, sometimes a limb from a tree and sometimes wid a fancy bush.

4. Was your master kind to you?

Yes, I was favored by being with my massy.

5. How many slaves were there on the same plantation and farm?

I don't know. There was plenty o' dem up in de hundreds, I reckon.

6. Do you remember what kind of cooking utensils your mother used?

Yes, dey had spiders an' big iron kettles that dey hung in de chimney by a long chain. When dey wanted to cook fast dey lowered de chain and when dey wanted to bake in the spiders, they's put them under de kettle can cover with coals until dey was hot. Dey'd put de pones in does double concerned spiders and turn them around when dey was done on one side.

7. What were your main foods and how were they cooked?

We had everything you could think of to eat.

8. Do you remember making imitation or substitute coffee by grinding up corn or peanuts?

No. We had real coffee.

9. Do you remember ever having, when you were young, any other kind of bread besides corn bread?

Yes, batter and white bread.

10. Do you remember evaporating sea water to get salt?

[TR: word illegible] did hit dat way.

11. When you were a child, what sort of stove do you

remember your mother having? Did they have a hanging pot in the fire place, and did they make their candles of their own tallow?

Always had fireplaces or open fires on the plantation, but after a long time while my massy had hearth stoves to cook on. De would give us slaves pot liquor to cook green in sometimes. Dey lit de fires with flint and steel, when it would go out. We all ate with wooden paddles for spoons. We made dem taller candles out of beef and mutton tallow, den we'd shoog 'em down into the candle sticks made of tin pans wid a handle on and a holder for the candle in the center. You know how.

12. Did you use an open well or pump to get the water?

We had a well with two buckets on a pulley to draw the water.

13. Do you remember when you first saw ice in regular form?

No. Ice would freeze in winter in our place.

14. Did your family work in the rice fields or in the cotton on the farm, or what sort of work did they do?

They did all kinds of work in the fields.

15. If they worked in the house or about the place, what sort of work did they do?

I was house maid and did everything they told me to do. Sometimes I'd sweep and work around all the time.

16. Do you remember ever helping tan and cure hides and pig hides?

This was done on the plantation. I took no part in it.

17. As a young person what sort of work did you do? If you helped your mother around the house or cut firewood or swept the yard, say so.

I helped do the housework and did what the mistress told me do.

18. When you were a child do you remember how people wove cloth, or spun thread, or picked out cotton seed, or weighed cotton or what sort of bag was used on the cotton bales?

No.

19. Do you remember what sort of soap they used? How did they get the lye for making the soap?

Yes, I'd help to make the ash lye and soft soap. Never seed and cake soap until I came here.

20. What did they use for dyeing thread and cloth and how did they dye them?

They used indigo for blue, copperas for yellow, and red oak chips for red.

21. Did your mother use big, wooden washtubs with cut-out holes on each side for the fingers?

Yes, and dey had smaller wooden keels. Never seed any tin tubs up there.

22. Do you remember the way they made shoes by hand in the country?

Yes, they made all our shoes on the plantation.

23. Do you remember saving the chicken feathers and goose feathers always for your featherbeds?

Yes.

23. Do you remember when women wore hoop [TR: illegible] in their skirts and when they stopped wearing them and wore narrow skirts?

Yes. My missus, she made me a pair of hoops, or I guess she bought it, but some of the slaves took thin limbs from trees and made their hoops. Others made them out of stiff paper and others would starch their skirts stiff with rice starch to make their skirts stand way out. We thought those hoops were just the thing for style.

25. Do you remember when you first saw your first windmill?

Yes. They didn't have them there.

26. Do you remember when you first saw bed springs instead of bed ropes?

I slept in a gunny bunk. My missus had a rope bed and she covered the ropes with a cow hide. We made hay and corn shuck mattresses for her. We'd cut the hay and shucks up fine and stuff the ticks with them. The cow hides were placed on top of the mattresses to protect them.

27. When did you see the first buggy and what did it look like?

It was a buggy like you see.

28. Do you remember your grandparents?

No. My mother was sold from me when I was small. I stayed in my uncle's shed at night.

29. Do you remember the money called "shin-plasters"?

No.

30. What interesting historical events happened during your youth, such as Sherman's army passing through your section? Did you witness the happenings and what was the reaction of the other Negroes to them?

I remember well when de war was on. I used to turn the big corn sheller and sack the shelled corn for the Confederate soldiers. They used to sell some of the corn and they gave some of it to the soldiers. Anyway the Yankees got some and they did not expect them to get it. It was this way: The Wheeler boys came through there ahead of Sherman's Army. Now, we thought the Wheeler boys were Confederates. They came down the road as happy as could be, a-singin'

"Hurrah, hurrah, hurrah
Hurrah for the Broke Book Boys
Hurrah for the Broke Brook Boys of South Carolina."

So of course we thought they were our soldiers a-singin' our songs. Well, they came an' tol' our boss that Sherman's soldiers were coming' and we'd better hide all our food and valuable things, for they'd take everything they wanted. So we "hoped" our Massy hide the tings. They dug holes and buried the potatoes and covered them with cotton seed and all that. Then our ma say give dem food and thanked them for their kindness and he set out wid two of the girls to tote them to safety, but before he got back after the missus the Yanks were on us.

Our missus had od[TR:?] led us together and told us what to say. "Now you beg for me. If they ask you whether I've been good to you, you tell 'em 'yes'. If they ask you if we give you meat, you say 'yes'." Now de res' didn't git any meat, but I did, 'cause I worked in the house. So I didn't tell a lie, for I did git meat.

So we begged, an' we say, "Our missus is good. Don't you kill her. Don't you take our meat away from us. Don't you hurt her. Don't you burn her house down." So they burned the stable and some of the other buildings, but they did not burn the house nor hurt us any. We saw the rest of the Yanks comin'. They never stopped for nothin'. Their horses would jump the worn rail fences and they come 'cross fields 'n everything. They bound our missus upstairs so she couldn't get away, then they came to the sheds and we begged and begged for her. Then they loosed her, but they took some of us for refugees and some of the slaves went off with them of their own will. They took all the things that were buried all the hams and everything they wanted. But they did not burn the house and our missus was saved.

31. Did you know any Negroes who enlisted or joined the northern army? Yes.

32. Did you know any Negroes who enlisted in the southern army?

Yes.

33. Did your master join the confederacy? What do you remember of his return from the war? Or was he wounded and killed?

Yes. Two boys went. One was killed and one came back.

34. Did you live in Savannah when Sherman and the Northern forces marched through the state, and do you remember the excitement in your town or around the plantation where you lived?

We lived north of Savannah. I don't know how far it was, but it was in South Carolina.

35. Did your master's house get robbed or burned during the time of Sherman's march?

We were robbed, but the house was not burned. We saved it for them.

36. What kind of uniforms did they wear during the civil war?

Blue and gray

37. What sort of medicine was used in the days just after the war? Describe a Negro doctor of that period.

She used to make tea out of the Devil's Shoe String that grew along on the ground. We used oil and turpentine. Put turpentine on sores.

38. What do you remember about northern people or outside people moving into the community after the war?

Yes. Mrs. Dermont, she taught white folks. I didn't go to school.

39. How did your family's life compare after Emancipation with it before?

I had it better and so did the rest.

40. Do you know anything about political meetings and clubs formed after the war?

You had to have a ticket to go to church or the paddle rollers.

41. Do you know anything regarding the letters and stories from Negroes who migrated north after the war?

No.

42. Were there any Negroes of your acquaintance who were skilled [TR: illegible] particular line of work?

Yes. In making shoes and furniture, they had to do most everything well or get paddled.

48

MATILDA BROOKS

FEDERAL WRITERS' PROJECT
American Guide, (Negro Writers' Unit)
Alfred Farrell, Field Worker
Monticello, Florida
January 12, 1937

A GOVERNOR'S SLAVES

Matilda Brooks, 79, who lives in Monticello, Fla., was once a slave of a South Carolina governor.

Mrs. Brooks was born in 1857 or 1858 in Edgefield, S.C. Her parents were Hawkins and Harriet Knox, and at the time of the birth of their daughter were slaves on a large plantation belonging to Governor Frank Pickens. On this plantation were raised cotton, corn, potatoes, tobacco, peas, wheat and truck products. As soon as Matilda was large enough to go into the fields she helped her parents with the farming.

The former slave describes Governor Pickens as being 'very good' to his slaves. He supervised them personally, although official duties often made this difficult. He saw to it that their quarters were comfortable and that they always had sufficient food. When they became ill he would himself doctor on them with pills, castor oil, turpentine other remedies. Their diet consisted largely of potatoes, corn bread, syrup, greens, peas, and occasionally ham, fowl and other meats or poultry. Their chief beverage was coffee made from parched corn.

Since there were no stoves during slavery, they cooked their foods in large iron pots suspended from racks built into the fireplaces. Fried foods were prepared in iron 'spiders', large frying pans with legs. These pans were placed over hot coals, and the seasoning was done with salt which they secured from evaporated sea-water. After the food was fried and while the coals were still glowing the fat of oxen and sheep was melted to make candles. Any grease left over was put into a large box, to be used later for soap-making.

Lye for the soap was obtained by putting oak ashes in a barrel and pouring water over them. After standing for several days—until the ashes had decayed—holes were drilled into the bottom of the barrell and the liquid drained off. This liquid was the lye, and it was then trickled into the pot into which the fat had been placed. The two were then boiled, and after cooling cut into squares of soap.

Water for cooking and other purposes was obtained from a well, which also served as a refrigerator at times. Matilda does not recall seeing ice until many years later.

In the evenings Matilda's mother would weave cloth on her spinning-jenny and an improvised loom. This cloth was sometimes dyed in various colors: blue from the indigo plant; yellow from the crocus and brown from the bark of the red oak. Other colors were obtained from berries and other plants.

In seasons other than picking-time for the cotton the children were usually allowed to play in the evenings, when cotton crops were large, however, they spent their evenings picking out seeds from the cotton bolls, in order that their parents might work uninterruptedly in the fields during the day. The cotton, after being picked and separated, would be weighed in balances and packed tightly in 'crocus' bags.

Chicken and goose feathers were jealously saved during these days. They were used for the mattresses that rested on the beds of wooden slats that were built in corners against the walls. Hoop skirts were worn at the time, but for how long afterward Matilda does not remember. She only recalls that they were disappearing 'about the time I saw a windmill for the first time'.

The coming of the Yankee soldiers created much excitement among the slaves on the Pickens plantation. The slaves were in ignorance of activities going on, and of their approach, but when the first one was sighted the news spread 'just like dry grass burning up a hill'. Despite the kindness of Governor Pickens the slaves were happy to claim their new-found freedom. Some of them even ran away to join the Northern armies before they were officially freed. Some attempted to show their loyalty to their old owners by joining the southern armies, but in this section they were not permitted to do so.

After she was released from slavery Matilda came with her parents to the Monticello section, where the Knoxes became paid house servants. The parents took an active part in politics in the section, and

Matilda was sent to school. White teachers operated the schools at first, and were later replaced by Negro teachers. Churches were opened with Negro ministers in the pulpits, and other necessities of community life eventually came to the vicinity.

Matilda still lives in one of the earlier homes of her parents in the area, now described as 'Rooster-Town' by its residents. The section is in the eastern part of Monticello.

BIBLIOGRAPHY
Interview with subject, Matilda Brooks; "Rooster-Town", eastern part of city, Monticello, Jefferson County, Fla.

TITUS I. BYNES

FEDERAL WRITERS' PROJECT
American Guide, (Negro Writers' Unit)
Alfred Farrell, Field Worker
John A. Simms, Editor
Titusville, Florida
September 25, 1936

Titus B. [TR: Titus I. above] Bynes, affectionately known as "Daddy Bynes", is reminiscent of Harriet Beecher Stowe's immortal "Uncle Tom" and Joel Chandler Harris' inimitable 'Uncle Remus' with his white beard and hair surrounding a smiling black face. He was born in November 1846 in what is now Clarendon County, South Carolina. Both his father, Cuffy, and mother, Diana, belonged to Gabriel Flowden who owned 75 or 80 slaves and was noted for his kindness to them.

Bynes' father was a common laborer, and his mother acted in the capacity of chambermaid and spinner. They had 12 children, seven boys—Abraham, Tutus[TR:?], Reese, Lawrence, Thomas, Billie, and Hamlet—and five girls—Charity, Chrissy, Fannie, Charlotte, and Violet.

When Titus was five or six years of age he was given to Flowden's wife who groomed him for the job of houseboy. Although he never received any education, Bynes was quick to learn. He could tell the time of day and could distinguish one newspaper from another.

He recalled an incident which happened when he was about eight years of age which led him to conceal his precociousness. One day while writing on the ground, he heard his mistress' little daughter tell her mother that he was writing about water. Mistress Flowden called him and told him that if he were caught writing again his right arm would be cut off. From then on his precociousness vanished. In regards to religion, Bynes can recall the Sunday services very vividly; and he tells how the Negroes who were seated in the gallery first heard a sermon by the white minister and then after these services they would gather on the main floor and hear a sermon by a Negro preacher.

Bynes served in the Civil War with his boss, and he can remember the regiment camp between Savannah, Georgia and Charleston, South Carolina. His mistress would not permit Bynes to accompany his master to Virginia to join the Hampton Legion on the grounds that it was too cold for him. And thus ended his war days! When he was 20 years of age, his father turned him loose. Young Bynes rented 14 acres of land from Arthur Harven and began farming.

In 1868 he left South Carolina and came to Florida. He settled in Enterprise (now Benson Springs), Velusia County where he worked for J.C. Hayes, a farmer, for one year, after which he homesteaded. He next became a carpenter and, as he says himself, "a jack of all trades and master of none." He married shortly after coming to Florida and is the father of three sons—"as my wife told me," he adds with a twinkle in his eyes. His wife is now dead. He was prevailed upon while very ill to enter the Titusville Poor Farm where he has been for almost two years. (2)

Della Bess Hilyard ("Aunt Bess")
Della Bess Hilyard, or "Aunt Bess" as she is better known, was born in Darlington, South Carolina in 1858, the daughter of Resier and Zilphy Hart, slaves of Gus Hiwards. Both her parents were cotton pickers and as a little girl Della often went with her parents into the fields. One day she stated that the Yankees came through South Carolina with Knapsacks on their shoulders. It wasn't until later that she learned the reason.

When asked if she received any educational training, "Aunt Bess" replied in the negative, but stated that the slaves on the Hiwards plantation were permitted to pick up what education they could without fear of being molested. No one bothered, however, to teach them anything.

In regards to religion, "Aunt Bess" said that the slaves were not told about heaven; they were told to honor their masters and mistresses and of the damnation which awaited them for disobedience.

After slavery the Hart family moved to Georgia where Della grew into womanhood and at an early age married Caleb Bess by whom she had two children. After the death of Bess, about fifteen years ago, "Aunt Bess" moved to Fort Pierce, Florida. While there she married Lonny Hilyard who brought her to Titusville where she now resides, a relic of bygone days. (3)

Taylor Gilbert

Taylor Gilbert was born in Shellman, Georgia, 91 years ago, of a colored mother and a white father, "which is why I am so white", he adds. He has never been known to have passed as white, however, in spite of the fact that he could do so without detection. David Ferguson bought Jacob Gilbert from Dr. Gilbert as a husband for Emily, Taylor's mother. Emily had nine children, two by a white man, Frances and Taylor, and seven by Jacob, only three of whom Gilbert remembers—Gettie, Rena, and Annis. Two of these children were sent to school while the others were obliged to work on the plantation. Emily, the mother, was the cook and washwoman while Jacob was the Butler.

Gilbert, a good sized lad when slavery was at its height, recalls vividly the cruel lashings and other punishments meted out to those who disobeyed their master or attempted to run away. It was the custom of slaves who wished to go from one plantation to another to carry passes in case they were stopped as suspected runaways. Frequently slaves would visit without benefit of passes, and as result they suffered severe torturing. Often the sons of the slaves' owners would go "nigger hunting" and nothing—not even murder was too horrible for them to do to slaves caught without passes. They justified their fiendish acts by saying the "nigger tried to run away when told to stop."

Gilbert cannot remember when he came to Florida, but he claims that it was many years ago. Like the majority of Negroes after slavery, he became a farmer which occupation he still pursues. He married once but "my wife got to messin' around with another man so I sent her home to her mother." He can be found in Miami, Florida, where he may be seen daily hobbling around on his cane. (4)

REFERENCES
1. Personal interview of field worker with subject.

2. Personal interview with subject.

3. Personal interview with subject.

4. Personal interview of field worker with subject.

United States. Work Projects Administration

PATIENCE CAMPBELL

FEDERAL WRITERS' PROJECT
American Guide, (Negro Writers' Unit)
James Johnson, Field Worker
Monticello, Florida
December 15, 1936

Patience Campbell, blind for 26 years, was-born in Jackson County, near Marianna, Florida about 1883[TR: incorrect date?], on a farm of George Bullock. Her mother Tempy, belonged to Bullock, while her father Arnold Merritt, belonged to Edward Merritt, a large plantation owner. According to Patience, her mother's owner was very kind, her father's very cruel. Bullock had very few slaves, but Merritt had a great many of them, not a few of whom he sold at the slave markets.

Patience spent most of her time playing in the sand when she was a child, while her parents toiled in the fields for their respective owners. Her grandparents on her mother's side belonged to Bullock, but of her father's people she knew nothing as "they didn't come to this country." When asked where they lived, she replied "in South Carolina."

Since she lived with her mother, Patience fared much better than had she lived with her father. Her main foods included meats, greens, rice, corn bread which was replaced by biscuits on Sunday morning. Coffee was made from parched corn or meal and was the chief drink. The food was cooked in large iron pots and pans in an open fireplace and seasoned with salt obtained by evaporating sea water.

Water for all purposes was drawn from a well. In order to get soap to wash with, the cook would save all the grease left from the cooking. Lye was obtained by mixing oak ashes with water and allowing them to decay; Tubs were made from large barrels.

When she was about seven or eight, Patience assisted other children about her age and older in picking out cotton seeds from the picked cotton. After the cotton was weighed on improved scales, it was bound in bags made of hemp.

Spinning and weaving were taught Patience when she was about ten. Although the cloth and thread were dyed various colors, she knows only how blue was obtained by allowing the indigo plant to rot in water and straining the result.

Patience's father was not only a capable field worker but also a finished shoemaker. After tanning and curing his hides by placing them in water with oak bark for several days and then exposing them to the sun to dry, he would cut out the uppers and the soles after measuring the foot to be shod. There would be an inside sole as well as an outside sole tacked together by means of small tacks made of maple wood. Sewing was done on the shoes by means of flax thread.

Patience remembers saving the feathers from all the fowl to make feather beds. She doesn't remember when women stopped wearing hoops in their skirts nor when bed springs replaced bed ropes. She does remember, however, that these things were used.

She saw her first windmill about 36 years ago, ten years before she went blind. She remembers seeing buggies during slavery time, little light carriages, some with two wheels and some with four. She never heard of any money called "shin-plasters," and she became money-conscious during the war when Confederate currency was introduced. When the slaves were sick, they were given castor oil, turpentine and medicines made from various roots and herbs.

Patience's master joined the confederacy, but her father's master did not. [Although Negroes could enlist in the Southern army if they desired,] none of them wished to do so but preferred to join northern forces and fight for the thing they desired most, freedom. When freedom was no longer a dream, but a reality, the Merritts started life on their own as farmers. Twelve-year old Patience entered one of the schools established by the Freedmen's Bureau. She recalls the gradual growth of Negro settlements, the churches and the rise and fall of the Negroes politically.

REFERENCE
1. Personal interview with Patience Campbell, 910 Cherry Street, Monticello, Florida

FLORIDA CLAYTON

FEDERAL WRITERS' PROJECT
American Guide, (Negro Writers' Unit)
Rachel A. Austin, Field Worker
Jacksonville, Florida
November 20, 1936

The life of Florida Clayton is interesting in that it illustrates the miscegenation prevalent during the days of slavery. Interesting also is the fact that Florida was not a slave even though she was a product of those turbulent days. Many years before her birth—March 1, 1854—Florida's great grandfather, a white man, came to Tallahassee, Florida from Washington, District of Columbia, with his children whom he had by his Negro slave. On coming to Florida, he set all of his children free except one boy, Amos, who was sold to a Major Ward. For what reason this was done, no one knew. Florida, named for the state in which she was born, was one of seven children born to Charlotte Morris (colored) whose father was a white man and David Clayton (white).

Florida, in a retrogressive mood, can recall the "nigger hunters" and "nigger stealers" of her childhood days. Mr. Nimrod and Mr. Shehee, both white, specialized in catching runaway slaves with their trained bloodhounds. Her parents always warned her and her brothers and sisters to go in someone's yard whenever they saw these men with their dogs lest the ferocious animals tear them to pieces. In regards to the "nigger stealers," Florida tells of a covered wagon which used to come to Tallahassee at regular intervals and camp in some secluded spot. The children, attracted by the old wagon, would be eager to go near it, but they were always told that "Dry Head and Bloody Bones," a ghost who didn't like children, was in that wagon. It was not until later years that Florida and the other children learned that the driver of the wagon was a "nigger stealer" who stole children and took them to Georgia to sell at the slave markets.

When she was 11 years old, Florida saw the surrender of Tallahassee to the Yankees. Three years later she came to Jacksonville to live with her sister. She married but is now divorced after 12 years of marriage.

Three years ago she entered the Old Folks Home at 1627 Franklin Street to live.

1. Personal Interview with Florida Clayton, 1627 Franklin Street, Jacksonville, Florida

"FATHER" CHARLES COATES

FEDERAL WRITERS' PROJECT
American Guide, (Negro Writers' Unit)
Viola B. Muse, Field Worker
Jacksonville, Florida
December 3, 1936

"Father" Charles Coates, as he is called by all who know him, was born a slave, 108 years ago at Richmond, Virginia, on the plantation of a man named L'Angle. His early boyhood days was spent on the L'Angle place filled with duties such as minding hogs, cows, bringing in wood and such light work. His wearing apparel consisted of one garment, a shirt made to reach below the knees and with three-quarter sleeves. He wore no shoes until he was a man past 20 years of age.

The single garment was worn summer and winter alike and the change in the weather did not cause an extra amount of clothes to be furnished for the slaves. They were required to move about so fast at work that the heat from the body was sufficient to keep them warm.

When Charles was still a young man Mr. L'Angle sold him on time payment to W.B. Hall; who several years before the Civil War moved from Richmond to Washington County, Georgia, carrying 135 grown slaves and many children. Mr. Hall made Charles his carriage driver, which kept him from hard labor. Other slaves on the plantation performed such duties as rail splitting, digging up trees by the roots and other hard work.

Charles Coates remembers vividly the cruelties practiced on the Hall plantation. His duty was to see that all the slaves reported to work on time. The bell was rung at 5:30 a.m. by one of the slaves. Charles had the ringing of the bell for three years; this was in addition to the carriage driving. He tells with laughter how the slaves would "grab a piece of meat and bread and run to the field" as no time was allowed to sit and eat breakfast. This was a very different way from that of the master he had before, as Mr. L'Angle was much better to his slaves.

Mr. Hall was different in many ways from Mr. L'Angle, "He was always pretending" says Charles that he did not want his slaves beaten unmercifully. Charles being close to Mr. Hall during work hours had opportunity to see and hear much about what was going on at the plantation. And he believes that Mr. Hall knew just how the overseer dealt with the slaves.

On the Hall plantation there was a contraption, similar to a gallows, where the slaves were suspended and whipped. At the top of this device were blocks of wood with chains run through holes and high enough that a slave when tied to the chains by his fingers would barely touch the ground with his toes. This was done so that the slave could not shout or twist his body while being whipped. The whipping was prolonged until the body of the slave covered with welts and blood trickled down his naked body. Women were treated in the same manner, and a pregnant woman received no more leniency than did a man. Very often after a severe flogging a slave's body was treated to a bath of water containing salt and pepper so that the pain would be more lasting and aggravated. The whipping was done with sticks and a whip called the "cat o' nine tails," meaning every lick meant nine. The "cat o' nine tails" was a whip of nine straps attached to a stick; the straps were perforated so that everywhere the hole in the strap fell on the flesh a blister was left.

The treatment given by the overseer was very terrifying. He relates how a slave was put in a room and locked up for two and three days at a time without water or food, because the overseer thought he hadn't done enough work in a given time.

Another offense which brought forth severe punishment was that of crossing the road to another plantation. A whipping was given and very often a slave was put on starvation for a few days.

One privilege given slaves on the plantation was appreciated by all and that was the opportunity to hear the word of God. The white people gathered in log and sometimes frame churches and the slaves were permitted to sit about the church yard on wagons and on the ground and listen to the preaching. When the slaves wanted to hold church they had to get special permission from the master, and at that time a slave hut was used. A white Preacher was called in and he would preach to them not to steal, lie or run away and "be sure and git all dem weeds outen dat corn in de field and your master will think a heap of you." Charles does not remember anything else the preacher told them about God. They learned more about God when they sat outside the church waiting to drive their masters and family back home.

Charles relates an incident of a slave named Sambo who thought himself very smart and who courted the favor of the master. The neighboring slaves screamed so loudly while being whipped that Sambo told his master that he knew how to make a contraption which, if a slave was put into while being whipped would prevent him from making a noise. The device was made of two blocks of wood cut to fit the head and could be fastened around the neck tightly. When the head was put in, the upper and lower parts were clamped together around the neck so that the slave could not scream. The same effect as choking. The stomach of the victim was placed over a barrel which allowed freedom of movement. When the lash was administered and the slave wiggled, the barrel moved.

Now it so happened that Sambo was the first to be put into his own invention for a whipping. The overseer applied the lash rather heavily, and Sambo was compelled to wiggle his body to relieve his feelings. In wiggling the barrel under his stomach rolled a bit straining Sambo's neck and breaking it. After Sambo died from his neck being broken the master discontinued the use of the device, as he saw the loss of property in the death of slaves.

Charles was still a carriage driver when freedom came. He had opportunity to see and hear many things about the master's private life. When the news of the advance of the Union Army came, Mr. Hall carried his money to a secluded spot and buried it in an iron pot so that the soldiers who were confiscating all the property and money they could, would not get his money. The slave owners were required to notify the slaves that they were free so Mr. Hall sent his son Sherard to the cabins to notify all the slaves to come into his presence and there he had his son to tell them that they were free. The Union soldiers took much of the slave owners' property and gave to the slaves telling them that if the owners' took the property back to write and tell them about it; the owners only laughed because they knew the slaves could not read nor write. After the soldiers had gone the timid and scared slaves gave up most of the land; some few however, fenced in a bit of land while the soldiers remained in the vicinity and they managed to keep a little of the land.

Many of the slaves remained with the owners. There they worked for small monthly wages and took whatever was left of cast off clothing and food and whatever the "old missus" gave them. A pair of old pants of the master was highly prized by them.

Charles Coates was glad to be free. He had been well taken care of and looked younger than 37 years of age at the close of slavery. He had not been married; had been put upon the block twice to be sold after belonging to Mr. Hall. Each time he was offered for sale, his master wanted so much for him, and refusing to sell him on time payments, he was always left on his master's hands. His master said "being tall, healthy and robust, he was well worth much money."

After slavery, Charles was rated as a good worker. He

at once began working and saving his money and in a short time he had accumulated "around $200."

The first sight of a certain young woman caused him to fall in love. He says the love was mutual and after a courtship of three weeks they were married. The girl's mother told Charles that she had always been very frail, but he did not know that she had consumption. Within three days after they were married she died and her death caused much grief for Charles.

He was reluctant to bury her and wanted to continue to stand and look at her face. A white doctor and a school teacher whose names he does not remember, told him to put his wife's body in alcohol to preserve it and he could look at it all the time. At that time white people who had plenty of money and wanted to see the faces of their deceased used this method.

A glass casket was used and the dressed body of the deceased was placed in alcohol inside the casket. Another casket made of wood held the glass casket and the whole was placed in a vault made of stone or brick. The walls of the vault were left about four feet above the ground and a window and ledge were placed in front, so when the casket was placed inside of the vault the bereaved could lean upon the ledge and look in at the face of the deceased. The wooden casket was provided with a glass top part of the way so that the face could easily be seen.

Although the process of preserving the body in alcohol cost $160, Charles did not regret the expense saying, "I had plenty of money at that time."

After the death of his wife, Charles left with his mother and father, Henrietta and Spencer Coates and went to Savannah, Georgia. He said they were so glad to go, that they walked to within 30 miles of Savannah, when they saw a man driving a horse and wagon who picked them up and carried them into Savannah. It was in that city that he met his present wife, Irene, and they were married about 1876.

There are nine grandchildren and eight great-grandchildren living and in March of 1936, when a party was given in honor of Father Coates' 108th birthday, one of each of the four generations of his family were present.

The party was given at the Clara White Mission, 615 West Ashley Street by Ertha M.M. White. Father Coates and his wife were very much honored and each spoke encouraging words to those present. On the occasion he said that the cause for his long life was due to living close to nature, rising early, going to bed early and not dissipating in any way.

He can "shout" (jumping about a foot and a half from the floor and knocking his heels together.) He does chores about his yard; looks years younger than he really is and enjoys good health. His hair is partly white; his memory very good and his chief delight is talking about God and his goodness. He has preached the gospel in his humble way for a number of years, thereby gaining the name of "Father" Coates.

REFERENCE
1. Personal interview with Charles Coates—2015 Windle Street, Jacksonville, Florida

IRENE COATES

FEDERAL WRITERS' PROJECT
American Guide, (Negro Writers' Unit)
Viola B. Muse, Field Worker
Jacksonville, Florida
December 16, 1936

Immediately after slavery in the United States, the southern white people found themselves without servants. Women who were accustomed to having a nurse, maid, cook and laundress found themselves without sufficient money to pay wages to all these. There was a great amount of work to be done and the great problem confronting married women who had not been taught to work and who thought it beneath their standing to soil their hands, found it very difficult.

There were on the other hand many Negro women who needed work and young girls who needed guidance and training.

The home and guidance of the aristocratic white people offered the best opportunity for the dependent un-schooled freed women; and it was in this kind of home that the ex-slave child of this story was reared.

Irene Coates of 2015 Windle Street, Jacksonville, Florida, was born in Georgia about 1859. She was close to six years of age when freedom was declared.

She was one among the many Negro children who

had the advantage of living under the direct supervision of kind whites and receiving the care which could only be excelled by an educated mother.

Jimmie and Lou Bedell were the names of the man and wife who saw the need of having a Negro girl come into their home as one in the family and at the same time be assured of a good and efficient servant in years to come.

When Irene was old enough, she became the nurse of the Bedell baby and when the family left Savannah, Georgia to come to Jacksonville, they brought Irene with them.

Although Irene was just about six years old when the Civil War ended, she has vivid recollection of happenings during slavery. Some of the incidents which happened were told her by her slave associates after slavery ended and some of them she remembers herself.

Two incidents which she considers caused respect for slaves by their masters and finally the Emancipation by Abraham Lincoln she tells in this order.

The first event tells of a young, strong healthy Negro woman who knew her work and did it well. "She would grab up two bags of guana (fertilizer) and tote 'em at one time," said Irene, and was never found shirking her work. The overseer on the plantation, was very hard on the slaves and practiced striking them across the back with a whip when he wanted to spur them on to do more work.

Irene says, one day a crowd of women were hoeing in the field and the overseer rode along and struck one of the women across the back with the whip, and the one nearest her spoke and said that if he ever struck her like that, it would be the day he or she would die. The overseer heard the remark and the first opportunity he got, he rode by the woman and struck her with the whip and started to ride on. The woman was hoeing at the time, she whirled around, struck the overseer on his head with the hoe, knocking him from his horse, she then pounced upon him and chopped his head off. She went mad for a few seconds and proceeded to chop and mutilate his body; that done to her satisfaction, she then killed his horse. She then calmly went to tell the master of the murder, saying "I've done killed de overseer," the master replied—"Do you mean to say you've killed the overseer?" she answered yes, and that she had killed the horse also. Without hesitating, the master pointing to one of his small cabins on the plantation said—"You see that house over there?" she answered yes—at the same time looking—"Well" said he, "take all your belongings and move into that house and you are free from this day and if the mistress wants you to do anything for her, do it if you want to." Irene related with much warmth the effect that incident had upon the future treatment of the slaves.

The other incident occured in Virginia. It was upon an occasion when Mrs. Abraham Lincoln was visiting in Richmond. A woman slaveowner had one of her slaves whipped in the presence of Mrs. Lincoln. It was easily noticed that the woman was an expectant mother. Mrs. Lincoln was horrified at the situation and expressed herself as being so, saying that she was going to tell the President as soon as she returned to the

White House. Whether this incident had any bearing upon Mr. Lincoln's actions or not, those slaves who were present and Irene says that they all believed it to be the beginning of the President's activities to end slavery.

Besides these incidents, Irene remembers that women who were not strong and robust were given such work as sewing, weaving and minding babies. The cloth from which the Sunday clothes of the slaves was made was called ausenburg and the slave women were very proud of this. The older women were required to do most of the weaving of cloth and making shirts for the male slaves.

When an old woman who had been sick, regained her strength, she was sent to the fields the same as the younger ones. The ones who could cook and tickle the palates of her mistress and master were highly prized and were seldon if ever offered for sale at the auction block.

The slaves were given fat meat and bread made of husk of corn and wheat. This caused them to steal food and when caught they were severely whipped.

Irene recalls the practice of blowing a horn whenever a sudden rain came. The overseer had a certain Negro to blow three times and if shelter could be found, the slaves were expected to seek it until the rain ceased.

The master had sheds built at intervals on the plantation. These accomodated a goodly number; if no shed was available the slaves stood under trees. If neither was handy and the slaves got wet, they could not go to the cabins to change clothes for fear of losing time from work. This was often the case; she says that slaves were more neglected than the cattle.

Another custom which impressed the child-mind of Irene was the tieing of slaves by their thumbs to a tree limb and whipping them. Women and young girls were treated the same as were men.

After the Bedells took Irene to live in their home they traveled a deal. After bringing her to Jacksonville, when Jacksonville was only a small port, they then went to Camden County, Georgia.

Irene married while in Georgia and came back to Jacksonville with her husband Charles, the year of the earthquake at Charleston, South Carolina, about 1888.

Irene and Charles Coates have lived in Jacksonville since that time. She relates many tales of happenings during the time that this city grew from a town of about four acres to its present status.

Irene is the mother of five children. She has nine grandchildren and eight great-grandchildren. Her health is fair, but her eyesight is poor. It is her delight to entertain visitors and is conversant upon matters pertaining to slavery and reconstruction days.

REFERENCE
1. Irene Coates, 2015 Windle Street, Jacksonville, Florida

NEIL COKER

FEDERAL WRITERS' PROJECT
American Guide, (Negro Writers' Unit)
Martin D. Richardson, Field Worker
Grandin, Florida

Interesting tales of the changes that came to the section of Florida that is situated along the Putnam-Clay County lines are told by Neil Coker, old former slave who lives two miles south of McRae on the road Grandin.

Coker is the son of a slave mother and a half-Negro. His father, he states, was Senator John Wall, who held a seat in the senate for sixteen years. He was born in Virginia, and received his family name from an old family bearing the same in that state. He was born, as nearly as he can remember, about 1857.

One of Coker's first reminiscences is of the road on which he still lives. During his childhood it was known as the 'Bellamy Road,' so called because it was built, some 132 years ago, by a man of that name who hailed from West Florida.

The 'Bellamy Road' was at one time the main route of traffic between Tallahassee and St. Augustine. (Interestingly enough, the road is at least 30 miles southwest of St. Augustine where it passes through Grandin; the reason for cutting it in such a wide circle,

Coker says was because of the ferocity of the Seminoles in the swamps north and west of St. Augustine.)

Wagons, carriages and stages passed along this road in the days before the War Between the States, Coker says. In addition to these he claims to have seen many travellers by foot, and not infrequently furtive escaped slaves, the latter usually under cover of an appropriate background of darkness.

The road again came into considerable use during the late days of the War. It was during these days that the Federal troops, both whites and Negroes, passed in seemingly endless procession on their way to or from encounters. On one occasion the former slave recounts having seen a procession of soldiers that took nearly two days to pass; they travelled on horse and afoot.

Several amusing incidents are related by the ex-slave of the events of this period. Dozens of the Negro soldiers, he says, discarded their uniforms for the gaudier clothing that had belonged to their masters in former days, and could be identified as soldiers as they passed only with difficulty. Others would pause on their trip at some plantation, ascertain the name of the 'meanest' overseer on the place, then tie him backward on a horse and force him to accompany them. Particularly retributive were the punishments visited upon Messrs. Mays and Prevatt—generally recognized as the most vicious slave drivers of the section.

Bellamy, Coker says built the road with slave labor and as an investment, realizing much money on tolls on it for many years. A remarkable feature of the road is that despite its age and the fact that County authorities have permitted its former good grading to deterierate to an almost impassable sand at some seasons, there is no mistaking the fact that this was once a major thoroughfare.

The region that stretches from Green Cove Springs in the Northeast to Grandin in the Southwest, the former slave claims, was once dotted with lakes, creeks, and even a river; few of the lakes and none of the other bodies still exist, however.

Among the more notable of the bodies of water was a stream—he does not now remember its name—that ran for about 20 miles in an easterly direction from Starke. This stream was one of the fastest that the former slave can remember having seen in Florida; its power was utilised for the turning of a power mill which he believes ground corn or other grain. The falls in the river that turned the water mill, he states, was at least five or six feet high, and at one point under the Falls a man named (or possibly nicknamed) "Yankee" operated a sawmill. Coker believes that this mill, too, derived its power from the little stream. He says that the stream has been extinct since he reached manhood. It ended in 'Scrub Pond,' beyond Grandin and Starke.

Some of the names of the old lakes of the section were these: "Brooklyn Lake; Magnolia Lake; Soldier Pond (near Keystone); Half-Moon Pond, near Putnam Hall; Hick's Lake" and others. On one of them was the large grist mill of Dr. McCray; Coker suggests that this might be the origin of the town of McRae of the present period.

To add to its natural water facilities, Coker points out, Bradford County also had a canal. This canal ran from the interior of the county to the St. John's River near Green Cove Springs, and with Mandarin on the other side of the river still a major shipping point, the canal handled much of the commerce of Bradford and Clay Counties.

Coker recalls vividly the Indians of the area in the days before 1870. These, he claims to have been friendly, but reserved, fellows; he does not recall any of the Indian women.

Negro slaves from the region around St. Augustine and what is now Hastings used to escape and use Bellamy's Road on their way to the area about Micanopy. It was considered equivalent to freedom to reach that section, with its friendly Indians and impenetrable forests and swamps.

The little town of Melrose probably had the most unusual name of all the strange ones prevalent at the time. It was call, very simply, "Shake-Rag." Coker makes no effort to explain the appelation.

REFERENCES
1. Interview with subject, Neil Coker, Grandin, Putnam County

YOUNG WINSTON DAVIS

FEDERAL WRITERS' PROJECT
American Guide, (Negro Writers' Unit)
Rachel Austin, Field Worker
Jacksonville, Florida

Young Winston Davis states that he was born in Ozark, Alabama, June 28, 1855 on the plantation of Charles Davis who owned about seven hundred slaves and was considered very wealthy. Kindness and consideration for his slaves, made them love him.

Reverend Davis was rather young during his years in slavery but when he was asked to tell something about the days of slavery, replied: "I remember many things about slavery, but know they will not come to me now; anyway, I'll tell what I can think of."

He tells of the use of iron pots, fireplaces with rods used to hold the pots above the fire for cooking peas, rice, vegetables, meats, etc.; the home-made coffee from meal, spring and well water, tanning rawhide for leather, spinning of thread from cotton and the weaving looms.

"There was no difference," he states, "in the treatment of men and women for work; my parents worked very hard and women did some jobs that we would think them crazy for trying now; why my mother helped build a railroad before she was married to my father. My mother's first husband was sold away from her; shucks, some of the masters didn't care how they treated husbands, wives, parents and children; any of them might be separated from the other. A good price for a 'nigger' was $1500 on down and if one was what was called a stallion (healthy), able to get plenty children he would bring about $2500.

"They had what was called legal money—I did have some of it but guess it was burned when I lost my house by fire a few years ago.

"Now, my master had three boys and two girls; his wife, Elizabeth, was about like the ordinary missus; Master Davis was good, but positive; he didn't allow other whites to bother his slaves.

"When the war came, his two boys went first, finally Master Davis went; he and one son never returned.

"The Yankees killed cows, etc., as they went along but did not destroy any property 'round where I was.

"We had preachers and doctors, but no schools; the white preachers told us to obey and would read the Bible (which we could not understand) and told us not to steal eggs. Most of the doctors used herbs from the woods and "Aunt Jane" and "Uncle Bob" were known for using "Samson's Snake Root," "Devil's shoestring" for stomach troubles and "low-bud Myrtle" for fevers; that's good now, chile, if you can get it.

"The 'nigger' didn't have a chance to git in politics during slavery, but after Emancipation, he went immediately into the Republican Party; a few into the Democratic Party; there were many other parties, too.

"The religions were Methodist and Baptist; my master was Baptist and that's what I am; we could attend church but dare not try to get any education, less we punished with straps.

"There are many things I remember just like it was yesterday—the general punishment was with straps—some of the slaves suffered terribly on the plantations; if the master was poor and had few slaves he was mean—the more wealthy or more slaves he had, the better he was. In some cases it was the general law that made some of the masters as they were; as, the law required them to have an overseer or foreman (he was called "boss man") by the 'niggers' and usually came from the lower or poorer classes of whites; he didn't like 'niggers' usually, and took authority to do as he pleased with them at times. Some plantations preferred and did have 'nigger riders' that were next to the overseer or foreman, but they were liked better than the foreman and in many instances were treated like foremen but the law would not let them be called "foremen." Some of the masters stood between the 'nigger riders' and foremen and some cases, the 'nigger' was really boss.

"The punishments, as I said were cruel—some masters would hang the slaves up by both thumbs so that their toes just touched the floor, women and men, alike. Many slaves ran away; others were forced by their treatment to do all kinds of mean things. Some slaves would dig deep holes along the route of the "Patrollers" and their horses would fall in sometimes breaking the leg of the horse, arm or leg of the rider; some slaves took advantage of the protection their masters would give them with the overseer or other plantation owners, would do their devilment and "fly" to their masters who did not allow a man from another plantation to bother his slaves. I have known pregnant women to go ten miles to help do some devilment. My mother was a very strong woman (as I told you she helped build a railroad), and felt that she could whip any ordinary man, would not get a passport unless she felt like it; once when caught on another plantation without a passport, she had all of us with her, made all of the children run, but wouldn't run herself—somehow she went upstream, one of the men's horse's legs was broken and she told him "come and get me" but she knew the master allowed no one to come on his place to punish his slaves.

"My father was a blacksmith and made the chains used for stocks, (like handcuffs), used on legs and hands. The slaves were forced to lay flat on their backs and were chained down to the board made for that purpose; they were left there for hours, sometimes through rain and cold; he might 'holler' and groan but that did not always get him released.

"The Race became badly mixed then; some Negro women were forced into association, some were beaten almost to death because they refused. The Negro men dare not bother or even speak to some of their women.

"In one instance an owner of a plantation threatened a Negro rider's sweetheart; she told him and he went crying to this owner who in turned threatened him and probably did hit the woman; straight to his master this sweetheart went and when he finished his story, his master immediately took his team and drove to the other plantation—drove so fast that one of his horses' dropped dead; when the owner came out he levelled his double-barrel shotgun at him and shot him dead. No, suh; some masters did not allow you to bother their slaves.

"A peculiar case was that of Old Jim who lived on another plantation was left to look out for the fires and do other chores around the house while 'marster' was at war. A bad rumor spread, and do you know those mean devils, overseers of nearby plantations came out and got her dug a deep hole, and despite her cries, buried her up to her neck—nothing was left out but her head and hair. A crowd of young 'nigger boys' saw it all and I was one among the crowd that helped dig her out.

"Oh, there's a lots more I know but just cant get it together. My mother's name was Caroline and my father Patrick; all took the name of Davis from our master. There were thirteen children—I am the only one alive."

Mr. Davis appears well preserved for his age; he has most of his teeth and is slightly gray; his health seems to be good, although he is a cripple and uses a cane for walking always; this condition he believes is the result of an attack of rheumatism.

He is a preacher and has pastored in Alabama, Texas and Florida. He has had several years of training in public schools and under ministers.

He has lived in Jacksonville since 1918 coming here from Waycross, Georgia.

He was married for the first and only time during his 62 years of life to Mrs. Lizzie P. Brown, November 19, 1935. There are no children. He gives no reason for remaining single, but his reason for marrying was "to give some lady the privilege and see how it feels to be called husband."

REFERENCES
1. Interview with Young Winston Davis, 742 W. 10th Street, Jacksonville, Florida

DOUGLAS DORSEY

FEDERAL WRITERS' PROJECT
American Guide, (Negro Writers' Unit)
James Johnson, Field Worker
South Jacksonville, Florida
January 11, 1937

In South Jacksonville, on the Spring Glen Road lives Douglas Dorsey, an ex-slave, born in Suwannee County, Florida in 1851, fourteen years prior to freedom. His parents Charlie and Anna Dorsey were natives of Maryland and free people. In those days, Dorsey relates there were people known as "Nigger Traders" who used any subterfuge to catch Negroes and sell them into slavery. There was one Jeff Davis who was known as a professional "Nigger Trader," his slave boat docked in the slip at Maryland and Jeff Davis and his henchmen went out looking for their victims. Unfortunately, his mother Anna and his father were caught one night and were bound and gagged and taken to Jeff Davis' boat which was waiting in the harbor, and there they were put into stocks. The boat stayed in port until it was loaded with Negroes, then sailed for Florida where Davis disposed of his human cargo.

Douglas Dorsey's parents were sold to Colonel Louis Matair, who had a large plantation that was cultivated by 85 slaves. Colonel Matair's house was of the pretentious southern colonial type which was quite prevalent during that period. The colonel had won his title because of his participation in the Indian War in Florida. He was the typical wealthy southern gentleman, and was very kind to his slaves. His wife, however was just the opposite. She was exceedingly mean and could easily be termed a tyrant.

There were several children in the Matair family and their home and plantation were located in Suwannee County, Florida.

Douglas' parents were assigned to their tasks, his mother was house-maid and his father was the mechanic, having learned this trade in Maryland as a free man. Charlie and Anna had several children and Douglas was among them. When he became large enough he was kept in the Matair home to build fires, assist in serving meals and other chores.

Mrs. Matair being a very cruel woman, would whip the slaves herself for any misdemeanor. Dorsey recalls an incident that is hard to obliterate from his mind, it is as follows: Dorsey's mother was called by Mrs. Matair, not hearing her, she continued with her duties, suddenly Mrs. Matair burst out in a frenzy of anger over the woman not answering. Anna explained that she did not hear her call, thereupon Mrs. Matair seized a large butcher knife and struck at Anna, attempting to ward off the blow, Anna received a long gash on the arm that laid her up for for some time. Young Douglas was a witness to this brutal treatment of his mother and he at that moment made up his mind to kill his mistress. He intended to put strychnine that was used to kill rats into her coffee that he usually served her.

Fortunately freedom came and saved him of this act which would have resulted in his death.

He relates another incident in regard to his mistress as follows: To his mother and father was born a little baby boy, whose complexion was rather light. Mrs. Matair at once began accusing Colonel Matair as being the father of the child. Naturally the colonel denied, but Mrs. Matair kept harassing him about it until he finally agreed to his wife's desire and sold the child. It was taken from its mother's breast at the age of eight months and auctioned off on the first day of January to the highest bidder. The child was bought by a Captain Ross and taken across the Suwannee River into Hamilton County. Twenty years later he was located by his family, he was a grown man, married and farming.

Young Douglas had the task each morning of carrying the Matair children's books to school. Willie, a boy of eight would teach Douglas what he learned in school, finally Douglas learned the alphabet and numbers. In some way Mrs. Matair learned that Douglas was learning to read and write. One morning after breakfast she called her son Willie to the dining room where she was seated and then sent for Douglas to come there too. She then took a quill pen the kind used at that time, and began writing the alphabet and numerals as far as ten. Holding the paper up to Douglas, she asked him if he knew what they were; he proudly answered in the affirmative, not suspecting anything. She then asked him to name the letters and numerals, which he did, she then asked him to write them, which he did. When he reached the number ten, very proud of his learning, she struck him a heavy blow across the face, saying to him "If I ever catch you making another figure anywhere I'll cut off your right arm." Naturally Douglas and also her son Willie were much surprised as each thought what had been done was quite an achievement. She then called Mariah, the cook to bring a rope and tying the two of them to the old colonial post on the front porch, she took a chair and sat between the two, whipping them on their naked backs for such a time, that for two weeks their clothes stuck to their backs on the lacerated flesh.

To ease the soreness, Willie would steal grease from the house and together they would slip into the barn and grease each other's backs.

As to plantation life, Dorsey said that the slaves lived in quarters especially built for them on the plantation. They would leave for the fields at "sun up" and remain until "sun-down," stopping only for a meal which they took along with them.

Instead of having an overseer they had what was called a "driver" by the name of Januray[TR:?]. His duties were to get the slaves together in the morning and see that they went to the fields and assigned them to their tasks. He worked as the other slaves, though, he had more priveliges. He would stop work at any time he pleased and go around to inspect the work of the others, and thus rest himself. Most of the orders from the master were issued to him. The crops consisted of cotton, corn, cane and peas, which was raised in abundance.

When the slaves left the fields, they returned to their

cabins and after preparing and eating of their evening meal they gathered around a cabin to sing and moan songs seasoned with African melody. Then to the tune of an old fiddle they danced a dance called the "Green Corn Dance" and "Cut the Pigeon wing." Sometimes the young men on the plantation would slip away to visit a girl on another plantation. If they were caught by the "Patrols" while on these visits they would be lashed on the bare backs as a penalty for this offense.

A whipping post was used for this purpose. As soon as one slave was whipped, he was given the whip to whip his brother slave. Very often the lashes would bring blood very soon from the already lacerated skin, but this did not stop the lashing until one had received their due number of lashes.

Occasionally the slaves were ordered to church to hear a white minister, they were seated in the front pews of the master's church, while the whites sat in the rear. The minister's admonition to them to honor their masters and mistresses, and to have no other God but them, as "we cannot see the other God, but you can see your master and mistress." After the services the driver's wife who could read and write a little would tell them that what the minister said "was all lies."

Douglas says that he will never forget when he was a lad 14 years of age, when one evening he was told to go and tell the driver to have all the slaves come up to the house; soon the entire host of about 85 slaves were gathered there all sitting around on stumps, some standing. The colonel's son was visibly moved as he told them they were free. Saying they could go anywhere they wanted to for he had no more to do with them, or that they could remain with him and have half of what was raised on the plantation.

The slaves were happy at this news, as they had hardly been aware that there had been a war going on. None of them accepted the offer of the colonel to remain, as they were only too glad to leaver the cruelties of the Matair plantation.

Dorsey's father got a job with Judge Carraway of Suwannee where he worked for one year. He later homesteaded 40 acres of land that he received from the government and began farming. Dorsey's father died in Suwannee County, Florida when Douglas was a young man and then he and his mother moved to Arlington, Florida. His mother died several years ago at a ripe old age.

Douglas Dorsey, aged but with a clear mind lives with his daughter in Spring Glen.

REFERENCE
1. Interview with Douglas Dorsey, living on Spring Glen Road, South Jacksonville, Florida

AMBROSE DOUGLASS

FEDERAL WRITERS' PROJECT
American Guide, (Negro Writers' Unit)
Martin D. Richardson, Field Worker
Brooksville, Florida

In 1861, when he was 16 years old, Ambrose Hilliard Douglass was given a sound beating by his North Carolina master because he attempted to refuse the mate that had been given to him—with the instructions to produce a healthy boy-child by her—and a long argument on the value of having good, strong, healthy children. In 1937, at the age of 92, Ambrose Douglass welcomed his 38th child into the world.

The near-centenarian lives near Brooksville, in Hernando County, on a run-down farm that he no longer attempts to tend now that most of his 38 children have deserted the farm for the more lucrative employment of the cities of the phosphate camps.

Douglass was born free in Detroit in 1845. His parents returned South to visit relatives still in slavery, and were soon reenslaved themselves, with their children. Ambrose was one of these.

For 21 years he remained in slavery; sometimes at the plantation of his original master in North Carolina, sometimes in other sections after he had been sold to different masters.

"Yassuh, I been sold a lot of times", the old man states. "Our master didn't believe in keeping a house, a horse or a darky after he had a chance to make some money on him. Mostly, though, I was sold when I cut up".

"I was a young man", he continues, "and didn't see why I should be anybody's slave. I'd run away every chance I got. Sometimes they near killed me, but mostly they just sold me. I guess I was pretty husky, at that."

"They never did get their money's worth out of me, though. I worked as long as they stood over me, then I ran around with the gals or sneaked off to the woods. Sometimes they used to put dogs on me to get me back.

"When they finally sold me to a man up in Suwannee County—his name was Harris—I thought it would be the end of the world. We had heard about him all the way up in Virginia. They said he beat you, starved you and tied you up when you didn't work, and killed you if you ran away.

"But I never had a better master. He never beat me, and always fed all of us. 'Course, we didn't get too much to eat; corn meal, a little piece of fat meat now and then, cabbages, greens, potatoes, and plenty of molasses. When I worked up at 'the house' I et just what the master et; sometimes he would give it to me his-self. When he didn't, I et it anyway.

"He was so good, and I was so scared of him, till I didn't ever run away from his place", Ambrose reminisces; "I had somebody there that I liked, anyway. When he finally went to the war, he sold me back to a man in North Carolina, in Hornett County. But the war was near over then; I soon was as free as I am now.

"I guess we musta celebrated 'Mancipation about twelve times in Hornett County. Every time a bunch of No'thern sojers would come through they would tell us we was free and we'd begin celebratin'. Before we would get through somebody else would tell us to go back to work, and we would go. Some of us wanted to jine up with the army, but didn't know who was goin' to win and didn't take no chances.

"I was 21 when freedom finally came, and that time I didn't take no chances on 'em taking it back again. I lit out for Florida and wound up in Madison County. I had a nice time there; I got married, got a plenty of work, and made me a little money. I fixed houses, built 'em, worked around the yards, and did everything. My first child was already born; I didn't know there was goin' to be 37 more, though. I guess I would have stopped right there....

"I stayed in Madison County until they started to working concrete rock down here. I heard about it and thought that would be a good way for me to feed all them two dozen children I had. So I came down this side. That was about 20 years ago.

"I got married again after I got here; right soon after. My wife now is 30 years old; we already had 13 children together. (His wife is a slight, girlish-looking woman; she says she was 13 when she married Douglass, had her first child that year. Eleven of her thirteen are still living.)

"Yossuh, I ain't long stopped work. I worked here in the phosphate mine until last year, when they started to paying pensions. I thought I would get one, but all I got was some PWA work, and this year they told me I was too old for that. I told 'em I wasn't but 91, but they didn't give nothin' else. I guess I'll get my pension soon, though. My oldest boy ought to get it, too; he's sixty-five."

FOLK STUFF, FLORIDA

Jules A. Frost
Tampa, Florida
May 19, 1937
"MAMA DUCK"

"Who is the oldest person, white or colored, that you know of in Tampa?"

"See Mama Duck," the grinning Negro elevator boy told me. "She bout a hunnert years old."

So down into the "scrub" I went and found the old woman hustling about from washpot to pump. "I'm mighty busy now, cookin breakfast," she said, "but if you come back in bout an hour I'll tell you what I can bout old times in Tampa."

On the return visit, her skinny dog met me with elaborate demonstrations of welcome.

"Guan way fum here Spot. Dat gemmen ain gwine feed you nothin. You keep your dirty paws offen his clothes."

Mama duck sat down on a rickety box, motioning me to another one on the shaky old porch. "Take keer you doan fall thoo dat old floor," she cautioned. "It's bout ready to fall to pieces, but I way behind in the rent, so I kaint ask em to have it fixed."

"I see you have no glass in the windows—doesn't it get you wet when it rains?"

"Not me. I gits over on de other side of de room. It didn't have no door neither when I moved in. De young folks frum here useta use it for a courtin-house."

"A what?"

"Courtin-house. Dey kept a-comin after I moved in, an I had to shoo em away. Dat young rascal comin yonder—he one of em. I clare to goodness—" and Mama Duck raised her voice for the trespasser's benefit, "I wisht I had me a fence to keep folks outa my yard."

"Qua-a-ck, quack, quack," the young Negro mocked, and passed on grinning.

"Dat doan worry me none; I doan let nothin worry me. Worry makes folks gray-headed." She scratched her head where three gray braids, about the length and thickness of a flapper's eyebrow, stuck out at odd angles.

"I sho got plenty chancet to worry ifen I wants to," she mused, as she sipped water from a fruit-jar foul with fingermarks. "Relief folks got me on dey black list. Dey won't give me rations—dey give rations to young folks whas workin, but won't give me nary a mouthful."

"Why is that?"

"Well, dey wanted me to go to de poor house. I was willin to go, but I wanted to take my trunk along an dey wouldn't let me. I got some things in dere I been havin nigh onta a hunnert years. Got my old blue-back Webster, onliest book I ever had, scusin my Bible. Think I wanna throw dat stuff away? No-o, suh!" Mama Duck pushed the dog away from a cracked pitcher on the floor and refilled her fruit-jar. "So day black list me, cause I won't kiss dey feets. I ain kissin nobody's feets—wouldn't kiss my own mammy's."

"Well, we'd all do lots of things for our mothers that we wouldn't do for anyone else."

"Maybe you would, but not me. My mammy put me in a hickry basket when I was a day an a half old, with nothin on but my belly band an diaper. Took me down in de cotton patch an sot me on a stump in de bilin sun."

"What in the world did she do that for?"

"Cause I was black. All de other younguns was bright. My granmammy done hear me bawlin an go fotch me to my mammy's house. 'Dat you mammy?' she ask, sweet as pie, when granmammy pound on de door.

"'Doan you never call me mammy no more,' granmammy say. 'Any woman what'd leave a poor lil mite like dis to perish to death ain fitten to be no datter o' mine.'

"So granmammy took me to raise. I ain never seen my mammy sincet, an I ain never wanted to."

"What did your father think of the way she treated you?"

"Never knew who my daddy was, an I reckon she didn't either."

"Do you remember anything about the Civil War?"

"What dat?"

"The Civil War, when they set the slaves free."

"Oh, you mean de fust war. I reckon I does—had three chillern, boys, borned fore de war. When I was old enough to work I was taken to Pelman, Jawja. Dey let me nust de chillern. Den I got married. We jus got married in de kitchen and went to our log house.

"I never got no beatins fum my master when I was a slave. But I seen collored men on de Bradley plantation git frammed out plenty. De whippin boss was Joe Sylvester. He had pets amongst de women folks, an let some of em off light when they deserved good beatins."

"How did he punish his 'pets'?"

"Sometimes he jus bop em crosst de ear wid a battlin stick."

"A what?"

"Battlin stick, like dis. You doan know what a battlin stick is? Well, dis here is one. Use it for washin clothes. You lift em outa de wash pot wid de battlin stick; den you lay em on de battlin block, dis here stump. Den you beat de dirt out wid de battlin stick."

"A stick like that would knock a horse down!"

"Wan't nigh as bad as what some of de others got. Some of his pets amongst de mens got it wusser dan de womens. He strap em crosst de sharp side of a barrel an give em a few right smart licks wid a bull whip."

"And what did he do to the bad ones?"

"He make em cross dere hands, den he tie a rope roun dey wrists an throw it over a tree limb. Den he pull em up so dey toes jus touch de ground an smack em on da back an rump wid a heavy wooden paddle, fixed full o' holes. Den he make em lie down on de ground while he bust all dem blisters wid a raw-hide whip."

"Didn't that kill them?"

"Some couldn't work for a day or two. Sometimes dey throw salt brine on dey backs, or smear on turputine to make it git well quicker."

"I suppose you're glad those days are over."

"Not me. I was a heap better off den as I is now. Allus had sumpun to eat an a place to stay. No sich thing as gittin on a black list. Mighty hard on a pusson old as me not to git no rations an not have no reglar job."

"How old are you?"

"I doun know, zackly. Wait a minnit, I didn't show you my pitcher what was in de paper, did I? I kaint read, but somebody say dey put how old I is under my pitcher in dat paper."

Mama Duck rummaged through a cigar box and brought out a page of a Pittsburgh newspaper, dated in 1936. It was so badly worn that it was almost illegible, but it showed a picture of Mama Duck and below it was given her age, 109.

Slave Narratives

FLORIDA FOLKLORE

Jules Abner Frost
May 19, 1937
"MAMA DUCK"

1. Name and address of informant, Mama Duck, Governor & India Sts., Tampa, Florida.

2. Date and time of interview, May 19, 1937, 9:30 A.M.

3. Place of interview, her home, above address.

4. Name and address of person, if any, who put you in touch with informant, J.D. Davis (elevator operator), 1623 Jefferson St., Tampa, Florida.

5. Name and address of person, if any accompanying you (none).

6. Description of room, house, surroundings, etc.

Two-room unpainted shack, leaky roof, most window panes missing, porch dangerous to walk on. House standing high on concrete blocks. Located in alley, behind other Negro shacks.

NOTE: Letter of Feb. 17, 1939, from Mr. B.A. Botkin to Dr. Corse states that my ex-slave story, "Mama Duck" is marred by use of the question and answer method. In order to make this material of use as American Folk Stuff material, I have rewritten it, using the first person, as related by the informant.

Personal History of Informant
[TR: Repetitive information removed.]

1. Ancestry: Negro.

2. Place and date of birth: Richard (probably Richmond), Va., about 1828.

3. Family: unknown.

4. Places lived in, with dates: Has lived in Tampa since about 1870.

5. Education, with dates: Illiterate.

6. Occupations and accomplishments, with dates: None. Informant was a slave, and has always performed common labor.

7. Special skills and interests: none.

8. Community and religious activities: none.

9. Description of informant: Small, emaciated, slightly graying, very thin kinky hair, tightly braided in small pigtails. Somewhat wrinkled, toothless. Active for her age, does washing for a living.

10. Other points gained in interview: Strange inability of local Old Age Pension officials to establish right of claimants to benefits. Inexplainable causes of refusal of direct relief.

MAMA DUCK
Gwan away f'm here, Po'-Boy; dat gemmen ain't gwine feed you nuthin. You keep yo' dirty paws offen his close.

Come in, suh. Take care you don't fall thoo dat ol' po'ch flo'; hit 'bout ready to go t' pieces, but I 'way behind on rent, so I cain't ask 'em to have hit fixed. Dis ol' house aint fitten fer nobody t' live in; winder glass gone an' roof leaks. Young folks in dese parts done be'n usin' it fer a co't house 'fore I come; you know—a place to do dey courtin' in. Kep' a-comin' atter I done move in, an' I had to shoo 'em away.

Dat young rascal comin' yondah, he one of 'em. I claiah to goodness, I wisht I had a fence to keep folks outa my yahd. Reckon you don't know what he be quackin' lak dat fer. Dat's 'cause my name's "Mama Duck." He doin' it jus' t' pester me. But dat don't worry me none; I done quit worryin'.

I sho' had plenty chance to worry, though. Relief folks got me on dey black list. Dey give rashuns to young folks what's wukkin' an' don't give me nary a mouthful. Reason fer dat be 'cause dey wanted me t' go t' de porehouse. I wanted t' take my trunk 'long, an' dey wouldn't lemme. I got some things in dere I be'n havin' nigh onto a hunnert years. Got my ol' blueback Webster, onliest book I evah had, 'scusin' mah Bible. Think I wanna th'ow dat away? No-o suh!

So dey black-list me, 'cause I won't kiss dey feets. I ain't kissin nobody's, wouldn't kiss my own mammy's.

I nevah see my mammy. She put me in a hick'ry basket when I on'y a day and a half old, with nuthin' on but mah belly band an' di'per. Took me down in de cotton patch an' sot de basket on a stump in de bilin sun. Didn't want me, 'cause I be black. All de otha youngins o' hers be bright.

Gran'mammy done tol' me, many a time, how she heah me bawlin' an' go an' git me, an' fotch me to mammy's house; but my own mammy, she say, tu'n me down cold.

"Dat you, Mammy" she say, sweet as pie, when gran'mammy knock on de do'.

"Dont you nevah call me 'Mammy' no mo'," gran'mammy tol' 'er. "Any woman what'd leave a po' li'l mite lak dat to perish to death ain't fitten t' be no dotter o' mine."

So gran'mammy tuk me to raise, an' I ain't nevah wanted no mammy but her. Nevah knowed who my daddy was, an' I reckon my mammy didn't know, neithah. I bawn at Richard, Vahjinny. My sistah an' brothah be'n dead too many years to count; I de las' o' de fam'ly.

I kin remember 'fore de fust war start. I had three chillen, boys, taller'n me when freedom come. Mah fust mastah didn't make de li'l chillen wuk none. All I done was play. W'en I be ol' enough t' wuk, dey tuk us to Pelman, Jawjah. I never wukked in de fiel's none, not den. Dey allus le me nuss de chillens.

Den I got married. Hit wa'nt no church weddin'; we got married in gran'mammy's kitchen, den we go to our own log house. By an' by mah mahster sol' me an' mah baby to de man what had de plantation nex' to ours. His name was John Lee. He was good to me, an' let me see my chillens.

I nevah got no beatin's. Onliest thing I evah got was a li'l slap on de han', lak dat. Didn't hurt none. But I'se seen cullud men on de Bradley plantation git tur'ble beatin's. De whippin' boss was Joe Sylvester, a white man. He had pets mongst de wimmen folks, an' used t' let 'em off easy, w'en dey desarved a good beatin'. Sometimes 'e jes' bop 'em crost de ear wid a battlin' stick, or kick 'em in de beehind.

You don't know what's a battlin' stick? Well, dis here be one. You use it fer washin' close. You lif's de close outa de wash pot wid dis here battlin' stick; den you tote 'em to de battlin' block—dis here stump. Den you beat de dirt out wid de battlin' stick.

De whippin' boss got pets 'mongst de mens, too, but dey got it a li'l wusser'n de wimmens. Effen dey wan't too mean, he jes' strap 'em 'crost de sharp side of a bar'l an' give 'em a few right smaht licks wid a bull whip.

But dey be some niggahs he whip good an' hard. If dey sass back, er try t' run away, he mek 'em cross dey han's lak dis; den he pull 'em up, so dey toes jes' tetch de ground'; den he smack 'em crost de back an' rump wid a big wood paddle, fixed full o' holes. Know what dem holes be for? Ev'y hole mek a blister. Den he mek 'em lay down on de groun', whilst he bus' all dem blisters wid a rawhide whip.

I nevah heard o' nobody dyin' f'm gittin' a beatin'. Some couldn't wuk fer a day or so. Sometimes de whippin' boss th'ow salt brine on dey backs, or smear on turpentine, to mek it well quicker.

I don't know, 'zackly, how old I is. Mebbe—wait a minute, I didn't show you my pitcher what was in de paper. I cain't read, but somebody say dey put down how old I is undah mah pitcher. Dar hit—don't dat say a hunndrt an' nine? I reckon dat be right, seein' I had three growed-up boys when freedom come.

Dey be on'y one sto' here when I come to Tampa. Hit b'long t' ol' man Mugge. Dey be a big cotton patch where Plant City is now. I picked some cotton dere, den I come to Tampa, an' atter a while I got a job nussin' Mister Perry Wall's chillen. Cullud folks jes' mek out de bes' dey could. Some of 'em lived in tents, till dey c'd cut logs an' build houses wid stick-an'-dirt chimbleys.

Lotta folks ask me how I come to be called "Mama Duck." Dat be jes' a devil-ment o' mine. I named my own se'f dat. One day when I be 'bout twelve year old, I come home an' say, "Well, gran'mammy, here come yo' li'l ducky home again." She hug me an' say, "Bress mah li'l ducky." Den she keep on callin' me dat, an' when I growed up, folks jes' put de "Mama" on.

I reckon I a heap bettah off dem days as I is now. Allus had sumpin t' eat an' a place t' stay. No sech thing ez gittin' on a black list dem days. Mighty hard on a pusson ol' az me not t' git no rashuns an' not have no reg'lar job.

WILLIS DUKES

FEDERAL WRITERS' PROJECT
American Guide, (Negro Writers' Unit)
Pearl Randolph, Field Worker
Madison, Florida
January 30, 1937

Born in Brooks County, Georgia, 83 years ago on February 24th, Willie[TR:?] Dukes jovially declares that he is "on the high road to livin' a hund'ed years."

He was one of 40 slaves belonging to one John Dukes, who was only in moderate circumstances. His parents were Amos and Mariah Dukes, both born on this plantation, he thinks. As they were a healthy pair they were required to work long hours in the fields, although the master was not actually cruel to them.

On this plantation a variety of products was grown, cotton, corn, potatoes, peas, rice and sugar cane. Nothing was thrown away and the slaves had only coarse foods such as corn bread, collard greens, peas and occasionally a little rice or white bread. Even the potatoes were reserved for the white folk and "house niggers."

As a child Willis was required to "tote water and wood, help at milking time and run errands." His clothing consisted of only a homespun shirt that was made on the plantation. Nearly everything used was grown or manufactured on the plantation. Candles were made in the big house by the cook and a batch of slaves from the quarters, all of them being required to bring fat and tallow that had been saved for this purpose. These candles were for the use of the master and mistress, as the slaves used fat lightwood torches for lighting purposes. Cotton was used for making clothes, and it was spun and woven into cloth by the slave women, then stored in the commisary for future use. Broggan shoes were made of tanned leather held together by tacks made of maple wood. Lye soap was made in large pots, cut into chunks and issued from the smoke house. Potash was secured from the ashes of burnt oak wood and allowed to set in a quantity of grease that had also been saved for the purpose, then boiled into soap.

The cotton was gathered in bags of bear grass and deposited in baskets woven with strips of white oak that had been dried in the sun.

Willis remembers the time when a slave on the plantation escaped and went north to live. This man managed to communicate with his family somehow, and it was whispered about that he was "living very high" and actually saving money with which to buy his family. He was even going to school. This fired all the slaves with an ambition to go north and this made them more than usually interested in the outcome of the war between the states. He was too young to fully understand the meaning of freedom but wanted very much to go away to some place where he could earn enough money to buy his mother a real silk dress. He confided this information to her and she was very proud of him but gave him a good spanking for fear he expressed this desire for freedom to his young master or mistress.

Prayer meetings were very frequent during the days of the war and very often the slaves were called in from the fields and excused from their labors so they could hold these prayer meetings, always praying God for the safe return of their master.

The master did not return after the war and when the soldiers in blue came through that section the frightened women were greatly dependent upon their slaves for protection and livelihood. Many of these black man chose loyalty to their dead masters to freedom and shouldered the burden of the support of their former mistresses cheerfully.

After the war Willis' father was one of those to remain with his widowed mistress. Other members of his family left as soon as they were freed, even his wife. They thus remained separated until her death.

Willis saw his first bedspring about 50 years ago and he still thinks a feather mattress superior to the store-bought variety. He recalls a humorous incident which occurred when he was a child and had been introduced for the first time to the task of picking a goose.

After demonstrating how it was done to a group of slave children, the person in charge had gone about his way leaving them busily engaged in picking the goose. They had been told that the one gathering the most feathers would receive a piece of money. Sometimes later the overseer returned to find a dozen geese that had been stripped of all the feathers. They had been told to pick only the pin feathers beneath the wings and about the bodies of the geese. Need we guess what happened to the over ambitious children?

He had heard of ice long before he looked upon it and he only thought of it as another wild experiment. Why buy ice, when watermelons and butter could be ley down into the well to keep cool?

One of Willis' happiest moments was when he earned enough money to buy his first pair of patern leather shoes. To possess a paid of store bought shoes had been his ambition since he was a child, when he had to shine the shoes of his master and those of the master's children.

He next owned a horse and buggy of which he was very proud. This increased his popularity with the girls and bye and bye he was married to Mary, a girl with whom he had been reared. Nobody was surprised but Mary, explained Mr. Dukes. "Me and everybody else knowed us ud get married some day. We didn't jump over no broom neither. We was married like white folks wid flowers and cake and everything."

Willis Dukes has been in Florida for "Lawd knows how long" and prefers this state to his home state. He still has a few relatives there but has never returned since leaving so long ago.

REFERENCE
1. Personal Interview with Willis Dukes, Valdosta Road, near Jeslamb Church, Madison, Florida

SAM AND LOUISA EVERETT

FEDERAL WRITERS' PROJECT
American Guide, (Negro Writers' Unit)
Pearl Randolph, Field Worker
John A. Simms, Editor
Mulberry, Florida
October 8, 1936

Sam and Louise Everett, 86 and 90 years of age respectively, have weathered together some of the worst experiences of slavery, and as they look back over the years, can relate these experiences as clearly as if they had happened only yesterday.

Both were born near Norfolk, Virginia and sold as slaves several times on nearby plantations. It was on the plantation of "Big Jim" McClain that they met as slave-children and departed after Emancipation to live the lives of free people.

Sam was the son of Peter and Betsy Everett, field hands who spent long back-breaking hours in the cotton fields and came home at nightfall to cultivate their small garden. They lived in constant fear that their master would confiscate most of their vegetables; he so often did.

Louisa remembers little about her parents and thinks that she was sold at an early age to a separate master. Her name as nearly as she could remember was Norfolk Virginia. Everyone called her "Nor." It was not until after she was freed and had sent her children to school that she changed her name to Louisa.

Sam and Norfolk spent part of their childhood on the plantation of "Big Jim" who was very cruel; often he would whip his slaves into insensibility for minor offences. He sometimes hung them up by their thumbs whenever they were caught attempting to escape—"er fer no reason atall."

On this plantation were more than 100 slaves who were mated indiscriminately and without any regard for family unions. If their master thought that a certain man and woman might have strong, healthy offspring, he forced them to have sexual relation, even though they were married to other slaves. If there seemed to be any slight reluctance on the part of either of the unfortunate ones "Big Jim" would make them consummate this relationship in his presence. He used the same procedure if he thought a certain couple was not producing children fast enough. He enjoyed these orgies very much and often entertained his friends in this manner; quite often he and his guests would engage in these debaucheries, choosing for themselves the prettiest of the young women. Sometimes they forced the unhappy husbands and lovers of their victims to look on.

Louisa and Sam were married in a very revolting manner. To quote the woman:

"Marse Jim called me and Sam ter him and ordered Sam to pull off his shirt—that was all the McClain niggers wore—and he said to me: 'Nor, do you think you can stand this big nigger?' He had that old bull whip flung acrost his shoulder, and Lawd, that man could hit so hard! So I jes said 'yassur, I guess so,' and tried to hide my face so I couldn't see Sam's nakedness, but he made me look at him anyhow."

"Well, he told us what we must git busy and do in his presence, and we had to do it. After that we were considered man and wife. Me and Sam was a healthy pair and had fine, big babies, so I never had another man forced on me, thank God. Sam was kind to me and I learnt to love him."

Life on the McClain plantation was a steady grind of work from morning until night. Slaves had to rise in the dark of the morning at the ringing of the "Big House" bell. After eating a hasty breakfast of fried fat pork and corn pone, they worked in the fields until the bell rang again at noon; at which time they ate boiled vegetables, roasted sweet potatoes and black molasses. This food was cooked in iron pots which had legs attached to their bottoms in order to keep them from resting directly on the fire. These utensils were either hung over a fire or set atop a mound of hot coals. Biscuits were a luxury but whenever they had white bread it was cooked in another thick pan called a "spider". This pan had a top which was covered with hot embers to insure the browning of the bread on top.

Slave women had no time for their children. These were cared for by an old woman who called them twice a day and fed them "pot likker" (vegetable broth) and skimmed milk. Each child was provided with a wooden laddle which he dipped into a wooden trough and fed himself. The older children fed those who were too young to hold a laddle.

So exacting was "Big Jim" that slaves were forced to work even when sick. Expectant mothers toiled in the fields until they felt their labor pains. It was not uncommon for babies to be born in the fields.

There was little time for play on his plantation. Even the very small children were assigned tasks. They hunted hen's eggs, gathered poke berries for dyeing, shelled corn and drove the cows home in the evening. Little girls knitted stockings.

There was no church on this plantation and itinerant ministers avoided going there because of the owner's cruelty. Very seldom were the slaves allowed to attend neighboring churches and still rarer were the opportunities to hold meetings among themselves. Often when they were in the middle of a song or prayer they would be forced to halt and run to the "Big House." Woe to any slave who ignored the ringing of the bell that summoned him to work and told him when he might "knock off" from his labors.

Louisa and Sam last heard the ringing of this bell in the fall of 1865. All the slaves gathered in front of the "Big House" to be told that they were free for the time being. They had heard whisperings of the War but did not understand the meaning of it all. Now "Big Jim" stood weeping on the piazza and cursing the fate that had been so cruel to him by robbing him of all his "niggers." He inquired if any wanted to remain until all the crops were harvested and when no one consented to do so, he flew into a rage; seizing his pistol, he began firing into the crowd of frightened Negroes. Some were killed outright and others were maimed for life. Finally he was prevailed upon to stop. He then attempted to take his own life. A few frightened slaves promised to remain with him another year; this placated him. It was necessary for Union soldiers to make another visit to the plantation before "Big Jim" would allow his former slaves to depart.

Sam and Louisa moved to Boston, Georgia, where they sharecropped for several years; they later bought a small farm when their two sons became old enough to help. They continued to live on this homestead until a few years ago, when their advancing ages made it necessary that they live with the children. Both of the children had settled in Florida several years previous and wanted their parents to come to them. They now live in Mulberry, Florida with the younger son. Both are pitifully infirm but can still remember the horrors they experienced under very cruel owners. It was with difficulty that they were prevailed upon to relate some of the gruesome details recorded here.

REFERENCES
1. Personal interview with Sam and Louisa Everett, P.O. Box 535 c/o E.P.J. Everett, Mulberry, Florida

United States. Work Projects Administration

DUNCAN GAINES

FEDERAL WRITERS' PROJECT
American Guide, (Negro Writers' Unit)
Pearl Randolph, Field Worker
Madison, Florida
November 24, 1936

Duncan Gaines, the son of George and Martha Gaines was born on a plantation in Virginia on March 12, 1853. He was one of four children, all fortunate enough to remain with their parents until maturity. They were sold many times, but Duncan Gaines best remembers the master who was known as "old man Beever."

On this plantation were about 50 slaves, who toiled all day in the cotton and tobacco fields and came home at dusk to cook their meals of corn pone, collards and sweet potatoes on the hearths of their one room cabins. Biscuits were baked on special occasions by placing hot coals atop the iron tops of long legged frying pans called spiders, and the potatoes were roasted in the ashes, likewise the corn pone. Their masters being more or less kind, there was pork, chicken, syrup and other foodstuffs that they were allowed to raise as their own on a small scale. This work was often done by the light of a torch at night as they had little time of their own. In this way slaves earned money for small luxuries and the more ambitious sometimes saved enough money to buy their freedom, although this was not encouraged very much.

The early life of Duncan was carefree and happy. With the exception of carrying water to the laborers and running errands, he had little to do. Most of the time of the slave children was spent in playing ball and wrestling and foraging the woods for berries and fruits and playing games as other children. They were often joined in their play by the master's children, who taught them to read and write and fired Duncan with the ambition to be free, so that he could "wear a frill on his colar and own a pair of shoes that did not have brass caps on the toes" and require the application of fat to make them shine.

Wearing his shoes shined as explained above and a coarse homespun suit dyed with oak bark, indigo or poke berries, he went to church on Sunday afternoons after the whites had had their services and listened to sermons delivered by white ministers who taught obedience to their masters. After the services, most of the slaves would remove their shoes and carry them in their hands, as they were unaccustomed to wearing shoes except in winter.

The women were given Saturday afternoons off to launder their clothes and prepare for Sunday's services. All slaves were required to appear on Monday mornings as clean as possible with their clothing mended and heads combed.

Lye soap was used both for laundering and bathing. It was made from fragments of fat meat and skins that were carefully saved for that purpose. Potash was secured from oak ashes. This mixture was allowed to set for a certain period of time, then cooked to a jelly-like consistency. After cooling, the soap was cut into square bars and "lowanced out" (allowance) to the slaves according to the number in each family. Once Duncan was given a bar of "sweet" soap by his mistress for doing a particularly nice piece of work of polishing the harness of her favorite mare and so proud was he of the gift that he put it among his Sunday clothes to make them smell sweet. It was the first piece of toilet sopa that he had ever seen; and it caused quite a bit of envy among the other slave children.

Duncan Gaines does not remember his grandparents but thinks they were both living on some nearby plantation. His father was the plantation blacksmith and Duncan liked to look on as plowshares, single trees, horse shoes, etc were turned out or sharpened. His mother was strong and healthy, so she toiled all day in the fields. Duncan always listened for his mother's return from the field, which was heraled by a song, no matter how tired she was. She was very fond of her children and did not share the attitude of many slave mother who thought of their children as belonging solely to the masters. She lived in constant fear that "old marse Seever" would meet with some adversity and be forced to sell them separately. She always whispered to them about "de war" and fanned to a flame their desire to be free.

At that time Negro children listened to the tales of Raw Head and Bloody Bones, various animal stories and such childish ditties as:

"Little Boy, Little Boy who made your breeches? Mamma cut 'em out and pappa sewed de stitches."

Children were told that babies were dug out of tree stumps and were generally made to "shut up" if they questioned their elders about such matters.

Children with long or large heads were thought to be marked to become "wise men." Everyone believed in ghosts and entertained all the superstitions that have been handed down to the present generation. There was much talk of "hoodooism" and anyone ill for a long time without getting relief from herb medicines was thought to be "fixed" or suffering from some sin that his father had committed.

Duncan was 12 years of age when freedom was declared and remembers the hectic times which followed. He and other slave children attended schools provided by the Freedmen' Aid and other social organizations fostered by Northerners. Most of the instructors were whites sent to the South for that purpose.

The Gaines were industrious and soon owned a prosperous farm. They seldom had any money but had plenty of foodstuffs and clothing and a fairly comfortable home. All of the children secured enough learning to enable them to read and write, which was regarded as very unusual in those days. Slaves had been taught that their brain was inferior to the whites who owned them and for this reason, many parents refused to send their children to school, thinking it a waste of time and that too much learning might cause some injury to the brain of their supposedly weak-minded children.

Of the various changes, Duncan remembers very little, so gradual did they occur in his section. Water was secured from the spring or well. Perishable foodstuffs were let down into the well to keep cool. Shoes were made from leather tanned by setting in a solution of red oak bark and water; laundering was done in wooden tubs, made from barrels cut in halves. Candles were used for lighting and were made from sheep and beef tallow. Lightwood torches were used by those not able to afford candles. Stockings were knitted by the women during cold or rainy weather. Weaving and spinning done by special slave women who were too old to work in the fields; others made the cloth into garments. Everything was done by hand except the luxuries imported by the wealthy.

Duncan Gaines is now a widower and fast becoming infirm. He looks upon this "new fangled" age with bare tolerance and feels that the happiest age of mankind has passed with the discarding of the simple, old fashioned way of doing things.

REFERENCE
1. Personal interview with Duncan Gaines, Second Street near Madison Training School for Negroes, Madison, Florida

CLAYBORN GANTLING

FEDERAL WRITERS' PROJECT
American Guide, (Negro Writers' Unit)
Rachel Austin, Secretary
Jacksonville, Florida
April 16, 1937

Clayborn Gantling was born in Dawson, Georgia, Terrell County, January 20, 1848 on the plantation of Judge Williams.

Judge Williams owned 102 heads of slaves and was known to be "tolable nice to 'em in some way and pretty rough on 'em in other ways" says Mr. Gantling. "He would'nt gi' us no coffee, 'cept on Sunday Mornings when we would have shorts or seconds of wheat, which is de leavins' of flour at mills, yu' know, but we had plenty bacon, corn bread, taters and peas.

"As a child I uster have to tote water to de old people on de farm and tend de cows an' feed de sheep. Now, I can' say right 'zackly how things wuz during slavery 'cause its been a long time ago but we had cotton and corn fields and de hands plowed hard, picked cotton grabbled penders, gathered peas and done all the other hard work to be done on de plantations. I wuz not big 'nuff to do all of dem things but I seed plenty of it done.

"Dey made lye soap on de farms and used indigo from

wood for dye. We niggers slept on hay piled on top of planks but de white folks had better beds.

"I don't 'member my grandparents but my mas was called Harriet Williams and my pa was called Henry Williams; dey wuz called Williams after my master. My mas and pa worked very hard and got some beatings but I don't know what for. Dey wuz all kinds of money, five and ten dollar bills, and so on then, but I didn't ever see them with any.

"When war came along and Sherman came through the old people wuz very skeered on account of the white owners but there was no fighting close to me. My master's sons Leo and Fletcher joined the army and lots of de other masters went; de servants wuz sent along to wait on de young white men. Guess you'd like to know if any were killed. 'I should smile,' two I know were killed.

"During those days for medicine, the old people used such things as butterfly root and butterfly tea, sage tea, red oak bark, hippecat—something that grow—was used for fevers and bathing children. They wuz white doctors and plenty of colored grannies.

"When de Yankees came they acted diffunt and was naturally better to servants than our masters had been; we colored folks done the best we could but that was not so good right after freedom. Still it growed on and growed on getting better.

"Before freedom we always went to white churches on Sundays with passes but they never mentioned God;

they always told us to be "good niggers and mind our missus and masters".

"Judge Williams had ten or twelve heads of children but I can' 'member the names of 'em now; his wife was called Mis' 'Manda and she was jes' 'bout lak Marse Williams. I had 'bout eighteen head of boys and five girls myself; dere was so many, I can' 'member all of dem."

Mr. Gantling was asked to relate some incidents that he could remember of the lives of slaves, and he continued:

"Well the horn would blow every morning for you to git up and go right to work; when the sun ris' if you were not in the field working, you would be whipped with whips and leather strops. I 'member Aunt Beaty was beat until she could hardly get along but I can' 'member what for but do you know she had to work along till she got better. My ma had to work pretty hard but my oldest sister, Judy, was too young to work much.

"A heap of de slaves would run away and hide in de woods to keep from working so hard but the white folks to keep them from running away so that they could not ketch 'em would put a chain around the neck which would hang down the back and be fastened on to another 'round the waist and another 'round the feet so they could not run, still they had to work and sleep in 'em, too; sometimes they would wear these chains for three or four months.

"When a slave would die they had wooden boxes to

put 'em in and dug holes and just put then in. A slave might go to a sister or brother's funeral.

"My recollection is very bad and so much is forgotten, but I have seen slaves sold in droves like cows; they called 'em 'ruffigees,' and white men wuz drivin' 'em like hogs and cows for sale. Mothers and fathers were sold and parted from their chillun; they wuz sold to white people in diffunt states. I tell you chile, it was pitiful, but God did not let it last always. I have heard slaves morning and night pray for deliverance. Some of 'em would stand up in de fields or bend over cotton and corn and pray out loud for God to help 'em and in time you see, He did.

"They had whut you call "pattyrollers" who would catch you from home and 'wear you out' and send you back to your master. If a master had slaves he jes' could not rule (some of 'em wuz hard and jes' would not mind de boss), he would ask him if he wanted to go to another plantation and if he said he did, then, he would give him a pass and that pass would read: "Give this nigger hell." Of course whan the "pattyrollers" or other plantation boss would read the pass he would beat him nearly to death and send him back. Of course the nigger could not read and did not know what the pass said. You see, day did not 'low no nigger to have a book or piece of paper of any kind and you know dey wuz not go teach any of 'em to read.

"De women had it hard too; women with little babies would have to go to work in de mornings with the rest, come back, nurse their chillun and go back to the field, stay two or three hours then go back and eat dinner; after dinner dey would have to go to de field and stay two or three more hours then go and nurse the chillun again, go back to the field and stay till night. One or maybe two old women would stay in a big house and keep all de chillun while their mothers worked in de fields.

"Now dey is a heap more I could tell maybe but I don't think of no more now."

Mr. Gantling came to Florida to Jennings Plantation near Lake Park and stayed two years, then went to Everett's Plantation and stayed one year. From there he went to a place called High Hill and stayed two or three years. He left there and went to Jasper, farmed and stayed until he moved his family to Jacksonville. Here he worked on public works until he started raising hogs and chickens which he continued up to about fourteen years ago. Now, he is too old to do anything but just "sit around and talk and eat."

He lives with his daughter, Mrs. Minnie Holly and her husband, Mr. Dany Holly on Lee Street.

Mr. Gantling cannot read or write, but is very interesting.

He has been a member of the African Methodist Episcopal Church for more than fifty years.

He has a very good appetite and although has lost his teeth, he has never worn a plate or had any dental work done. He is never sick and has had but little medical attention during his lifetime. His form is bent and he walks with a cane; although his going is confined to his home, it is from choice as he seldom wears shoes on account of bad feet. His eyesight is very good and his hobby is sewing. He threads his own needles without assistance of glasses as he has never worn them.

Mr. Gantling celebrated his 89th birthday on the 20th day of November 1936.

He is very small, also very short; quite active for his age and of a very genial disposition, always smiling.

REFERENCE
1. Interview with Mr. Clayborn Gantling, 1950 Lee Street, Jacksonville, Florida

ARNOLD GRAGSTON

FEDERAL WRITERS PROJECT
American Guide, (Negro Writers' Unit)
Martin Richardson, Field Worker
Eatonville, Florida

Verbatim Interview with Arnold Gragston, 97-year-old ex-slave whose early life was spent helping slaves to freedom across the Ohio River, while he, himself, remained in bondage. As he puts it, he guesses he could be called a 'conductor' on the underground railway, "only we didn't call it that then. I don't know as we called it anything—we just knew there was a lot of slaves always a-wantin' to get free, and I had to help 'em."

"Most of the slaves didn't know when they was born, but I did. You see, I was born on a Christmas mornin'— it was in 1840; I was a full grown man when I finally got my freedom."

"Before I got it, though, I helped a lot of others get theirs. Lawd only knows how many; might have been as much as two-three hundred. It was 'way more than a hundred, I know."

"But that all came after I was a young man—'grown' enough to know a pretty girl when I saw one, and to go chasing after her, too. I was born on a plantation that b'longed to Mr. Jack Tabb in Mason County, just across the river in Kentucky."

"Mr. Tabb was a pretty good man. He used to beat us, sure; but not nearly so much as others did, some of his own kin people, even. But he was kinda funny sometimes; he used to have a special slave who didn't have nothin' to do but teach the rest of us—we had about ten on the plantation, and a lot on the other plantations near us—how to read and write and figger. Mr. Tabb liked us to know how to figger. But sometimes when he would send for us and we would be a long time comin', he would ask us where we had been. If we told him we had been learnin' to read, he would near beat the daylights out of us—after gettin' somebody to teach us; I think he did some of that so that the other owners wouldn't say he was spoilin' his slaves."

"He was funny about us marryin', too. He would let us go a-courtin' on the other plantations near anytime we liked, if we were good, and if we found somebody we wanted to marry, and she was on a plantation that b'longed to one of his kin folks or a friend, he would swap a slave so that the husband and wife could be together. Sometimes, when he couldn't do this, he would let a slave work all day on his plantation, and live with his wife at night on her plantation. Some of the other owners was always talking about his spoilin' us."

"He wasn't a Dimmacrat like the rest of 'em in the county; he belonged to the 'know-nothin' party' and he was a real leader in it. He used to always be makin' speeches, and sometimes his best friends wouldn't be speaking to him for days at a time."

"Mr. Tabb was always specially good to me. He used

to let me go all about—I guess he had to; couldn't get too much work out of me even when he kept me right under his eyes. I learned fast, too, and I think he kinda liked that. He used to call Sandy Davis, the slave who taught me, 'the smartest Nigger in Kentucky.'

"It was 'cause he used to let me go around in the day and night so much that I came to be the one who carried the runnin' away slaves over the river. It was funny the way I started it too."

"I didn't have no idea of ever gettin' mixed up in any sort of business like that until one special night. I hadn't even thought of rowing across the river myself."

"But one night I had gone on another plantation 'courtin,' and the old woman whose house I went to told me she had a real pretty girl there who wanted to go across the river and would I take her? I was scared and backed out in a hurry. But then I saw the girl, and she was such a pretty little thing, brown-skinned and kinda rosy, and looking as scared as I was feelin', so it wasn't long before I was listenin' to the old woman tell me when to take her and where to leave her on the other side."

"I didn't have nerve enough to do it that night, though, and I told them to wait for me until tomorrow night. All the next day I kept seeing Mister Tabb laying a rawhide across my back, or shootin' me, and kept seeing that scared little brown girl back at the house, looking at me with her big eyes and asking me if I wouldn't just row her across to Ripley. Me and Mr.

Tabb lost, and soon as dust settled that night, I was at the old lady's house."

"I don't know how I ever rowed the boat across the river the current was strong and I was trembling. I couldn't see a thing there in the dark, but I felt that girl's eyes. We didn't dare to whisper, so I couldn't tell her how sure I was that Mr. Tabb or some of the others owners would 'tear me up' when they found out what I had done. I just knew they would find out."

"I was worried, too, about where to put her out of the boat. I couldn't ride her across the river all night, and I didn't know a thing about the other side. I had heard a lot about it from other slaves but I thought it was just about like Mason County, with slaves and masters, overseers and rawhides; and so, I just knew that if I pulled the boat up and went to asking people where to take her I would get a beating or get killed."

"I don't know whether it seemed like a long time or a short time, now—it's so long ago; I know it was a long time rowing there in the cold and worryin'. But it was short, too, 'cause as soon as I did get on the other side the big-eyed, brown-skin girl would be gone. Well, pretty soon I saw a tall light and I remembered what the old lady had told me about looking for that light and rowing to it. I did; and when I got up to it, two men reached down and grabbed her; I started tremblin' all over again, and prayin'. Then, one of the men took my arm and I just felt down inside of me that the Lord had got ready for me. 'You hungry, Boy?' is what he asked me, and if he hadn't been holdin' me I think I would have fell backward into the river."

"That was my first trip; it took me a long time to get over my scared feelin', but I finally did, and I soon found myself goin' back across the river, with two and three people, and sometimes a whole boatload. I got so I used to make three and four trips a month.

"What did my passengers look like? I can't tell you any more about it than you can, and you wasn't there. After that first girl—no, I never did see her again—I never saw my passengers. I would have to be the "black nights" of the moon when I would carry them, and I would meet 'em out in the open or in a house without a single light. The only way I knew who they were was to ask them; "What you say?" And they would answer, "Menare." I don't know what that word meant—it came from the Bible. I only know that that was the password I used, and all of them that I took over told it to me before I took them.

"I guess you wonder what I did with them after I got them over the river. Well, there in Ripley was a man named Mr. Rankins; I think the rest of his name was John. He had a regular station there on his place for escaping slaves. You see, Ohio was a free state and once they got over the river from Kentucky or Virginia. Mr. Rankins could strut them all around town, and nobody would bother 'em. The only reason we used to land quietly at night was so that whoever brought 'em could go back for more, and because we had to be careful that none of the owners had followed us. Every once in a while they would follow a boat and catch their slaves back. Sometimes they would shoot at whoever was trying to save the poor devils.

"Mr. Rankins had a regular 'station' for the slaves. He

had a big lighthouse in his yard, about thirty feet high and he kept it burnin' all night. It always meant freedom for slave if he could get to this light.

"Sometimes Mr. Rankins would have twenty or thirty slaves that had run away on his place at the time. It must have cost him a whole lots to keep them and feed 'em, but I think some of his friends helped him.

"Those who wanted to stay around that part of Ohio could stay, but didn't many of 'em do it, because there was too much danger that you would be walking along free one night, feel a hand over your mouth, and be back across the river and in slavery again in the morning. And nobody in the world ever got a chance to know as much misery as a slave that had escaped and been caught.

"So a whole lot of 'em went on North to other parts of Ohio, or to New York, Chicago or Canada; Canada was popular then because all of the slaves thought it was the last gate before you got all the way inside of heaven. I don't think there was much chance for a slave to make a living in Canada, but didn't many of 'em come back. They seem like they rather starve up there in the cold than to be back in slavery.

"The Army soon started taking a lot of 'em, too. They could enlist in the Union Army and get good wages, more food than they ever had, and have all the little gals wavin' at 'em when they passed. Them blue uniforms was a nice change, too.

"No, I never got anything from a single one of the people I carried over the river to freedom. I didn't want anything; after had made a few trips I got to like it, and even though I could have been free any night myself, I figgered I wasn't getting along so bad so I would stay on Mr. Tabb's place and help the others get free. I did it for four years.

"I don't know to this day how he never knew what I was doing; I used to take some awful chances, and he knew I must have been up to something; I wouldn't do much work in the day, would never be in my house at night, and when he would happen to visit the plantation where I had said I was goin' I wouldn't be there. Sometimes I think he did know and wanted me to get the slaves away that way so he wouldn't have to cause hard feelins' by freein 'em.

"I think Mr. Tabb used to talk a lot to Mr. John Fee; Mr. Fee was a man who lived in Kentucky, but Lord! how that man hated slavery! He used to always tell us (we never let our owners see us listenin' to him, though) that God didn't intend for some men to be free and some men be in slavery. He used to talk to the owners, too, when they would listen to him, but mostly they hated the sight of John Fee.

"In the night, though, he was a different man, for every slave who came through his place going across the river he had a good word, something to eat and some kind of rags, too, if it was cold. He always knew just what to tell you to do if anything went wrong, and sometimes I think he kept slaves there on his place 'till they could be rowed across the river. Helped us a lot.

"I almost ran the business in the ground after I had

been carrying the slaves across for nearly four years. It was in 1863, and one night I carried across about twelve on the same night. Somebody must have seen us, because they set out after me as soon as I stepped out of the boat back on the Kentucky side; from that time on they were after me. Sometimes they would almost catch me; I had to run away from Mr. Tabb's plantation and live in the fields and in the woods. I didn't know what a bed was from one week to another. I would sleep in a cornfield tonight, up in the branches of a tree tomorrow night, and buried in a haypile the next night; the River, where I had carried so many across myself, was no good to me; it was watched too close.

"Finally, I saw that I could never do any more good in Mason County, so I decided to take my freedom, too. I had a wife by this time, and one night we quietly slipped across and headed for Mr. Rankin's bell and light. It looked like we had to go almost to China to get across that river: I could hear the bell and see the light on Mr. Rankin's place, but the harder I rowed, the farther away it got, and I knew if I didn't make it I'd get killed. But finally, I pulled up by the lighthouse, and went on to my freedom—just a few months before all of the slaves got their's. I didn't stay in Ripley, though; I wasn't taking no chances. I went on to Detroit and still live there with most of 10 children and 31 grandchildren.

"The bigger ones don't care so much about hearin' it now, but the little ones never get tired of hearin' how their grandpa brought Emancipation to loads of slaves he could touch and feel, but never could see."

REFERENCES

1. Interview with subject, Arnold Gragston, present address, Robert Hungerford College Campus, Eatonville (P.O. Maitland) Florida

(Subject is relative of President of Hungerford College and stays several months in Eatonville at frequent intervals. His home is Detroit, Michigan).

HARRIETT GRESHAM

FEDERAL WRITERS' PROJECT
American Guide, (Negro Writers' Unit)
Pearl Randolph, Field Worker
Jacksonville, Florida
December 18, 1936

Born on December 6, 1838, Harriett Gresham can recall quite clearly the major events of her life as a slave, also the Civil War as it affected the slaves of Charleston and Barnwell, South Carolina.

She was one of a, group of mulattoes belonging to Edmond Bellinger, a wealthy plantation owner of Barnwell. With her mother, the plantation seamstress and her father, a driver, she lived in the "big house" quarters, and was known as a "house nigger." She played with the children of her mistress and seldom mixed with the other slaves on the plantation.

To quote some of her quaint expressions: "Honey I aint know I was any diffrunt fum de chillen o' me mistress twel atter de war. We played and et and fit togetter lak chillen is bound ter do all over der world. Somethin allus happened though to remind me dat I was jist a piece of property."

"I heard der gun aboomin' away at Fort Sumpter and fer de firs' time in my life I knowed what it was ter fear anythin' cept a sperrit. No, I aint never seed one myself but—"

"By der goodness o'God I done lived ter waltz on der citadel green and march down a ile o' soldiers in blue, in der arms o' me husban', and over me haid de bay'nets shined."

"I done lived up all my days and some o' dem whut mighta b'longed ter somebody else is dey'd done right in der sight o' God." "How I know I so old?" "I got documents ter prove it." The documents is a yellow sheet of paper that appears to be stationery that is crudely decorated at the top with crissed crossed lines done in ink. Its contents in ink are as follows:

Harriett Pinckney, born September 25, 1790. Adeline, her daughter, born October 1, 1809. Betsy, her daughter, born September 11, 1811. Belinda, her daughter, born October 4, 1813. Deborah, her daughter, born December 1, 1815. Stephen, her son, born September 1, 1818.

Harriett's Grandchildren
Bella, the daughter of Adeline born July 5, 1827. Albert, son of Belinda born August 19, 1833. Laurence, son of Betsy born March 1, 1835. Sarah Ann Elizabeth, daughter of Belinda born January 3, 1836. Harriett, daughter of Belinda born December 6, 1838. (This record was given Harriett by Mrs. Harriett Bellinger, her mistress. Each slave received a similar one on being freed.)

As a child Harriett played about the premises of the Bellinger estate, leading a very carefree life as did all the slave children belonging to Edmond Bellinger. When she was about twelve years old she was given small tasks to do such as knitting a pair of stockings or dusting the furniture and ample time was given for each of these assignments.

This was a very large plantation and there was always something for the score of slaves to do. There were the wide acres of cotton that must be planted, hoed and gathered by hand. A special batch of slave women did the spinning and weaving, while those who had been taught to sew, made most of the clothing worn by slaves at that time.

Other products grown here were rice, corn, sugarcane, fruits and vegetables. Much of the food grown on the plantation was reserved to feed the slaves. While they must work hard to complete their tasks in a given time, no one was allowed to go hungry or forced to work if the least ill.

Very little had to be bought here. Candles ware made in the kitchen of the "big house," usually by the cook who was helped by other slaves. These were made of beeswax gathered on the plantation. Shoes were made of tanned dried leather and re-inforced with brass caps; the large herds of cattle, hogs and poultry furnished sufficient meat. Syrup and sugar were made from the cane that was carried to a neighboring mill.

Harriett remembers her master as being exceptionally kind but very severe when his patience was tried too far. Mrs. Bellinger was dearly loved by all her slaves because she was very thoughtful of them. Whenever there was a wedding, frolic or holiday or quilting bee, she was sure to provide some extra "goody" and so dear to the hearts of the women were the cast off clothes she so often bestowed upon them on these occasions.

The slaves were free to invite those from the neighboring plantations to join in their social gatherings. A Negro preacher delivered sermons on the plantation. Services being held in the church used by whites after their services on Sunday. The preacher must always act as a peacemaker and mouthpiece for the master, so they were told to be subservient to their masters in order to enter the Kingdom of God. But the slaves held secret meetings and had praying grounds where they met a few at a time to pray for better things.

Harriett remembers little about the selling of slaves because this was never done on the Bellinger plantation. All slaves were considered a part of the estate and to sell one, meant that it was no longer intact.

There were rumors of the war but the slaves on the Bellinger place did not grasp the import of the war until their master went to fight on the side of the Rebel army. Many of them gathered about their mistress and wept as he left the home to which he would never return. Soon after that it was whispered among the slaves that they would be free, but no one ran away.

After living in plenty all their lives, they were forced to do without coffee, sugar salt and beef. Everything available was bundled off to the army by Mrs. Bellinger who shared the popular belief that the soldiers must have the best in the way of food and clothing.

Harriett still remembers very clearly the storming of Fort Sumpter. The whole countryside was thrown into confusion and many slaves were mad with fear. There were few men left to establish order and many women loaded their slaves into wagons and gathered such belongings as they could and fled. Mrs. Bellinger was one of those who held their ground.

When the Union soldiers visited her plantation they found the plantation in perfect order. The slaves going about their tasks as if nothing unusual had happened. It was necessary to summon them from the fields to give them the message of their freedom.

Harriett recalls that her mistress was very frightened but walked upright and held a trembling lip between her teeth as they waited for her to sound for the last time the horn that had summoned several generations of human chattel to and from work.

Some left the plantation; others remained to harvest the crops. One and all they remembered to thank God for their freedom. They immediately began to hold meetings, singing soul stirring spirituals. Harriett recalls one of these songs. It is as follows:

T'ank ye Marster Jesus, t'ank ye,
T'ank ye Marster Jesus, t'ank ye,
T'ank ye Marster Jesus, t'ank ye
Da Heben gwinter be my home.
No slav'ry chains to tie me down,
And no mo' driver's ho'n to blow fer me
No mo' stocks to fasten me down
Jesus break slav'ry chain, Lord
Break slav'ry chain Lord,
Break slav'ry chain Lord,
Da Heben gwinter be my home.

Harriett's parents remained with the widowed woman for a while. Had they not remained, she might not have met Gaylord Jeannette, the knight in Blue, who later became her husband. He was a member of Company "I", 35th Regiment. She is still a bit breathless when she relates the details of the military wedding that followed a whirlwind courtship which had its beginning on the citadel green, where the soldiers stationed there held their dress parade. After these parades there was dancing by the soldiers and belles who had bedecked themselves in their Sunday best and come out to be wooed by a soldier in blue.

Music was furnished by the military band which offered many patriotic numbers that awakened in the newly freed Negroes that had long been dead—patriotism. Harriett recalls snatches of one of these songs to which she danced when she was 20 years of age. It is as follows:

Don't you see the lightning flashing in the cane brakes,
Looks like we gonna have a storm
Although you're mistaken its the Yankee soldiers
Going to fight for Uncle Sam.
Old master was a colonel in the Rebel army
Just before he had to run away—
Look out the battle is a-falling
The darkies gonna occupy the land.

Harriett believes the two officers who tendered congratulations shortly after her marriage to have been Generals Gates and Beecher. This was an added thrill to her.

As she lived a rather secluded life, Harriett Gresham can tell very little about the superstitions of her people during slavery, but knew them to be very reverent of various signs and omens. In one she places much credence herself. Prior to the Civil War, there were hordes of ants and everyone said this was an omen of war, and there was a war.

She was married when schools were set up for Negroes, but had no time for school. Her master was adamant on one point and that was the danger of teaching a slave to read and write, so Harriett received little "book learning."

Harriett Gresham is the mother of several children, grandchildren and great grandchildren. Many of them are dead. She lives at 1305 west 31st Street, Jacksonville, Florida with a grand daughter. Her second husband is also dead. She sits on the porch of her shabby cottage and sews the stitches that were taught her by her mistress, who is also dead. She embroiders, crochets, knits and quilts without the aid of glasses. She likes to show her handiwork to passersby who will find themselves listening to some of her reminiscences if they linger long enough to engage her in conversation—for she loves to talk of the past.

She still corresponds with one of the children of her mistress, now an old woman living on what is left of a once vast estate at Barnwell, South Carolina. The two old women are very much attached to each other and each in her letters helps to keep alive the memories of the life they shared together as mistress and slave.

REFERENCE
1. Personal interview with Harriett Gresham, 1305 West 31st, Street, Jacksonville, Florida

BOLDEN HALL

FEDERAL WRITERS' PROJECT
American Guide, (Negro Writers' Unit)
Alfred Farrell, Field Worker
John A. Simms, Editor
Dive Oak, Florida
August 30, 1936

Bolden Hall was born in Walkino, Florida, a little town in Jefferson County, on February 13, 1853, the son of Alfred and Tina Hall. The Halls who were the slaves of Thomas Lenton, owner of seventy-five or a hundred slaves, were the parents of twenty-one children. The Halls, who were born before slavery worked on the large plantation of Lenton which was devoted primarily to the growing of cotton and corn and secondarily to the growing of tobacco and pumpkins. Lenton was very good to his slaves and never whipped them unless it was absolutely necessary—which was seldom! He provided them with plenty of food and clothing, and always saw to it that their cabins were liveable. He was careful, however, to see that they received no educational training, but did not interfere with their religious quest. The slaves were permitted to attend church with their masters to hear the white preacher, and occasionally the master—supposedly un-beknown to the slaves—would have an itinerant colored minister preach to the slaves, instructing them to obey their master and mistress at all times. Although freedom came to the slaves in January, Master Lenton kept them until May in order to help him with his crops. When actual freedom was granted to the slaves, only a few of the young ones left the Lenton plantation. In 1882 Bolden Hall came to Live Oak where he has resided ever since. He married but his wife is now dead, and to that union one child was born.

Charlotte Martin

Charlotte Mitchell Martin, one of twenty children born to Shepherd and Lucinda Mitchell, eighty-two years ago, was a slave of Judge Wilkerson on a large plantation in Sixteen, Florida, a little town near Madison. Shepherd Mitchell was a wagoner who hauled whiskey from Newport News, Virginia for his owner. Wilkerson was very cruel and held them in constant fear of him. He would not permit them to hold religious meetings or any other kinds of meetings, but they frequently met in secret to conduct religious services. When they were caught, the "instigators"—known or suspected—were severely flogged. Charlotte recalls how her oldest brother was whipped to death for taking part in one of the religious ceremonies. This cruel act halted the secret religious services.

Wilkerson found it very profitable to raise and sell slaves. He selected the strongest and best male and female slaves and mated them exclusively for breeding. The huskiest babies were given the best of attention in order that they might grow into sturdy youths, for it was those who brought the highest prices at the slave markets. Sometimes the master himself had sexual relations with his female slaves, for the products of miscegenation were very remunerative. These offsprings were in demand as house servants.

After slavery the Mitchells began to separate. A few of the children remained with their parents and eked out their living from the soil. During this period Charlotte began to attract attention with her herb cures. Doctors sought her out when they were stumped by difficult cases. She came to Live Oak to care for an old colored woman and upon whose death she was given the woman's house and property. For many years she has resided in the old shack, farming, making quilts, and practicing her herb doctoring. She has outlived her husband for whom she bore two children. Her daughter is feebleminded—her herb remedies can't cure her!

Sarah Ross
Born in Benton County, Mississippi nearly eighty years ago, Sarah is the daughter of Harriet Elmore and William Donaldson, her white owner. Donaldson was a very cruel man and frequently beat Sarah's mother because she would not have sexual relations with the overseer, a colored man by the name of Randall. Sarah relates that the slaves did not marry, but were forced—in many cases against their will—to live together as man and wife. It was not until after slavery that they learned about the holy bonds of matrimony, and many of them actually married.

Cotton, corn, and rice were the chief products grown on the Donaldson plantation. Okra also was grown, and from this product coffee was made. The slaves arose with the sun to begin their tasks in the fields and worked until dusk. They were beaten by the overseer if they dared to rest themselves. No kind of punishment was too cruel or severe to be inflicted upon these souls in bondage. Frequently the thighs of the male slaves were gashed with a saw and salt put in the wound as a means of punishment for some misdemeanor. The female slaves often had their hair cut off, especially those who had long beautiful hair. If a female slave was pregnant and had to be punished, she was whipped about the shoulders, not so much in pity as for the protection of the unborn child. Donaldson's wife committed suicide because of the cruelty not only to the slaves but to her as well.

The slaves were not permitted to hold any sort of meeting, not even to worship God. Their work consumed so much of their time that they had little opportunity to congregate. They had to wash their clothes on Sunday, the only day which they could call their own. On Sunday afternoon some of the slaves were sent for to entertain the family and its guests.

Sarah remembers the coming of the Yankees and the destruction wrought by their appearance. The soldiers stripped the plantation owners of their meats, vegetables, poultry and the like. Many plantation owners took their own lives in desperation. Donaldson kept his slaves several months after liberation and defied them to mention freedom to him. When he did give them freedom, they lost no time in leaving his plantation which held for them only unpleasant memories. Sarah came to Florida thirty-five years ago. She has been married twice, and is the mother of ten children, eight of whom are living.

REFERENCES

1. Personal interview with Bolden Hall, living near the Masonic Hall, in the Eastern section of Live Oak, Florida

2. Personal interview with Charlotte Martin, living near Greater Bethel African Methodist Episcopal Church, in the Eastern section of Live Oak, Florida

3. Sarah Ross, living near Greater Bethel African Methodist Episcopal church, Live Oak, Florida

REBECCA HOOKS

FEDERAL WRITERS' PROJECT
American Guide, (Negro Writers' Unit)
Pearl Randolph, Field Worker
Lake City, Florida
January 14, 1937

Rebecca Hooks, age 90 years, is one of the few among the fast-thinning ranks of ex-slaves who can give a clear picture of life "befo' de wah."

She was born in Jones County, Georgia of Martha and Pleasant Lowe, who were slaves of William Lowe. The mother was the mulatto offspring of William Lowe and a slave woman who was half Cherokee. The father was also a mulatto, purchased from a nearby plantation.

Because of this blood mixture Rebecca's parents were known as "house niggers," and lived on quarters located in the rear of the "big house." A "house nigger" was a servant whose duties consisted of chores around the big house, such as butler, maid, cook, stableman, gardner and personal attendant to the man who owned him.

These slaves were often held in high esteem by their masters and of course fared much better than the other slaves on the plantation. Quite often they were mulattoes as in the case of Rebecca's parents. There seemed to be a general belief among slave owners that mulattoes could not stand as much laborious work as pure blooded Negro slaves. This accounts probably for the fact that the majority of ex-slaves now alive are mulattoes.

The Lowes were originally of Virginia and did not own as much property in Georgia as they had in Virginia. Rebecca estimates the number of slaves on this plantation as numbering no more than 25.

They were treated kindly and cruelly by turns, according to the whims of a master and mistress who were none too stable in their dispositions. There was no "driver" or overseer on this plantation, as "Old Tom was devil enough himself when he wanted to be," observes Rebecca. While she never felt the full force of his cruelties, she often felt sorry for the other slaves who were given a task too heavy to be completed in the given time; this deliberately, so that the master might have some excuse to vent his pentup feelings. Punishment was always in the form of a severe whipping or revocation of a slave's privilege, such as visiting other plantations etc.

The Lowes were not wealthy and it was necessary for them to raise and manufacture as many things on the plantation as possible. Slaves toiled from early morning until night in the corn, cotton sugar cane and tobacco fields. Others tended the large herds of cattle from which milk, butter, meat and leather was produced. The leather was tanned and made into crude shoes for the slaves for the short winter months. No one wore shoes except during cold weather and on Sundays. Fruit orchards and vegetables were also grown, but not given as much attention as the cotton and corn, as these were the main money crops.

As a child Rebecca learned to ape the ways of her mistress. At first this was considered very amusing. Whenever she had not knitted her required number of socks during the week, she simply informed them that she had not done it because she had not wanted to—besides she was not a "nigger." This stubbornness accompanied by hysterical tantrums continued to cause Rebecca to receive many stiff punishments that might have been avoided. Her master had given orders that no one was ever to whip her, so devious methods were employed to punish her, such as marching her down the road with hands tied behind her back, or locking her in a dark room for several hours with only bread and water.

Rebecca resembled very much a daughter of William Lowe. The girl was really her aunt, and very conscious of the resemblance. Both had brown eyes and long dark hair. They were about the same height and the clothes of the young mistress fitted Rebecca "like a glove." To offset this likeness, Rebecca's hair was always cut very short. Finally Rebecca rebelled at having her hair all cut off and blankly refused to submit to the treatment any longer. After this happening, the girls formed a dislike for each other, and Rebecca was guilty of doing every mean act of which she was capable to torment the white girl. Rebecca's mother aided and abetted her in this, often telling her things to do. Rebecca did not fear the form of punishment administered her and she had the cunning to keep "on the good side of the master" who had a fondness for her "because she was so much like the Lowes." The mistress' demand that she be sold or beaten was always turned aside with "Dear, you know the child can't help it; its that cursed Cherokee blood in her."

There seemed to be no very strong opposition to a slave's learning to read and write on the plantation, so Rebecca learned along with the white children. Her father purchased books for her with money he was allowed to earn from the sale of corn whiskey which he made, or from work done on some other plantation during his time off. He was not permitted to buy his freedom, however.

On Sundays Rebecca attended church along with the other slaves. Services were held in the white churches after their services were over. They were taught to obey their masters and work hard, and that they should be very thankful for the institution of slavery which brought them from darkest Africa.

On the plantation, the doctor was not nearly as popular as the "granny" or midwife, who brewed medicines for every ailment. Each plantation had its own "granny" who also served the mistress during confinement. Some of her remedies follows:

For colds: Horehound tea, pinetop tea, lightwood drippings on sugar. For fever: A tea made of pomegranate seeds and crushed mint. For whooping cough: A tea made of sheep shandy (manure); catnip tea. For spasms: garlic; burning a garment next to the skin of the patient having the fit.

Shortly before the war, Rebecca was married to Solomon, her husband. This ceremony consisted of simply jumping over a broom and having some one read a few words from a book, which may or may not have been the Bible. After the war, many couples were remarried because of this irregularity.

Rebecca had learned of the war long before it ended and knew its import. She had confided this information to other slaves who could read and write. She read the small newspaper that her master received at irregular intervals. The two sons of William Lowe had gone to fight with the Confederate soldiers (One never returned) and everywhere was felt the tension caused by wild speculation as to the outcome of the war.

Certain commodities were very scarce Rebecca remembers drinking coffee made of okra seed, that had been dried and parched. There was no silk, except that secured by "running the blockade," and this was very expensive. The smokehouse floors were carefully scraped for any morsel of salt that might be gotten. Salt had to be evaporated from sea water and this was a slow process.

There were no disorders in that section as far as Rebecca remembers, but she thinks that the slaves were kept on the Lowe plantation a long time after they had been freed. It was only when rumors came that Union soldiers were patrolling the countryside for such offenders, that they were hastily told of their freedom. Their former master predicted that they would fare much worse as freemen, and so many of them were afraid to venture into the world for themselves, remaining in virtual slavery for many years afterward.

Rebecca and her husband were among those who left the plantation. They share-cropped on various plantations until they came to Florida, which is more than fifty years ago. Rebecca's husband died several years ago and she now lives with two daughters, who are very proud of her.

REFERENCE
Personal interview with Rebecca Hooks, 1604 North Marion Street, Lake City, Florida.

REV. SQUIRES JACKSON

FEDERAL WRITERS' PROJECT
American Guide, (Negro Writers' Unit)
Samuel Johnson
September 11, 1937

Lying comfortably in a bed encased with white sheets, Rev. Squires Jackson, former slave and minister of the gospel living at 706 Third Street cheerfully related the story of his life.

Born in a weather-beaten shanty in Madison, Fla. September 14, 1841 of a large family, he moved to Jacksonville at the age of three with the "Master" and his mother.

Very devoted to his mother, he would follow her into the cotton field as she picked or hoed cotton, urged by the thrashing of the overseer's lash. His master, a prominent political figure of that time was very kind to his slaves, but would not permit them to read and write. Relating an incident after having learned to read and write, one day as he was reading a newspaper, the master walked upon him unexpectingly and demanded to know what he was doing with a newspaper. He immediately turned the paper upside down and declared "Confederates done won the war." The master laughed and walked away without punishing him. It la interesting to know that slaves on this plantation were not allowed to sing when they were at work, but with all the vigilance of the overseers, nothing could stop those silent songs of labor and prayers for freedom.

On Sundays the boys on the plantation would play home ball and shoot marbles until church time. After church a hearty meal consisting of rice and salt picked pork was the usual Sunday fare cooked in large iron pots hung over indoor hearths. Sometimes coffee, made out of parched corn meal, was added as an extra treat.

He remembers the start of the Civil war with the laying of the Atlantic Cable by the "Great Eastern" being nineteen years of age at the time. Hearing threats of the War which was about to begin, he ran away with his brother to Lake City, many times hiding in trees and groves from the posse that was looking for him. At night he would cover up his face and body with spanish moss to sleep. One night he hid in a tree near a creek, over-slept himself, in the morning a group of white women fishing near the creek saw him and ran to tell the men, fortunately however he escaped.

After four days of wearied travelling being guided by the north star and the Indian instinct inherited from his Indian grandmother, he finally reached Lake City. Later reporting to General Scott, he was informed that he was to act as orderly until further ordered. On Saturday morning, February 20, 1861, General Scott called him to his tent and said "Squire; I have just had you appraised for $1000 and you are to report to Col. Guist in Alachua County for service immediately." That very night he ran away to Wellborn where the Federals were camping. There in a horse stable were wounded colored soldiers stretched out on the filthy ground. The sight of these wounded men and the feeble medical attention given them by the Federals was so repulsive to him, that he decided that he didn't want to join the Federal Army. In the silent hours of the evening he stole away to Tallahassee, throughly convinced that War wasn't the place for him. While in the horse shed make-shift hospital, a white soldier asked one of the wounded colored soldiers to what regiment he belonged, the negro replied "54th Regiment, Massachusetts."

At that time, the only railroad was between Lake City and Tallahassee which he had worked on for awhile. At the close of the war he returned to Jacksonville to begin work as a bricklayer. During this period, Negro skilled help was very much in demand.

The first time he saw ice was in 1857 when a ship brought some into this port. Mr. Moody, a white man, opened an icehouse at the foot of Julia Street. This was the only icehouse in the city at that time.

On Sundays he would attend church. One day he thought he heard the call of God beseeching him to preach. He began to preach in 1868, and was ordained an elder in 1874.

Some of the interesting facts obtained from this slave of the fourth generation were: (1) Salt was obtained by evaporating sea water, (2) there were no regular stoves, (3) cooking was done by hanging iron pots on rails in the fireplaces, (4) an open well was used to obtain water, (5) flour was sold at $12.00 a barrell, (6) "shin-plasters" was used for money, (7) the first buggy was called "rockaways" due to the elasticity of the leather-springs, (8) Rev. Jackson saw his first buggy as described, in 1851.

During the Civil War, cloth as well as all other commodities were very high. Slaves were required to weave the cloth. The women would delight in dancing as they marched to and fro in weaving the cloth by hand. This was one kind of work the slaves enjoyed doing. Even Cotton seeds was picked by hand, hulling the seeds out with the fingers, there was no way of ginning it by machine at that time. Rev. Jackson vividly recalls the croker-sacks being used around bales of the finer cotton, known as short cotton. During this same period he made all of the shoes he wore by hand from cow hides. The women slaves at that time wore grass shirts woven very closely with hoops around on the inside to keep from contacting the body.

Gleefully he told of the Saturday night baths in big wooden washtubs with cut out holes for the fingers during his boyhood, of the castor oil, old fashion paragoric, calomel, and burmo chops used for medicine at that time. The herb doctors went from home to home during times of illness. Until many years after the Civil War there were no practicing Negro physicians. Soap was made by mixing bones and lard together, heating and then straining into a bucket containing alum, turpentine, and rosin. Lye soap was made by placing burnt ashes into straw with corn shucks placed into harper, water is poured over this mixture and a trough is used to sieze the liquid that drips into the tub and let stand for a day. Very little moss was used for mattresses, chicken feathers and goose feathers were the principal constituents during his boyhood. Soot mixed with water was the best medicine one could use for the stomach ache at that time.

Rev. Jackson married in 1882 and has seven sons and seven daughters. Owns his own home and plenty of other property around the neighborhood. Ninety-six years of age and still feels as spry as a man of fifty, keen of wit, with a memory as good can be expected. This handsome bronze piece of humanity with snow-white beard over his beaming face ended the interview saying, "I am waiting now to hear the call of God to the promise land." He once was considered as a candidate for senator after the Civil war but declined to run. He says that the treatment during the time of slavery was very tough at times, but gathering himself up he said, "no storm lasts forever" and I had the faith and courage of Jesus to carry me on, continuing, "even the best masters in slavery couldn't be as good as the worst person in freedom, Oh, God, it is good to be free, and I am thankful."

REFERENCE
Personal interview with subject, Rev. Squires Jackson, 706 Third Street, Jacksonville, Florida.

United States. Work Projects Administration

"PROPHET" JOHN HENRY KEMP

FEDERAL WRITERS' PROJECT
American Guide, (Negro Writers' Unit)
L. Rebecca Baker, Field Worker
Daytona Beach, Florida
January 11, 1937

A long grey beard, a pair of piercing owl-like eyes and large bare feet, mark "Prophet" Kemp among the citizenry of Daytona Beach, Florida. The "Prophet", christened John Henry—as nearly as he can remember—is an 80 year old ex-slave whose remininiscences of the past, delight all those who can prevail upon him to talk of his early life on the plantation of the section.

"Prophet" Kemp does not talk only of the past, however, his conversation turns to the future; he believes himself to be equally competent to talk of the future, and talks more of the latter if permitted.

Oketibbeha County, Mississippi was the birthplace of the "Prophet". The first master he can remember was John Gay, owner of a plantation of some 2,700 acres and over 100 slaves and a heavy drinker. The "Prophet" calls Gay "father", and becomes very vague when asked if this title is a blood tie or a name of which he is generally known.

According to Kemp—Gay was one of the meanest plantation owners in the entire section, and frequently voiced his pride in being able to employ the cruelest overseers that could be found in all Mississippi. Among these were such men as G.T. Turner, Nels T. Thompson, Billy Hole, Andrew Winston and other men with statewide reputations for brutality. When all of the cruelties of one overseer had been felt by the slaves on the Gay plantation and another meaner man's reputation was heard of on the Gay plantation, the master would delight in telling his slaves that if they did not behave, he would send for this man. "Behaving"—the "Prophet" says, meant living on less food than one should have; mating only at his command and for purposes purely of breeding more and stronger slaves on his plantation for sale. In some cases with women—subjecting to his every demand if they would escape hanging by the wrists for half a day or being beaten with a cowhide whip.

About these whippings, the "Prophet" tells many a blood-curdling tale.

"One day when an old woman was plowing in the field, an overseer came by and reprimanded her for being so slow—she gave him some back talk, he took out a long closely woven whip and lashed her severely. The woman became sore and took her hoe and chopped him right across his head, and child you should have seen how she chopped this man to a bloody death."

"Prophet" Kemp will tell you that he hates to tell these things to any investigator, because he hates for people to know just how mean his "fahter" really was.

So great was the fear in which Gay was held that when Kemp's mother, Arnette Young, complained to Mrs. Gay, that her husband was constantly seeking her for a mistress and threatening her with death if she did not submit, even Mrs. Gay had to advise the slaves to do as Gay demanded, saying—"My husband is a dirty man and will find some reason to kill you if you don't." "I can't do a thing with him." Since Arnette worked at the "big house" there was no alternative, and it was believed that out of the union with her master, Henry was born. A young slave by the name of Broxton Kemp was given to the woman as husband at the time John Kemp was born, it is from this man that "Prophet" took his name.

Life on the plantation held nothing but misery for the slaves of John Gay. A week's allowance of groceries for the average small family consisted of a package of about ten pounds containing crudely ground meal, a slab of bacon—called side-meat and from a pint to a quart of syrup made from sorghum, depending upon the season.

All slaves reported for work a 5 o'clock in the morning, except those who cared for the overseer, who began their work an hour earlier to enable the overseer to be present at the morning checkup. This checkup determined which slaves were late or who had committed some offense late on the day before or during the night. These were singled out and before the rest of the slaves began their work they were treated to the sight of these delinquents being stripped and beaten until blood flowed; women were no exception to the rule.

The possible loss of his slaves upon the declaration of freedom on January 1, 1866 caused Gay considerable concern. His liquor-ridden mind was not long in finding a solution, however, he barred all visitors from his plantation and insisted that his overseers see to the carrying out of this detail. They did, with such efficiency that it was not until May 8, when the government finally learned of the condition and sent a marshall to the plantation, that freedom came to Gay's slaves. May 8, is still celebrated in this section of Mississippi, as the official emancipation day.

Relief for the hundreds of slaves of Gay came at last with the declaration of freedom for them. The government officials divided the grown and growing crops; and some land was parcelled out to the former slaves.

Kemp may have gained the name "Prophet" from his constant reference to the future and to his religion. He says he believes on one faith, one Lord and one religion, and preaches this belief constantly. He claims to have turned his back on all religions that "do not do as the Lord says."

In keeping this belief he says he represents the "True Primitive Baptist Church", but does not have any connection with that church, because he believes it has not lived exactly up to what the Lord expects of him.

Kemp claims the ability to read the future with ease; even to help determine what it will bring in some cases. He reads it in the palms of those who will believe in him; he determines the good and bad luck; freedom from sickness; success in love and other benefits it will bring from the use of charms, roots, herbs and magical incantations and formulae. He has recently celebrated what he believes to be his 80th birthday, and says he expects to live at least another quarter of a century.

REFERENCE
1. Personal interview with John Henry Kemp, Daytona Beach, Florida

United States. Work Projects Administration

CINDY KINSEY

Barbara Darsey
SLAVE INTERVIEW
With
FORMER SLAVE
About 86 Years of Age

"Yes maam, chile, I aint suah ezackly, but I think I bout 85 mebby 86 yeah old. Yes maam, I wus suah bahn in de slavery times, an I bahn right neah de Little Rock in Arkansas, an dere I stay twell I comed right from dere to heah in Floridy bout foah yeah gone.

"Yes maam, my people de liv on a big plantation neah de Little Rock an we all hoe cotton. My Ma? Lawzy me, chile, she name Zola Young an my pappy he name Nelson Young. I had broddehs Danel, Freeman, George, Will, and Henry. Yes maam, Freeman he de younges an bahn after we done got free. An I had sistehs by de name ob Isabella, Mary, Nora,—dat aint all yet, you want I should name em all? Well then they was too Celie, Sally, and me Cindy but I aint my own sisteh is I, hee, hee, hee.

"My Ole Massa, he name Marse Louis Stuart, an my Ole Missy, dat de real ole one you know, she name,— now—let-me-see, does—I—ricollek, lawzy me, chile, I suah fin it hard to member some things. O! yes,—her name hit war Missy Nancy, an her chilluns dey name Little Marse Sammie an Little Missy Fanny. I don know huccum my pappy he go by de name Young when Ole Massa he name Marse Stuart lessen my pappy he be raised by nother Massa fore Marse Louis got him, but I disrememba does I eber heerd him say.

"Yes maam, chile I suah like dem days. We had lot ob fun an nothin to worrify about, suah wish dem days wus now, chile, us niggahs heaps better off den as now. Us always had plenty eat and plenty wearin close too, which us aint nevah got no more. We had plenty cahn pone, baked in de ashes too, hee, hee, hee, it shore wus good, an we had side meat, an we had other eatin too, what ever de Ole Marse had, but I like de side meat bes. I had a good dress for Sunday too but aint got none dese days, jes looky, chile, dese ole rags de bes I got. My Sunday dress? Lawzy me, chile, hit were alway a bright red cotton. I suah member dat color, us dye de cotton right on de plantation mostly. Other close I dont ezackly ricollek, but de mostly dark, no colahs.

"My ma, she boss all de funerls ob de niggahs on de plantation an she got a long white veil for wearin, lawzy me, chile, she suah look bootiful, jes lak a bride she did when she boss dem funerls in dat veil. She not much skeered nether fo dat veil hit suah keep de hants away. Wisht I had me dat veil right now, mout hep cure dis remutizics in ma knee what ailin me so bad. I disrememba, but I sposen she got buried in dat veil, chile. She hoe de cotton so Ole Marse Louis he always let her off fo de buryings cause she know how to manage de other niggahs and keep dem quiet at de funerls.

"No maam, chile, we didn't hab no Preacher-mans much, hit too fah away to git one when de niggah die. We sung songs and my ma she say a Bible vurs what Ole Missy don lernt her. Be vurs, lawsy me, chile, suah wish I could member hit for you. Dem songs? I don jes recollek, but hit seem lak de called 'Gimme Dem Golden Slippahs', an a nother one hit wah 'Ise Goin To Heben In De Charot Ob Fiah', suah do wish I could recollek de words an sing em foh you, chile, but I caint no more, my min, hit aint no good lak what it uster be.

"Yes maam, chile, I suah heerd ob Mr. Lincoln but not so much. What dat mans wanter free us niggahs when we so happy an not nothin to worrify us. No, maam, I didn't see none dem Yankee sojers but I heerd od[TR: of?] dem an we alwy skeerd dey come. Us all cotch us rabbits an weah de lef hine foots roun our nek wif a bag ob akkerfedity, yessum I guess dat what I mean, an hit shore smell bad an hit keep off de fevah too, an if a Yankee cotch you wif dat rabbit foots an dat akkerfedity bag roun youh nek, he suah turn you loose right now.

"Yes maam, chile, Ise a Baptis and sho proud ob it. Praise de Lord and go to Church, dat de onliest way to keep de debbil offen youh trail and den sometime he almos kotch up wif you. Lawsy me, chile, when de Preacher-mans baptiz me he had duck me under de wateh twell I mos dron, de debbil he got such a holt on me an jes wont let go, but de Preacher-mans he kep a duckin me an he finaly shuck de debbil loose an he aint bother me much sence, dat is not very much, an dat am a long time ago.

"Yes maam, chile, some ob de niggahs dey run off

from Ole Marse Louis, but de alway come back bout stahved, hee, hee, hee, an do dey eat, an Ole Marse, he alway take em back an give em plenty eatins. Yes maam, he alway good to us and he suah give us niggahs plenty eatins all de time. When Crismus come, you know chile, hit be so cole, and Old Marse, he let us make a big fiah, a big big fiah in de yahd roun which us live, an us all dance rounde fiah, and Ole Missy she brang us Crismus Giff. What war de giff? Lawzy me, chile, de mostly red woolen stockings and some times a pair of shoeses, an my wus we proud. An Ole Marse Louis, he giv de real old niggahs, both de mens an de owmans, a hot toddy, hee, hee, hee. Lawzy me, chile, dem wus de good days, who give an ole niggah like me a hot toddy dese days? an talkin you bout dem days, chile, sho mek me wish dey was now."

RANDALL LEE

FEDERAL WRITERS' PROJECT
American Guide, (Negro Writers' Unit)
Viola B. Muse, Field Worker
Palatka, Florida

Randall Lee of 500 Branson Street, Palatka, Florida, was born at Camden, South Carolina about seventy-seven years ago, maybe longer.

He was the son of Robert and Delhia Lee, who during slavery were Robert and Delhia Miller, taking the name of their master, as was the custom.

His master was Doctor Miller and his mistress was Mrs. Camilla Miller. He does not know his master's given name as no other name was ever heard around the plantation except Doctor Miller.

Randall was a small boy when the war between the states broke out, but judging from what he remembers he must have been a boy around six or seven years of age.

During the few years he spent in slavery, Randall had many experiences which made such deep impressions upon his brain that the memory of them still remains clear.

The one thing that causes one to believe that he must have been around seven years of age is the statement that he was not old enough to have tasks of any importance placed upon him, yet he was trusted along with another boy about his own age, to carry butter from the plantation dairy two miles to the 'big house.' No one would trust a child younger than six years of age to handle butter for fear of it being dropped into the dirt. He must have at least reached the age when he was sent two miles with a package and was expected to deliver the package intact. He must have understood the necessity of not playing on the way. He stated that he knew not to stop on the two-mile journey and not to let the butter get dirty.

Randall had the pleasure of catching the pig for his father for Doctor Miller gave each of his best Negro men a pig to raise for himself and family. He was allowed to build a pen for it and raise and fatten it for killing. When killing time came he was given time to butcher it and grind all the sausage he could make to feed his family. By that method it helped to solve the feeding problem and also satisfied the slaves.

It was more like so many families living around a big house with a boss looking over them, for they were allowed a privilege that very few masters gave their slaves.

On the Miller plantation there was a cotton gin. Doctor Miller owned the gin and it was operated by his slaves. He grew the cotton, picked it, ginned it and wove it right there. He also had a baler and made the bagging to bale it with. He only had to buy the iron bands that held the bales intact.

Doctor Miller was a rich man and had a far reaching

sight into how to work slaves to the best advantage. He was kind to them and knew that the best way to get the best out of men was to keep them well and happy. His arrangement was very much the general way in that he allowed the young men and women to work in the fields and the old women and a few old men to work around the house, in the gin and at the loom. The old women mostly did the spinning of thread and weaving of cloth although in some instances Doctor Miller found a man who was better adapted to weaving than any of his women slaves.

Everyone kept his plantation under fence and men who were old but strong and who had some knowledge of carpentry were sent out to keep the fence in repair and often to build new ones. The fences were not like those of today. They were built of horizontal rails about six or seven feet long, running zig-zag fashion. Instead of having straight line fences and posts at regular points they did not use posts at all. The bottom rails rested upon the ground and the zigzag fashion in which they were laid gave strength to the fence. No nails were used to hold the rails in place. If stock was to be let in or out of the places the planks were unlocked so to speak, and the stock allowed to enter after which they were laid back as before.

Boys and girls under ten years of age were never sent into the field to work on the Miller plantation but were required to mind the smaller children of the family and do chores around the "big house" for the mistress and her children. Such work as mending was taught the domestic-minded children and tending food on the pots was alloted others with inborn ability to cook. They were treated well and taught 'manners' and later was used as dining room girls and nurses.

Randall's father and mother were considered lucky. His father was overseer and his mother was a waitress.

Doctor Miller was a kind and considerate owner; never believed in punishing slaves unless in extreme cases. No overseer, white or colored could whip his slaves without first bringing the slave before him and having a full understanding as to what the offense was. If it warranted whipping them it had to be given in his presence so he could see that it was not given unmercifully. He indeed was a doctor and practised his profession in the keeping of his slaves from bodily harm as well as keeping them well. He gave them medicine when they did not feel well and saw to it that they took needed rest if they were sick and tired.

Now, Robert Lee, Randall's father, was brought from Virginia and sold to Doctor Miller when he was a young man. The one who sold him told Doctor Miller, "Here's a nigger who wont take a whipping. He knows his work and will do it and all you will need to do is tell him what you want and its as good as done." Robert Lee never varied from the recommendation his former master gave when he sold him.

The old tale of corn bread baked on the hearth covered with ashes and sweet potatoes cooked in like manner are vivid memories upon the mind of Randall. Syrup water and plenty of sweet and butter milk, rice and crackling bread are other foods which were plentiful around the cabin of Randall's parents.

Cows were numerous and the family of Doctor Miller did not need much for their consumption. While they sold milk to neighboring plantations, the Negroes were not denied the amount necessary to keep all strong and healthy. None of the children on the plantation were thin and scrawny nor did they ever complain of being hungry.

The tanning yard was not far from the house Doctor Miller. His own butcher shop was nearby. He had his cows butchered at intervals and when one died of unnatural causes it was skinned and the hide tanned on the place.

Randall as a child delighted in stopping around the tanning yard and watching the men salt the hide. They, after salting it dug holes and buried it for a number of days. After the salting process was finished it was treated with a solution of water and oak bark. When the oak bark solution had done its work it was ready for use. Shoes made of leather were not dyed at that time but the natural color of the finished hide was thought very beautiful and those who were lucky enough to possess a pair were glad to get them in their natural color. To dye shoes various colors is a new thing when the number of years leather has been dyed is compared with the hundreds of years people knew nothing about it, especially American people.

Randall's paternal grandparents were also owned by Doctor Miller and were not sold after he bought them. Levi Lee was his grandfather's name. He was a fine worker in the field but was taken out of it to be taught the shoe-makers trade. The master placed him under a white shoemaker who taught him all the fine points. If there were any, he knew about the trade. Dr. Miller had an eye for business who could make shoes was a great saving to him. Levi made all the shoes and boots the master, mistress and the Miller family wore. Besides, he made shoes for the slaves who wore them. Not all slaves owned a pair of shoes. Boys and girls under eighteen went bare-footed except in winter. Doctor Miller had compassion for them and did not allow them to suffer from the cold by going bare-footed in winter.

Another good thing to be remembered was the large number of chickens, ducks and geese which the slaves raised for the doctor. Every slave family could rest his tired body upon a feather bed for it was allowed him after the members of the master's family were supplied. Moss mattresses also were used under the feather beds and slaves did not need to have as thick a feather bed on that account. They were comfortable though and Randall remembers how he and the other children used to fall down in the middle of the bed and become hidden from view, so soft was the feather mattress. It was especially good to get in bed in winter but not so pleasant to get up unless 'pappy' had made the fire early enough for the large one-room cabin to get warm. The children called their own parents 'pappy' and 'mammy' in slavery time.

Randall remembers how after a foot-washing in the old wooden tub, (which, by the way, was simply a barrel cut in half and holes cut in the two sides for fingers to catch a hold) he would sit a few minutes with his feet held to the fire so they could dry. He also said his 'mammy' would rub grease under the soles of his feet to keep him from taking cold.

It seemed to the child that he had just gone to bed when the old tallow candle was lighted and his 'pappy' arose and fell upon his knees and prayed aloud for God's blessings and thanked him for another day. The field hands were to be in the field by five o'clock and it meant to rise before day, summer and winter. Not so bad in summer for it was soon day but in winter the weather was cold and darkness was longer passing away. When daylight came field hands had been working an hour or more. Robert Lee, Randall's father was an overseer and it meant for him to be up and out with the rest of the men so he could see if things were going allright.

The Randall children were not forced up early because they did not eat breakfast with their 'pappy'. Their mother was dining-room girl in her mistress' house, so fed the children right from the Miller table. There was no objection offered to this.

Doctor Miller was kind but he did not want his slaves enlightened too much. Therefore, he did not allow much preaching in the church. They could have prayer meeting all they wanted to, but instructions from the Bible were thought dangerous for the slaves. He did not wish them to become too wise and get it into their heads to ran away and get free.

There was talk about freedom and Doctor Miller knew it would be only a matter of time when he would loose all his slaves. He said to Randall's mother one day, "Delhia you'll soon be as free as I am." She said.

"Sho' nuf massy?" and he answered. "You sure will." Nothing more was said to any of the slaves until Sherman's army came through notifying the slaves they were free.

The presence of the soldiers caused such a comotion around the plantation that Randall's mind was indelibly impressed with their doings.

The northern soldiers took all the food they could get their hands on and took possession of the cattle and horses and mules. Levi, the brother of Randall, and who was named after his paternal grandfather, was put on a mule and the mule loaded with provisions and sent two miles to the soldier's camp. Levi liked that, for beside being well treated he received several pieces of money. The federal soldiers played with him and gave him all the food he wanted, although the Miller slaves and their children were fed and there was no reason for the child to be hungry.

Levi Lee, the grandfather of young Levi and Randall, had a dream while the soldiers were encamped round about the place. He dreamed that a pot of money was buried in a certain place; the person who showed it to him told him to go dig for it on the first rainy night. He kept the dream a secret and on the first rainy night he went, dug, and found the pot of money right where his dream had told him it would be. He took the pot of money to his cabin and told no one anything about it. He hid it as securely as possible, but when the soldiers were searching for gold and silver money they did not leave the Negro's cabin out of the search. When they found the money they thought Levi's master had given him the money to hide as they took it from him.

Levi mourned a long time about the loss of his money and often told his grandchildren that he would have been well fixed when freedom came if he had not been robbed of his money.

"Paddyroles" as the men were called who were sent by the Rebels to watch the slaves to prevent their escaping during war times, were very active after freedom. They intimidated the Negroes and threatened them with loss of life if they did not stay and work for their former masters. Doctor Miller did not want any of his slaves treated in such manner. He told them they were free and could take whatever name they desired.

Robert Lee, during slavery was Robert Miller, as were all of the doctor's slaves. After slavery was ended he chose the name Lee. His brother Aaron took the name Alexander not thinking how it looked for two brothers of the same parents to have different surnames. There are sons of each brother living in Palatka now, one set Lees and the others, Alexander.

Randall, as was formerly stated, spent a very little time in slavery. Most of his knowledge concerning customs which long ago have been abandoned and replaced by more modern ones, is of early reconstruction days. Just after the Civil War, when his father began farming on his own plantation, his mother remained home and cared for her house and children. She was of fair complexion, having been the daughter of a half-breed Indian and Negro mother. Her father was white. Her native state was Virginia and she bore some of the aristocratic traits so common among those born in that state of such parentage. She often boasted of her "blue blood Virginia stock."

Robert Lee, Randall's father was very prosperous in early reconstruction days. He owned horses, mules and a plow. The plow was made of point iron with a wooden handle, not like plows of today for they are of cast iron and steel.

Chickens, ducks and geese were raised in abundance and money began accumulating rapidly for Robert and Delhia Lee. They began improving their property and trying to give their children some education. It was very hard for those living in small towns and out in the country to go to school even though they had money to pay for their education. The north sent teachers down but not every hamlet was favored with such. (1)

Randall was taught to farm and he learned well. He saved his money as he worked and grew to manhood. Years after freedom he left South Carolina and went to Palatka, Florida, where he is today. He bought some land and although most of it is hammock land and not much good he has at intervals been offered good prices for it. Some white people during the "boom" of 1925-26 offered him a few dollars an acre for it but he refused to sell thinking a better price would be offered if he held on. (2)

Today finds Randall Lee, an old man with fairly good health; he stated that he had not had a doctor for years and his thinking faculties are in good order. His eyesight is failing but he does not allow that to handicap him in getting about. He talks fluently about what he remembers concerning slavery and that which his parents told him. He is between a mulatto and brown skin with good, mixed gray and black hair. His features are regular, not showing much Negro blood. He is tall and looks to weigh about one hundred and sixty-five pounds. His wife lives with him in their two-story frame house which shows that they have had better days financially. The man and wife both show interest in the progress of the Negro race and possess some books about the history of the Negro. One book of particular interest, and of which the wife of Randall Lee thinks a great deal, was written, according to her story, by John Brown. It is called "The History of the Colored Race in America." She could not find but a few pages of it when interviewed but declared she had owned the entire book for years. The pages she had and showed with such pride were 415 to 449 inclusive. The book was written in the year 1836 and the few pages produced by her gave information concerning the Negro, Lovejoy of St. Louis, Missouri. It is the same man for whom the city of Lovejoy, Illinois is named. The other book she holds with pride and guards jealously is "The College of Life" by Henry Davenport Northrop D.D., Honorable Joseph R. Gay and Professor I. Garland Penn. It was entered, according to the Act of Congress in the year 1900 by Horace C. Fry, in the office of the Librarian of Congress at Washington, D.C. (3)

REFERENCES
1. Randall Lee, 600 Brunson Street, Palatka, Florida

2. Mrs. Bessie Bates, 412 South Eleventh Street, Palatka, Florida

3. Observation of Field Worker

EDWARD LYCURGAS

FEDERAL WRITERS' PROJECT
American Guide, (Negro Writers' Unit)
Pearl Randolph, Field Worker
Jacksonville, Florida
December 5, 1936

"Pap tell us 'nother story 'bout do war—and 'bout de fust time you saw mamma."

It has been almost 60 years since a group of children gathered about their father's knee, clamoring for another story. They listened round-eyed to stories they already knew because "pap" had told them so many times before. These narratives along with the great changes he has seen, were carefully recorded in the mind of Edward, the only one of this group now alive.

"Pap" was always ready to oblige with the story they never tired of. He could always be depended upon to begin at the beginning, for he loved to tell it.

"It all begun with our ship being took off the coast of Newport News, Virginia. We wuz runnin' the blockade—sellin' guns and what-not to them Northerners. We aint had nothin' to do wid de war, unnerstand, we English folks was at'ter de money. Whose War? The North and South's, of course. I hear my captain say many a time as how they was playin' ball wid the poor niggers. One side says 'You can't keep your niggers lessen you pay em and treat em like other folks.' Mind you dat wasn't de rale reason, they was mad at de South but it was one of de ways dey could be hurted—to free de niggers."

"De South says 'Dese is our niggers and we'll do dum as we please,' and so de rumpus got wuss dan it was afore. The North had all do money, and called itself de Gov'ment. The South aint had nothin', but a termination not to be out-did, so we dealt wid de North. De South was called de Rebels."

"So when dey see a ship off they coast, they hailed it and when we kep goin', they fired at us. 'Twan't long afore we was being unloaded and marched off to the lousiest jail I ever been in. My captain kep tellin' em we was English subjects and could not be helt. Me, I was a scairt man, cause I was always free, and over here dey took it for granted dat all black men should be slaves."

"The jailer felt of my muscles one day, when he had marched me out at the point of his musket to fill de watering troughs for de horses. He wanted to know who I blong ter, and offered to buy me. When nobody claimed me, they was forced to let me go long wid de other Britishers and as our ship had been destroyed, we had to git back home best we could. Dey didn't dare hold us no longer."

"As de war was still being fit, we was forced to separate, cause a lot of us would cause spicion, traipsing 'bout do country. Me—I took off southward and way from de war belt, traveling as far as Saint Augustine. It was a dangerous journey, as anybody was liable to pick me off for a runaway slave. I was forced to hide in de day time if I was near a settlement and travel at night. I met many runaway slaves. Some was trying to get North and fight for de freeing of they people; others was jes runnin' way cause dey could. Many of dem didn't had no idea where dey was goin' and told of havin' good marsters. But one and all dey had a good strong notion ter see what it was like to own your own body."

"I felt worlds better when I reached Saint Augustine. Many ships landed there and I knowed I could get my way back at least to de West Indies, where I come frum. I showed my papers to everybody dat mounted ter anything and dey knowed I was a free nigger. I had plenty of money on me and I made a big ter do mong de other free men I met. One day I went to the slave market and watched em barter off po niggers lake dey was hogs. Whole families sold together and some was split—mother gone to one marster and father and children gone to others."

"They'd bring a slave out on the flatform and open his mouth, pound his chest, make him harden his muscles so the buyer could see what he was gittin'. Young men was called 'bucks' and young women 'wenches'. The person that offered the best price was de buyer. And dey shore did git rid uf some pretty gals. Dey always looked so shame and pitiful up on dat stand wid all dem men standin' dere lookin' at em wid what dey had on dey minds shinin' in they eyes One little gal walked up and left her mammy mourning so pitiful cause she had to be sold. Seems like dey all belong in a family where nobody ever was sold. My she was a pretty gal."

"And dats why your mamma's named Julia stead of Mary Jane or Hannah or somethin' else—She cost me $950.00 and den my own freedom. But she was worth it—every bit of it!"

"After that I put off my trip back home and made her home my home for three years. Den with our two young children we left Floridy and went to the West Indies to live. We traveled bout a bit gettin as far as England. We got letters from your ma's folks and dey jes had to see her or else somebody would'er died, so we sailed back into de war."

"Freedom was declared soon after we got back to dis country and de whole country was turned upside down. De po niggers went mad. Some refused to work and dey didn't stay in one place long 'nough to do a thing. De crops suffered and soon we had starvation times for 'bout two years. After dat everybody lernt to think of a rainy day and things got better."

Edward recalls of hearing his father tell of eating wild hog salad and cabbage palms. It was a common occurence to see whole families subsisting on any wild plant not known to be poisonous if it contained the least food value. The freedmen helped those who were newly liberated to gain a footing. Prior to Emancipation they had not been allowed to associate with slaves for fear they might engender in them the desire to be free. The freedmen bore the brunt of the white man's suspicion whenever there was a slave uprising. They were always accusing them of being instigators. Edward often heard his mother tell of the "patter-rollers", a group of white men who caught and administered severe whippings to these unfortunate slaves. They also corraled slaves back to their masters if they were caught out after nine o'clock at night without a pass from their masters.

George Lycurgas was born at Liverpool, England and became a seaman at an early age. Edward thinks he might have had a fair education if he had had the chance. The mother, Julia Gray, Lycurgas, was the daughter of Barbara and David Gray, slaves of the Flemings of Clay County, Florida.

These slaves were inherited from generation to generation and no one ever thought to sell one except for punishment or in dire necessity. They were treated kindly and like most slaves of the wealthy, had no knowledge of the real cruelties of slavery, but upon the death of their owner it became necessary to parcel the slaves out to different heirs, some of whom did not believe in holding these unfortunates. These would-be abolitionists were not averse to placing at auction their share of the slaves, however.

It was on this occasion that George Lycurgas saw and bought the girl who was to become his wife. Both are now dead, also all of the several children except Edward who tells their story here.

Edward Lycurgas was born on October 28, 1872, at Saint Augustine, Florida shortly after the return of the family from the West Indies. He lived on his father's farm sharing at an early age the hard work that seemed always in abundance, and listening in awe to the stories of the recent war. He heard his elders give thanks for their freedom when they attended church and wondered what it was all about.

No one failed to attend church on Sundays and all work ceased in a vicinity where a camp meeting was held. Farmers flocked to the meeting from all parts of Saint Johns County. They brought food in their large baskets. Some owned buggies but most of them hauled their families in wagons or walked. The camp meetings would sometimes last for several days according to the spiritual fervor exhibited by those attending.

Lycurgas recalls the stirring sermons and spirituals that rang through the woods and could be heard for several miles on a clear day. And the river baptisms! These climaxed the meetings and were attended by large crowds of whites in the neighborhood. All candidates were dressed in white gowns, stockings and towels would about their heads bandana fashion. Tow by two they marched to the river from the spot where they had dressed. There was always some stiring song to accompany their slow march to the river. "Take me to the water to be baptized" was the favorite spiritual for this occasion.

As in all things, some attended camp meetings for the opportunity it afforded them to indulge in illicit love making. Others went to show their finery and there was plenty of it according to Lycurgas' statement. There seemed to be beautiful clothing, fine teams and buggies everywhere—a sort of reaction from the restraint upon them in slavery. Many wore clothing they could not afford.

There seemed to be a deeper interest in politics during these times. Mass meetings, engineered by "carpet baggers" were often held and largely attended, although the father of Edward did not hold with these activities very much. He often heard the preacher point out Negroes who attended the meetings and attained prominence in politics as an example for members of his flock to follow. He believes he recalls hearing the name of Joseph Gibbs.

Next to the preacher, the Negro school teacher was held in greatest respect. Until the year of the "shake" (earthquake of 1886) there were no Negro school teachers on Saint John's County and no school buildings. They attended classes at the fort and were taught by a white woman who had come from "up nawth" for this purpose. Edward was able to learn very little from his blue back Webster because his help was needed on the farm.

He was a lover of home, very shy and did not care much for courting. He remained with his parents until their deaths and did not leave the vicinity for many years. He is still unmarried and resides at the Clara White Mission, Jacksonville, Florida, where he receives a email salary for the piddling jobs about the place that he is able to do.

REFERENCE
1. Personal interview with Edward Lycurgas, 611 West Ashley Street, Jacksonville, Florida

United States. Work Projects Administration

AMANDA MCCRAY

FEDERAL WRITERS' PROJECT
American Guide, (Negro Writers' Unit)
Pearl Randolph, Field Worker
Madison, Florida
November 13, 1936

Mrs. McCray was sitting on her porch crooning softly to herself and rocking so gently that one might easily have thought the wind was swaying her chair. Her eyes were closed, her hands incredibly old and workworn were slowly folding and unfolding on her lap.

She listened quietly to the interviewer's request for some of the "high lights" of her life and finally exclaimed: "Chile, why'ny you look among the living fer the high lights?"

There was nothing resentful in this expression; only the patient weariness of one who has been dragged through the boundaries of a yesterday from which he was inseparable and catapulted into a present with which he has nothing in common. After being assured that her life story was of real interest to some one she warmed up and talked quite freely of the life and times as they existed in her day.

How old was she? She confessed quite frankly that she never "knowed" her age. She was a grownup during the Civil War when she was commandered by Union soldiers invading the country and employed as a cook. Her owner, one Redding Pamell, possessed a hundred or more slaves and was, according to her statement very kind to them. It was on his plantation that she was born. Amanda McCray is one of several children born to Jacob and Mary Williams, the latter being blind since Amanda could remember.

Children on the Pamell plantation led a carefree existence until they were about 12 years of age, when they were put to light chores like carrying water and food, picking seed from cotton lint (there were no cotton gins), and minding the smaller children. They were duly schooled in all the current superstitions and listened to the tales of ghosts and animals that talked and reasoned, tales common to the Negro today. Little Mandy believes to this day that hogs can see the wind and that all animals talk like men on Christmas morning at a certain time. Children wore moles feet and pearl buttons around their necks to insure easy teething and had their legs bathed in a concoction of wasp nest and vinegar if they were slow about learning to walk. This was supposed to strengthen the weak limbs. It was a common occurence to see a child of two or three years still nursing at the mother's breast. Their masters encouraged the slaves to do this, thinking it made strong bones and teeth.

At Christmas time the slave children all trouped to "de big house" and stood outside crying "Christmas gift" to their master and mistress. They were never disappointed. Gifts consisted mostly of candies, nuts and fruits but there was always some useful article of clothing included, something they were not accustomed to having. Once little Mandy received a beautiful silk dress from her young mistress, who knew how much she liked beautiful clothes. She was a very happy child and loved the dress so much that she never wore it except on some special occasion.

Amanda was trained to be a house servant, learning to cook and knit from the blind mother who refused to let this handicap affect her usefulness. She liked best to sew the fine muslins and silks of her mistress, making beautiful hooped dresses that required eight and ten yards of cloth and sometimes as many as seven petticoats to enhance their fullness.

Hoops for these dresses were made of grape-vines that were shaped while green and cured in the sun before using. Beautiful imported laces were used to trim the petticoats and pantaloons of the wealthy.

The Pamell slaves had a Negro minister who could hold services any time he chose, so long as he did not interfere with the work of the other slaves. He was not obliged to do hard menial labors and went about the plantation "all dressed up" in a frock coat and store-bought shoes. He was more than a little conscious of this and was held in awe by the others. He often visited neighboring plantations to hold his services. It was from this minister that they first heard of the Civil War. He held whispered prayers for the success of the Union soldiers, not because freedom was so desirable to them, but for other slaves who were treated so cruelly. There was a praying ground where "the grass never had a chancet ter grow fer the troubled knees that kept it crushed down."

Amanda was an exceptionally good cook and so widespread was this knowledge that the Union soldiers employed her as a cook in their camp for a short while. She does not remember any of their officers and thinks they were no better nor worse than the others. These soldiers committed no depredations in her section except to confiscate whatever they wanted in the way of food and clothing. Some married southern girls.

Mr. Pamell made land grants to all slaves who wanted to remain with him; few left, so kind had he been to them all.

Life went on in much the same manner for Amanda's family except that the children attended school where a white teacher instructed them from a "blue back Webster." Amanda was a young woman but she managed to learn to read a little. Later they had colored teachers who followed much the same routine as the whites had. They were held in awe by the other Negroes and every little girl yearned to be a teacher, as this was about the only professional field open to Negro women at that time.

"After de war Negroes blossomed out with fine phaetons (buggies) and ceiled houses, and clothes—oh my!"

Mrs. McCray did not keep up with the politics of her time but remembers hearing about Joe Gibbs, member of the Florida Legislature. There was much talk then of Booker T. Washington, and many thought him a fool for trying to start a school in Alabama for Negroes. She recalls the Negro post master who served two or three terms at Madison. She could not give his name.

There have been three widespread "panics" (depressions) during her lifetime but Mrs. McCray thinks this is the worst one. During the Civil War, coffee was so dear that meal was parched and used as a substitute but now, she remarked, "you can't hardly git the meal for the bread."

Her husband and children are all dead and she lives with a niece who is no longer young herself. Circumstances are poor here. The niece earns her living as laundress and domestic worker, receiving a very poor wage. Mrs. McCray is now quite infirm and almost blind. She seems happiest talking of the past that was a bit kinder to her.

At present she lives on the northeast corner of First and Macon Streets. The postoffice address is #11, Madison, Florida.

REFERENCE
1. Personal interview with Amanda McCray, First and Macon Streets, Madison, Florida

HENRY MAXWELL

FEDERAL WRITERS' PROJECT
American Guide, (Negro Writers' Unit)
Alfred Farrell, Field Worker
John A. Simms, Editor
Titusville, Florida
September 25, 1936

"Up from Slavery" might well be called this short biographical sketch of Henry Maxwell, who first saw the light of day on October 17, 1859 in Lownes County, Georgia. His mother Ann, was born in Virginia, and his father, Robert, was born in South Carolina. Captain Peters, Ann's owner, bought Robert Maxwell from Charles Howell as a husband for Ann. To this union were born seven children, two girls—Elizabeth and Rosetta—and five boys—Richard, Henry, Simms, Solomon and Sonnie. After the death of Captain Peters in 1863, Elizabeth and Richard were sold to the Gaines family. Rosetta and Robert (the father) were purchased from the Peters' estate by Isham Peters, Captain Peters' son, and Henry and Simms were bought by James Bamburg, husband of Izzy Peters, daughter of Captain Peters. (Solomon and Sonnie were born after slavery.)

Just a tot when the Civil War gave him and his people freedom, Maxwell's memories of bondage-days are vivid through the experiences related by older Negroes. He relates the story of the plantation owner who trained his dogs to hunt escaped slaves. He had a Negro youth hide in a tree some distance away, and then he turned the pack loose to follow him. One day he released the bloodhounds too soon, and they soon overtook the boy and tore him to pieces. When the youth's mother heard of the atrocity, she burst into tears which were only silenced by the threats of her owner to set the dogs on her. Maxwell also relates tales of the terrible beatings that the slaves received for being caught with a book or for trying to run away.

After the Civil War the Maxwell family was united for a short while, and later they drifted apart to go their various ways. Henry and his parents resided for a while longer in Lownes County, and in 1880 they came to Titusville, with the two younger children, Solomon and Sonnie. Here Henry secured work with a farmer for whom he worked for $12 a month. In 1894 he purchased a small orange grove and began to cultivate oranges. Today he owns over 30 acres of orange groves and controls nearly 200 more acres. He is said to be worth around $250,000 and is Titusville's most influential and respected colored citizen. He is married but has no children.

[TR: Interview of **Titus Bynes**, including sections about Della Bess Hilyard ("Aunt Bess") and Taylor Gilbert repeated here. References to them deleted below.]

REFERENCES
1. Personal interview of field worker with subject

CHRISTINE MITCHELL

FEDERAL WRITERS' PROJECT
American Guide, (Negro Writers' Unit)
Martin Richardson, Field Worker
Saint Augustine, Florida
November 10, 1936

An interesting description of the slave days just prior to the War Between the States is given by Christine Mitchell, of Saint Augustine.

Christine was born in slavery at Saint Augustine, remaining on the plantation until she was about 10 years old.

During her slave days she knew many of the slaves on plantations in the Saint Augustine vicinity. Several of these plantations, she says, were very large, and some of them had as many as 100 slaves.

The ex-slave, who is now 84 years old, recalls that at least three of the plantations in the vicinity were owned or operated by Minorcans. She says that the Minorcans were popularly referred to in the section as "Turnbull's Darkies," a name they apparently resented. This caused many of them, she claims, to drop or change their names to Spanish or American surnames.

Christine moved to Fernandina a few years after her freedom, and there lived near the southern tip of Amelia Island, where Negro ex-slaves lived in a small settlement all their own. This settlement still exists, although many of its former residents are either dead or have moved away.

Christine describes the little Amelia Island community as practically self-sustaining, its residents raising their own food, meats, and other commodities. Fishing was a favorite vocation with them, and some of then established themselves as small merchants of sea foods.

Several of the families of Amelia Island, according to the ex-slave, were large ones, and her own relatives, the Drummonds, were among the largest of these.

Christine Mitchell regards herself as one of the oldest remaining ex-slaves in the Saint Augustine section, and is very well known in the neighborhood of her home at St. Francis and Oneida Streets.

REFERENCES
1. Interview with subject, Christine Drummond Mitchell, Oneida street corner Saint Francis, Saint Augustine, Florida

LINDSEY MOORE

FEDERAL WRITERS PROJECT
American Guide, (Negro Unit)
Martin Richardson, Field Worker
Palatka, Florida
January 13, 1937

AN EX-SLAVE WHO WAS RESOURCEFUL

In a little blacksmith shop at 1114 Madison Street, Palatka, is a busy little horse-shoer who was born in slavery eighty-seven years ago. Lindsey Moore, blacksmith, leather-tanner ex-marble shooting champion and a number of other things, represents one of the most resourceful former slaves yet found in the state.

Moore was born in 1850 on the plantation of John B. Overtree, in Forsythe County, Georgia. He was one of the six children of Eliza Moore; all of them remained the property of Overtree until freed.

On the Overtree plantation the slave children were allowed considerable time for play until their tenth or twelfth years; Lindsey took full advantage of this opportunity and became very skillful at marble-shooting. It was here that he first learned to utilize his talents profitably. 'Massa Overtree' discovered the ability of Lindsey and another urchin to shoot marbles, and began taking them into town to compete with the little slaves of other owners. There would be betting on the winners.

Mr. Overtree won some money in this manner, Lindsey and his companion being consistent winners. But Lindsey saw possibilities other than the glory of his victories in this new game; with pennies that some of the spectators tossed him he began making small wagers of his own with his competitors, and soon had amassed quite a small pile of silver for those days.

Although shoes were unheard-of in Lindsey's youth, he used to watch carefully whenever a cow was skinned and its hide tanned to make shoes for the women and the 'folks in the big house'. Through his attention to the tanning operations he learned everything about tanning except one solution that he could not discover. It was not until years later that he learned that the jealously-guarded ingredient was plain salt and water. By the time he had learned it, however, he had so mastered the tanning operations that he at once added it to his sources of livelihood.

Lindsey escaped much of the farm work on the Overtree place by learning to skillfully assist the women who made cloth out of the cotton from the fields. He grew very fast at cleaning 'rods', clearing the looms and other operations; when, at thirteen, it became time for him to pick cotton he had become so fast at helping with spinning and weighing the cotton that others had picked that he almost entirely escaped the picking himself.

Soap-making was another of the plantation arts that Lindsey mastered early. His ability to save every possible ounce of grease from the meats he cooked added many choice bits of pork to his otherwise meatless fare; he was able to spend many hours in the shade pouring water over oak ashes that other young slaves were passing picking cotton or hoeing potatoes in the burning sun.

Lindsey's first knowledge of the approach of freedom came when he heard a loud brass band coming down the road toward the plantation playing a strange, lively tune while a number of soldiers in blue uniforms marched behind. He ran to the front gate and was ordered to take charge of the horse of one of the officers in such an abrupt tone until he 'begin to shaking in my bare feet! There followed much talk between the officers and Lindsey's mistress, with the soldiers finally going into encampment a short distance away from the plantation.

The soldiers took command of the spring that was used for a water supply for the plantation, giving Lindsey another opportunity to make money. He would be sent from the plantation to the spring for water, and on the way back would pass through the camp of the soldiers. These would be happy to pay a few pennies for a cup of water rather than take the long hike to the Spring themselves; Lindsey would empty bucket after bucket before finally returning to the plantation. Out of his profits he bought his first pair of shoes—though nearly a grown man.

The soldiers finally departed, with all but five of the Overtree slaves joyously trooping behind them. Before leaving, however, they tore up the railroad and its station, burning the ties and heating the rails until red then twisting them around tree-trunks. Wheat fields were trampled by their horses, and devastation left on all sides.

Lindsey and his mother were among those who stayed at the plantation. When freedom became general his father began farming on a tract that was later turned over to Lindsey. Lindsey operated the farm for a while, but later desired to learn horseshoeing, and apprenticed himself to a blacksmith. At the end of three years he had become so proficient that his former master rewarded him with a five-dollar bonus for shoeing one horse.

Possessing now the trades of blacksmithing, tanning and weaving-and-spinning, Lindsey was tempted to follow some of his former associates to the North, but was discouraged from doing so by a few who returned, complaining bitterly about the unaccustomed cold and the difficulty of making a living. He moved South instead and settled in the area around Palatka.

He is still in the section, being recognized as an excellent blacksmith despite his more than four-score years.

BIBLIOGRAPHY
Interview with subject, Lindsey Moore, 1114 Madison Street, Palatka, Fla.

MACK MULLEN

FEDERAL WRITERS' PROJECT
American Guide, (Negro Writers' Unit)
J.M. Johnson, Field Worker
John A. Simms, Editor
Jacksonville, Florida
September 18, 1936

Mack Mullen, a former slave who now lives at 521 W. First Street, Jacksonville, Florida, was born in Americus, Georgia in 1857, eight years before Emancipation, on a plantation which covered an area of approximately five miles. Upon this expansive plantation about 200 slaves lived and labored. At its main entrance stood a large white colonial mansion.

In this abode lived Dick Snellings, the master, and his family. The Snellings plantation produced cotton, corn, oats, wheat, peanuts, potatoes, cane and other commodities. The live stock consisted primarily of hogs and cattle. There was on the plantation what was known as a "crib," where oats, corn and wheat were stored, and a "smoke house" for pork and beef. The slaves received their rations weekly, it was apportioned according to the number in the family.

Mack Mullen's mother was named Ellen and his father Sam. Ellen was "house woman" and Sam did the blacksmithing, Ellen personally attended Mrs. Snellings, the master's wife. Mack being quite young did not have any particular duties assigned to him, but stayed around the Snellings mansion and played. Sometimes "marster" Snellings would take him on his knee and talk to him. Mack remembers that he often told him that some day he was going to be a noble man. He said that he was going to make him the head overseer. He would often give him candy and money and take him in his buggy for a ride.

Plantation Life: The slaves lived in cabins called quarters, which were constructed of lumber and logs. A white man was their overseer, he assigned the slaves their respective tasks. There was also a slave known as a "caller." He came around to the slave cabins every morning at four o'clock and blew a "cow-horn" which was the signal for the slaves to get up and prepare themselves for work in the fields.

All of them on hearing this horn would arise and prepare their meal; by six o'clock they were on their way to the fields. They would work all day, stopping only for a brief period at midday to eat. Mack Mullen says that some of the most beautiful spirituals were sung while they labored.

The women wore towels wrapped around their heads for protection from the sun, and most of them smoked pipes. The overseer often took Mack with him astride his horse as he made his "rounds" to inspect the work being done. About sundown, the "cow-horn" of the caller was blown and all hands stopped work, and made their way back to their cabins. One behind the other they marched singing "I'm gonna wait 'til Jesus Comes." After arriving at their cabins they would prepare their meals; after eating they would sometimes gather in front of a cabin and dance to the tunes played on the fiddle and the drum. The popular dance at that time was known as the "figure dance." At nine p.m. the overseer would come around; everything was supposed to be quiet at that hour. Some of the slaves would "turn in" for the night while others would remain up as long as they wished or as long as they were quiet.

The slaves were sometimes given special holidays and on those days they would give "quilting" parties (quilt making) and dances. These parties were sometimes held on their own plantation and sometimes on a neighboring one. Slaves who ordinarily wanted to visit another plantation had to get a permit from the master. If they were caught going off the plantation without a permit, they were severely whipped by the "patrolmen" (white men especially assigned to patrol duty around the plantation to prevent promiscuous wandering from plantations and "runaways.")

Whipping: There was a white man assigned only to whip the slaves when they were insubordinate; however, they were not allowed to whip them too severely as "Marster" Snellings would not permit it. He would say "a slave is of no use to me beaten to death."

Marriage: When one slave fell in love with another and wanted to marry they were given a license and the matrimony was "sealed." There was no marriage ceremony performed. A license was all that was necessary to be considered married. In the event that the lovers lived on separate plantations the master of one of them would buy the other lover or wedded one so that they would be together. When this could not be arranged they would have to visit one another, but live on their respective plantations.

Religion: The slaves had a regular church house, which was a small size building constructed of boards. Preaching was conducted by a colored minister especially assigned to this duty. On Tuesday evenings prayer meeting was held; on Thursday evenings, preaching; and on Sundays both morning and evening preaching. At these services the slaves would "get happy" and shout excitedly. Those desiring to accept Christ were admitted for baptism.

Baptism: On baptismal day, the candidates attired in white robes which they had made, marched down to the river where they were immersed by the minister. Slaves from neighboring plantations would come to witness this sacred ceremony. Mack Mullen recalls that many times his "marster" on going to view a baptism took him along in his buggy. It was a happy scene, he relates. The slaves would be there in great numbers scattered about over the banks of the river. Much shouting and singing went on. Some of the "sisters" and "brothers" would get so "happy" that they would lose control of themselves and "fall out." It was then said that the Holy Ghost had "struck 'em." The other slaves would view this phenomena with awe and reverence, and wait for them to "come out of it." "Those were happy days and that was real religion," Mack Mullen said.

Education: The slaves were not given any formal education, however, Mullen's master was not as rigid as some of the slave-holders in prohibiting the slaves from learning to read and write. Mrs. Snellings, the mistress, taught Mack's mother to read and write a little, and Mr. Snellings also taught Mack's father how to read, write and figure. Having learned a little they would in turn impart their knowledge to their fellow slaves.

Freedom: Mullen vividly recalls the day that they heard of their emancipation; loud reports from guns were heard echoing through the woods and plantations; after awhile "Yankee" soldiers came and informed them that they were free. Mr. Snellings showed no resistance and he was not harmed. The slaves on hearing this good news of freedom burst out in song and praises to God: it was a gala day. No work was done for a week; the time was spent in celebrating. The master told his slaves that they were free and could go wherever they wanted to, or they could remain with him if they wished. Most of his 200 slaves refused to leave him because he was considered a good master.

They were thereafter given individual farms, mules and farm implements with which to cultivate the land; their former master got a share out of what was raised. There was no more whipping, no more forced labor and hours were less drastic.

Mack Mullen's parents were among those slaves who remained; they lived there until Mr. Snellings died, and then moved to Isonvillen, near Americus, Georgia, where his father opened a black-smith shop, and made enough money to buy some property. Another child was added to the family, a girl named Mariah. By this time Mack had become a young man with a strong desire to travel, so he bade his parents farewell and headed for Tampa, Florida. After living there awhile he came to Jacksonville, Florida. At the time of his arrival in Jacksonville, Bay Street was paved with blocks and there were no hard surfaced streets in the city.

He was one of the construction, foremen of the Windsor Hotel. Mack Mullen is tall, grey haired, sharp featured and of Caucasian strain (his mother was a mulatto) with a keen mind and an appearance that belies his 75 years. He laments that he was freed because his master was good to his slaves; he says "we had everything we wanted; never did I think I'd come to this—got to get relief." (1)

REFERENCE
1. From an interview with Mack Mullen, a former slave at his residence, 521 West First Street, Jacksonville, Florida

LOUIS NAPOLEON

FEDERAL WRITERS' PROJECT
American Guide, (Negro Writers' Unit)
J.M. Johnson, Field Worker
Jacksonville, Florida
November 17, 1936

About three miles from South Jacksonville proper down the old Saint Augustine Road lives one Louis Napoleon an ex-slave, born in Tallahassee, Florida about 1857, eight years prior to Emancipation.

His parents were Scipio and Edith Napoleon, being originally owned by Colonel John S. Sammis of Arlington, Florida and the Floyd family of Saint Marys, Georgia, respectively.

Scipio and Edith were sold to Arthur Randolph, a physician and large plantation owner of Fort Louis, about five miles from the capital at Tallahassee. On this large plantation that covered and area of about eight miles and composed approximately of 90 slaves is where Louis Napoleon first saw the light of day.

Louis' father was known as the wagoner. His duties were to haul the commodities raised on the plantation and other things that required a wagon. His mother Edith, was known as a "breeder" and was kept in the palatial Randolph mansion to loom cloth for the Randolph family and slaves. The cloth was made from the cotton raised on the plantation's fertile fields. As Louis was so young, he had no particular duties, only to look for hen nests, gather eggs and play with the master's three young boys. There were seven children in the Randolph family, three young boys, two "missy" girls and two grown sons. Louis would go fishing and hunting with the three younger boys and otherwise engage with them in their childish pranks.

He says that his master and mistress were very kind to the slaves and would never whip them, nor would he allow the "driver" who was a white man named Barton to do so. Barton lived in a home especially built for him on the plantation. If the "driver" whipped any of them, all that was necessary for the slave who had been whipped was to report it to the master and the "driver" was dismissed, as he was a salaried man.

Plantation Life. The slaves lived in log cabins especially built for them. They were ceiled and arranged in such a manner as to retain the heat in winter from the large fireplaces constructed therein.

Just before the dawn of day, the slaves were aroused from their slumber by a loud blast from a cow-horn that was blown by the "driver" as a signal to prepare themselves for the fields. The plantation being so expansive, those who had to go a long distance to the area where they worked, were taken in wagons, those working nearby walked. They took their meals along with them and had their breakfast and dinner on the fields. An hour was allowed for this purpose. The slaves worked while they sang spirituals to break the monotony of long hours of work. At the setting of the sun, with their day's work all done, they returned to their cabins and prepared their evening's meal. Having finished this, the religious among them would gather at one of the cabin doors and give thanks to God in the form of long supplications and old fashioned songs. Many of them being highly emotional would respond in shouts of hallelujahs sometimes causing the entire group to become "happy" concluding in shouting and praise to God. The wicked slaves expended their pent up emotions in song and dance. Gathering at one of the cabin doors they would sing and dance to the tunes of a fife, banjo or fiddle that was played by one of their number. Finished with this diversion they would retire to await the dawn of a new day which indicated more work. The various plantations had white men employed as "patrols" whose duties were to see that the slaves remained on their own plantations, and if they were caught going off without a permit from the master, they were whipped with a "raw hide" by the "driver." There was an exception to this rule, however, on Sundays the religious slaves were allowed to visit other plantations where religious services were being held without having to go through the matter of having a permit.

Religion. There was a free colored man who was called "Father James Page," owned by a family of Parkers of Tallahassee. He was freed by them to go and preach to his own people. He could read and write and would visit all the plantations in Tallahassee, preaching the gospel. Each plantation would get a visit from him one Sunday of each month. The slaves on the Randolph plantation would congregate in one of the cabins to receive him where he would read the Bible and preach and sing. Many times the services were punctuated by much shouting from the "happy ones." At these services the sacrament was served to those who had accepted Christ, those who had not, and were willing to accept Him were received and prepared for baptism on the next visit of "Father Page."

On the day of baptism, the candidates were attired in long white flowing robes, which had been made by one of the slaves. Amidst singing and praises they marched, being flanked on each side by other believers, to a pond or lake on the plantation and after the usual ceremony they were "ducked" into the water. This was a day of much shouting and praying.

Education. The two "missy" girls of the Randolph family were dutiful each Sunday morning to teach the slaves their catechism or Sunday School lesson. Aside from this there was no other training.

The War and Freedom. Mr. Napoleon relates that the doctor's two oldest sons went to the war with the Confederate army, also the white "driver," Barton. His place was filled by one of the slaves, named Peter Parker.

At the closing of the war, word was sent around among the slaves that if they heard the report of a gun, it was the Yankees and that they were free.

It was in May, in the middle of the day, cotton and corn being planted, plowing going on, and slaves busily engaged in their usual activities, when suddenly the loud report of a gun resounded, then could be heard the slaves crying almost en-masse, "dems de Yankees." Straightway they dropped the plows, hoes and other farm implements and hurried to their cabins. They put on their best clothes "to go see the Yankees." Through the countryside to the town of Tallahassee they went. The roads were quickly filled with these happy souls. The streets of Tallahassee were clustered with these jubilant people going here and there to get a glimpse of the Yankees, their liberators. Napoleon says it was a joyous and un-forgetable occasion.

When the Randolph slaves returned to their plantation, Dr. Randolph told them that they were free, and if they wanted to go away, they could, and if not, they could remain with him and he would give them half of what was raised on the farms. Some of them left, however, some remained, having no place to go, they decided it was best to remain until the crops came off, thus earning enough to help them in their new venture in home seeking. Those slaves who were too old and not physically able to work, remained on the plantation and were cared for by Dr. Randolph until their death.

Napoleon's father, Scipio, got a transfer from the government to his former master, Colonel Sammis of Arlington, and there he lived for awhile. He soon got employment with a Mr. Hatee of the town and after earning enough money, bought a tract of land from him there and farmed. There his family lived and increased. Louis being the oldest of the children obtained odd jobs with the various settlers, among them being Governor Reid of Florida who lived in South Jacksonville. Governor Reid raised cattle for market and Napoleon's job was to bring them across the Saint Johns River on a litter to Jacksonville, where they were sold.[HW:?]

Louis Napoleon is now aged and infirm, his father and mother having died many years ago. He now lives with one of his younger brothers who has a fair sized orange grove on the south side of Jacksonville. He retains the property that his father first bought after freedom and on which they lived in Arlington. His hair white and he is bent with age and ill health but his mental faculties are exceptionally keen for one of his age. He proudly tells you that his master was good to his "niggers" and cannot recall but one time that he saw him whip one of them and that when one tried to run away to the Yankees. Only memories of a kind master in his days of servitude remain with him as he recalls the dark days of slavery.

REFERENCES
Personal interview with Louis Napoleon, South Jacksonville, Florida

MARGRETT NICKERSON

FEDERAL WRITERS' PROJECT
American Guide, (Negro Writers' Unit)
Rachel A. Austin, Field Worker
Jacksonville, Florida
December 5, 1936

In her own vernacular, Margrett Nickerson was "born to William A. Carr, on his plantation near Jackson, Leon County, many years ago."

When questioned concerning her life on this plantation, she continues: "Now honey, its been so long ago, I don' 'member ev'ything, but I will tell you whut I kin as near right as possible; I kin 'member five uf Marse Carr's chillun; Florida, Susan, 'Lijah, Willie and Tom; cose Carr never 'lowed us to have a piece uf paper in our hands."

"Mr. Kilgo was de fust overseer I 'member; I was big enough to tote meat an' stuff frum de smokehouse to de kitchen and to tote water in and git wood for granny to cook de dinner and fur de sucklers who nu'sed de babies, an' I carried dinners back to de hands."

"On dis plantation dere was 'bout a hunnerd head; cookin' was done in de fireplace in iron pots and de meals was plenty of peas, greens, cornbread burnt co'n for coffee—often de marster bought some coffee fur us; we got water frum de open well. Jes 'fore de big gun fiahed dey fotched my pa frum de bay whar he was makin' salt; he had heerd dam say 'de Yankees is coming and wuz so glad."

"Dere wuz rice, cotton, co'n, tater fields to be tended to and cowhides to be tanned, thread to be spinned, and thread wuz made into ropes for plow lines."

"Ole Marse Carr fed us, but he did not care what an' whar, jes so you made dat money and when yo' made five and six bales o' cotton, said: 'Yo' ain don' nuthin'."

"When de big gun fiahed on a Sattidy me and Cabe and Minnie Howard wuz settin' up co'n fur de plowers to come 'long and put dirt to 'em; Carr read de free papers to us on Sunday and de co'n and cotton had to be tended to—he tole us he wuz goin' to gi' us de net proceeds (here she chuckles), what turned out to be de co'n and cotton stalks. Den he asked dem whut would stay wid him to step off on de right and dem dat wuz leavin' to step off on da left."

"My pa made soap frum ashes when cleaning new ground—he took a hopper to put de ashes in, made a little stool side de house put de ashes in and po'red water on it to drip; at night after gittin' off frum work he'd put in de grease and make de soap—I made it sometime and I make it now, myself."

"My step-pa useter make shoes frum cowhides fur de farm han's on de plantation and fur eve'body on de plantation 'cept ole Marse and his fambly; dey's wuz diffunt, fine."

"My grandma wus Pheobie Austin—my mother wuz name Rachel Jackson and my pa wus name Edmund

Jackson; my mother and uncle Robert and Joe wus stol' frum Virginia and fetched here. I don' know no niggers dat 'listed in de war; I don' 'member much 'bout de war only when de started talking 'bout drillin' men fur de war, Joe Sanders was a lieutenant. Marse Carr's sons, Tom and Willie went to de war."

"We didn' had no doctors, only de grannies; we mos'ly used hippecat (ipecac) fur medicine."

"As I said, Kilgo was de fust overseer I ricollec', then Sanders wuz nex' and Joe Sanders after him; John C. Haywood came in after Sanders and when de big gun fiahed old man Brockington wus dere. I never saw a nigger sold, but dey carried dem frum our house and I never seen 'em no mo'."

"We had church wid de white preachers and dey tole us to mind our masters and missus and we would be saved; if not, dey said we wouldn'. Dey never tole us nothin' 'bout Jesus. On Sunday after workin' hard all de week dey would lay down to sleep and be so tired; soon ez yo' git sleep, de overseer would come an' wake you up an' make you go to church."

"When de big gun fiahed old man Carr had six sacks uf confederate money whut he wuz carrying wid him to Athens Georgia an' all de time if any uf us gals whar he wuz an' ax him 'Marse please gi us some money' (here she raises her voice to a high, pitiful tone) he says' I aint got a cent' and right den he would have a chis so full it would take a whol' passle uv slaves to move it. He had plenty corn, taters, pum'kins, hogs, cows ev'ything, but he didn' gi us nuthin but strong plain close and plenty to eat; we slept in ole common beds and my pa made up little cribs and put hay in dem fur de chillun."

"Now ef you wanted to keep in wid Marster Carr don' drap you shoes in de field an' leave 'em—he'd beat you; you mus' tote you' shoes frum one field to de tother, didn' a dog ud be bettern you. He'd say 'You gun-haided devil, drappin' you' shoes and eve'thin' over de field'."

"Now jes lis'en, I wanna tell you all I kin, but I wants to tell it right; wait now, I don' wanna make no mistakes and I don' wanna lie on nobody—I ain' mad now and I know taint no use to lie, I takin' my time. I done prayed an' got all de malice out o' my heart and I ain' gonna tell no lie fer um and I ain' gonna tell no lie on um. I ain' never seed no slaves sold by Marster Carr, he wuz allus tellin' me he wuz gonna sell me but he never did—he sold my pa's fust wife though."

"Dere wuz Uncle George Bull, he could read and write and, chile, de white folks didn't lak no nigger whut could read and write. Carr's wife Miss Jane useter teach us Sunday School but she did not 'low us to tech a book wid us hands. So dey useter jes take uncle George Bull and beat him fur nothin; dey would beat him and take him to de lake and put him on a log and shev him in de lake, but he always swimmed out. When dey didn' do dat dey would beat him tel de blood run outen him and den trow him in de ditch in de field and kivver him up wid dirt, head and years and den stick a stick up at his haid. I wuz a water toter and had stood and seen um do him dat way more'n once and I stood and looked at um tel dey went 'way to de other rows and den I grabbed de dirt ofen him and he'd bresh de dirt off and say 'tank yo', git his hoe and go on back to work. Dey beat him lak dat and he didn' do a thin' to git dat sort uf treatment."

"I had a sister name Lytie Holly who didn' stand back on non' uv em; when dey'd git behin' her, she'd git behin' dem; she wuz dat stubbo'n and when dey would beat her she wouldn' holler and jes take it and go on. I got some whuppin's wid strops but I wanter tell you why I am cripple today:

"I had to tote tater vines on my haid, me and Fred'rick and de han's would be a callin fur em all over de field but you know honey, de two uv us could' git to all uvum at once, so Joe Sanders would hurry us up by beatin' us with strops and sticks and run us all over de tater ridge; he cripple us both up and den we couldn' git to all uv em. At night my pa would try to fix me up cose I had to go back to work nex' day. I never walked straight frum dat day to dis and I have to set here in dis chair now, but I don' feel mad none now. I feels good and wants to go to he'ven—I ain' gonna tel no lie on white nor black cose taint no use."

"Some uv de slaves run away, lots uv um. Some would be cot and when dey ketched em dey put bells on em; fust dey would put a iron ban' 'round dey neck and anuder one 'round de waist and rivet um together down de back; de bell would hang on de ban' round de neck so dat it would ring when de slave walked and den dey wouldn' git 'way. Some uv dem wore dese bells three and four mont'n and when dey time wuz up dey would take em off 'em. Jake Overstreet, George Bull, John Green, Ruben Golder, Jim Bradley and a hos' uv others wore dem bells. Dis is whut I know, not whut somebody else say. I seen dis myself. En missus, when de big gun fiahed, de runerway slaves comed out de woods frum all directions. We wuz in de field when it fiahed, but I 'members dey wuz all very glad."

"After de war, we worked but we got pay fur it."

"Ole man Pierce and others would call some kin' of a perlitical (political) meetin' but I could never understan' whut dey wuz talkin' 'bout. We didn' had no kin' uv schools and all I knows but dem is dat I sent my chillums in Leon and Gadsden Counties."

"I had lots uv sisters and brothers but I can't 'member de names of none by Lytie, Mary, Patsy and Ella; my brothers, is Edmond and Cornelius Jackson. Cornelius is livin' now somewhere I think but I don' never see him."

"When de big gun fiahed I was a young missy totin' cotton to de scales at de ginhouse; ef de ginhouse wuz close by, you had to tote de cotton to it, but ef it wuz fur 'way wagins ud come to de fields and weigh it up and take it to de ginhouse. I was still livin' near Lake Jackson and we went to Abram Bailey's place near Tallahassee. Carr turned us out without nuthin and Bailey gi'd us his hammoc' and we went dere fur a home. Fust we cut down saplin's fur we didn' had no house, and took de tops uv pines and put on de top; den we put dirt on top uv dese saplin's and slep' under dem. When de rain would come, it would wash all de dirt right down in our face and we'd hafter buil' us a house all over ag'in. We didn' had no body to buil' a house fur us, cose pa was gone and ma jes had us gals and we cut de saplin's fer de man who would buil' de house fer us. We live on Bailey's place a long time and fin'lly buil' us a log cabin and den we went frum dis cabin to Gadsden County to a place name Concord and dere I stay tel I come here 'fore de fiah."

"I had twelve chillun but right now missus, I can only 'member dese names: Robert, 'Lijah, Edward, Cornelius, Littie, Rachel and Sophie."

"I was converted in Leon County and after freedom I joined de Methodist church and my membership is now in Mount Zion A.M.E. Church in Jacksonville, Florida."

"My fust husban was Nelson Walker and de las' one was name Dave Nickerson. I don' think I was 20 years old when de big gun fiahed, but I was more' 17—I reckon I wuz a little older den Flossie May (a niece who is 17 years of age) is now." (1)

Mrs. Nickerson, according to her information must be about 89 or 90 years of age, sees without glasses having never used them; she does not read or write but speaks in a convincing manner. She has most of her teeth and a splendid appetite. She spends her time sitting in a wheel-chair sewing on quilts. She has several quilts that she has pieced, some from very small scraps which she has cut without the use of any particular pattern. She has a full head of beautiful snowy white hair and has the use of her limbs, except her legs, and is able to do most things for herself. (2)

She lives with her daughter at 1600 Myrtle Avenue, Jacksonville, Florida.

REFERENCES

1. Personal interview with Margrett Nickerson, 1600 Myrtle Avenue, Jacksonville, Florida

2. Sophia Nickerson Starke, 1600 Myrtle Avenue, daughter of Margrett Nickerson, Jacksonville, Florida

[TR: References moved from beginning of interview.]

DOUGLAS PARISH

FEDERAL WRITERS' PROJECT
American Guide, (Negro Writers' Unit)
Rachel A. Austin, Field Worker
Monticello, Florida
November 10, 1936

Douglas Parish was born in Monticello, Florida, May 7, 1850, to Charles and Fannie Parish, slaves of Jim Parish. Fannie had been bought from a family by the name of Palmer to be a "breeder", that is a bearer of strong children who could bring high prices at the slave markets. A "breeder" always fared better than the majority of female slaves, and Fannie Parish was no exception. All she had to do was raise children. Charles Parish labored in the cotton fields, the chief product of the Parish plantation.

As a small boy Douglas used to spend his time shooting marbles, playing ball, racing and wrestling with the other boys. The marbles were made from lumps of clay hardened in the fireplace. He was a very good runner, and as it was a custom in those days for one plantation owner to match his "nigger" against that of his neighbor, he was a favorite with Parish because he seldom failed to win the race. Parish trained his runners by having them race to the boundary of his plantation and back again. He would reward the winner with a jack-knife or a bag of marbles.

Just to be first was an honor in itself, for the fastest

runner represented his master in the Fourth of July races when runners from all over the country competed for top honors, and the winner earned a bag of silver for his master. If Parish didn't win the prize, he was hard to get along with for several days, but gradually he would accept his defeat with resolution. Prizes in less important races ranged from a pair of fighting cocks to a slave, depending upon the seriousness of the betting.

Douglas' first job was picking cotton seed from the cotton. When he was about 12 years of age, he became the stable boy, and soon learned about the care and grooming of horses from an old slave who had charge of the Parish stables. He was also required to keep the buggies, surreys, and spring-wagons clean. The buggies were light four-wheeled carriages drawn by one horse. The surreys were covered four-wheeled carriages, open at the sides, but having curtains that may be rolled down. He liked this job very much because it gave him an opportunity to ride on the horses, the desire of all the boys on the plantation. They had to be content with chopping wood, running errands, cleaning up the plantation, and similar tasks. Because of his knowledge of horses, Douglas was permitted to travel to the coast with his boss and other slaves for the purpose of securing salt from the sea water. It was cheaper to secure salt by this method than it was to purchase it otherwise.

Life in slavery was not all bad, according to Douglas. Parish fed his slaves well, gave them comfortable quarters in which to live, looked after them when they were sick, and worked them very moderately. The food was cooked in the fireplace in large iron pots, pans and ovens. The slaves had greens, potatoes, corn, rice, meat, peas, and corn bread to eat. Occasionally the corn bread was replaced by flour bread. The slaves drank an imitation coffee made from parched corn or meal. Since there was no ice to preserve the left-over food, only enough for each meal was prepared.

Parish seldom punished his slaves, and never did he permit his overseer to do so. If the slaves failed to do their work, they were reported to him. He would warn them and show his black whip which was usually sufficient. He had seen overseers beat slaves to death, and he did not want to risk losing the money he had invested in his. After his death, his son managed the plantation in much the same manner as his father.

But the war was destined to make the Parishes lose all their slaves by giving them their freedom. Even though they were free to go, many of the slaves elected to remain with their mistress who had always been kind to them. The war swept away much of the money which her husband had left her; and although she would liked to have kept all of her slaves, she found it impossible to do so. She allowed the real old slaves to remain on the premises and kept a few of the younger ones to work about the plantation. Douglas and his parents were among those who remained on the plantation. His father was a skilled bricklayer and carpenter, and he was employed to make repairs to the property. His mother cooked for the Parishes.

Many of the Negroes migrated North, and they wrote back stories of the "new country" where "de white folks let you do jes as you please." These stories influenced a great number of other Negroes to go North and begin life anew as servants, waiters, laborers and cooks. The Negroes who remained in the South were forced to make their own living. At the end of the war, foods and commodities had gone up to prices that were impossible for the Negro to pay. Ham, for example, cost 40¢ and 50¢ a pound; lard was 25¢; cotton was two dollars a bushel.

Douglas' father taught him all that he knew about carpentry and bricklaying, and the two were in demand to repair, remodel, or build houses for the white people. Although he never attended school, Charles Parish could calculate very rapidly the number of bricks that it would take to build a house. After the establishing of schools by the Freedmen's Bureau, Douglas' father made him go, but he did not like the confinement of school and soon dropped out. The teachers for the most part, were white, who were concerned only with teaching the ex-slaves reading, writing, and arithmetic. The few colored teachers went into the community in an effort to elevate the standards of living. They went into the churches where they were certain to reach the greatest number of people and spoke to them of their mission. The Negro teachers were cordially received by the ex-slaves who were glad to welcome some "Yankee niggers" into their midst.

Whereas the white teachers did not bother with the Negroes except in the classroom, other white men came who showed a decided interest in them. They were called "carpetbaggers" because of the type of traveling bag which they usually carried, and this term later became synonymous with "political adventurer." These men sought to advance their political schemes by getting the Negroes to vote for certain men who would be favorable to them. They bought the Negro votes or put a Negro in some unimportant office to obtain the goodwill of the ex-slaves. They used the ignorant colored minister to further their plans, and he was their willing tool. The Negro's unwise use of his ballot plunged the South further and further into debt and as a result the South was compelled to restrict his privileges.

REFERENCE
1. Personal interview with Douglas Parish, Monticello, Florida

United States. Work Projects Administration

GEORGE PRETTY

FEDERAL WRITERS' PROJECT
American Guide, (Negro Writers' Unit)
Viola B. Muse, Field Worker
Palatka, Florida
November 9, 1936

George Pretty of Vero Beach and Gifford, Florida, was born a free man, at Altoona, Pennsylvania, January 30, 1852. His father Isaac Pretty was also free born. His maternal grand-father Alec McCoy and his paternal grand-father George Pretty were born slaves who lived in the southern part of Pennsylvania.

He does not know how his father came to be born free but knows that he was told that from early childhood.

In Altoona, according to George, there were no slaves during his life there but in southern Pennsylvania slavery existed for a time. His grand-parents moved from southern Pennsylvania during slavery but whether they bought their freedom or ran away from their masters was never known to George.

As in most of the southland, the customs of the Negro in Altoona abounded in superstition and ignorance. They had about the same beliefs and looked upon life with about the same degree of intelligence as Negroes in the south.

The north being much colder than the south naturally had long ago used coal for fuel. Open grates were used for cooking just as open fireplaces were used in the south. Iron skillets or spiders as they called them, were used for cooking many foods, meats, vegetables, pies puddings and even cakes were baked over the fire.

The old familiar, often referred to as southern ash cake, was cooked on the hearth under the grate, right in Altoona, Pennsylvania. The north because of its rapid advance in the use of modern ways of cooking and doing many other things has been thought by many people to have escaped the crude methods of cooking, but not so. George told how a piece of thick paper was placed on the hearth under the grate and corn dough put upon it to bake. Hot ashes were raked over it and it was left to cook and brown. When it had remained a long enough time, the ashes were shaken off, the cake brushed clean with a cloth and no grit was encountered when it was eaten.

Isaac Pretty, George's father owned a large harness shop at Altoona and made and sold hundreds of dollars worth of saddles and harness to both northern and southern plantation owners. (1)

There was a constant going and coming of northern and southern owners; southern ones seeking places to buy implements for farming and other inventions as well as trying to locate runaway slaves.

Abolitionists were active in the north and there were those who assisted slaves across the boundary lines between free and slave states.

Negroes in the north who were free and had intelligence enough saw the gravity in assisting their slave brothers in the south. Some risked their lives in spreading propaganda which they thought would aid the enslaved Negroes in becoming free.

In and around Altoona, Negroes were very progressive and appreciated their freedom, and had a great deal of sympathy for their fellows and did all they could to demonstrate their attitude toward the slave traffic. Money was solicited and freely given to help abolitionists spread propaganda about freedom.

It is striking to note the similarity of living conditions in Pennsylvania and Georgia, Florida and the Carolinas. Ex-slaves who live in Florida now but who came here since the Emancipation of the Negro tell of living conditions of their respective states; they are very similar to the modes of living in Altoona, during slavery. (2)

Soap was made from grease and lye just as it was made in the south. Shin-plaster (paper money similar to green back, which represented amounts less than a dollar) were very plentiful and after the Civil War confederate money of all kinds was as so much trash.

Food stuffs which were raised on the farm at Altoona were: corn, peanuts, white potatoes and peas. Enough peas were raised to feed the stock and take care of the family for 18 months. Potatoes were raised in large quantities and after they were dug they were banked for the winter. By banked, it is meant, large holes were dug in the cellar of the house or under the house or inside of an outhouse; pine straw was put into this pit and the potatoes piled in; more straw was laid on and more potatoes piled in until all were in the pit. Dirt was shoveled over the lot and it was left until for using them. Northern people used and still use a large amount of white, or Irish potatoes.

In curing hides of cows for making leather the same method was employed as that used in the south. Hides were first salted and water was poured over them. They were covered with dirt and left to soak a few days. A solution of red oak bark was made by soaking the bark in water and this solution was poured over the hides. After it soaked a few days the hair was scraped off with a stiff brush and when it dried leather was ready for making shoes and harness.

George's father dealt extensively in leather and when he could not get enough cured himself, he bought of others who could supply him.

Now George's mother was very handy at the spinning wheel and loom. He remembers how the bunch of cotton was combed in preparation for spinning. Cards with teeth were arranged on the spinning wheel and the mass of cotton was combed through it to separate it into fibers. The fibers were rolled between the fingers and then put upon the spinning wheel to be spun into thread. As it was spun, it was wound upon spools. After the spools were filled they were taken off and put on the loom. Threads were strung across the loom some above others and the shuttle running back and forth through the threads would make cloth. All that was done by hand power. A person working at the loom regularly soon became proficient and George's mother was one who bore the name of being a very good weaver of cloth. Most of the clothes the family wore were home spun.

Underwear and sleeping garments were made of the natural colored homespun cloth. When colored cloth was wanted a dye was made to dip them in so as to get the desired color. Dyes were made by soaking red oak bark in water. Another was made of elder berries and when a real blood red was desired polk berries were used. Polk berries made a blood red dye and was considered very beautiful. Walnut hulls were used to make brown dye and it was lasting in its effects.

In making dye hold its color, the cloth and dye were boiled together. After it had "taken" well, the cloth was removed from the dye and rinsed well, the rinse water was salted so as to set the color.

Tubs for washing clothes and bathing purposes were made of wood. Some were made from barrels out in tew parts. In cutting a stay was left longer on each side and holes were cut length wise in it so there would be sufficient room for all of the fingers to fit. That was for lifting the tub about.

A very interesting side of George's life was depicted in his statement of the longevity of his innocence. We may call it ignorance but it seems to be more innocence when compared to the incident of Adam and Eve as told in the Holy Bible in the book of Genesis. He was 33 years of age before he knew he was a grown man, or how life was given humans. In plain words he did not know where babies came from, nor how they were bred.

Whenever George's mother was expecting to be confined with a baby's birth, his father would say to all the children together, large and small alike, "your mother has gone to New York, Baltimore, Buffalo" or any place he would think of at the time. There was an upstairs room in their home and she would stay there six weeks. She would go up as soon as signs of the coming child would present themselves. A midwife came, cooked three meals a day, fed the children and helped keep the place in order.

In older times people taught their children to respect older persons. They obeyed everyone older than themselves. The large children were just as obedient as the small ones so that it was not hard to maintain peace and order within any home.

The midwife in this case simply told all of the children that she did not want any of them to go upstairs, as she had important papers spread out all over the floor and did not want them disturbed. No questions were asked, she was obeyed.

George does not remember having heard a single cry the whole time they were being born in that upper room, and he said many a baby was born there. Decorum reigned throughout the household for six weeks or until their mother was ready to come down. When the time was up for mother to come down, his father would casually say, "children your ma is coming home today and what do you recon, someone has given her another baby." The children would say, almost in concert, "what you say pa, is it a boy or girl?" He would tell them which it was and nothing more was said nor any further inquiry made into the happening.

The term "broke her leg" was used to convey the meaning of pregnancy. George relates how his mother told him and his sister not to have any thing more to do with Mary Jones, "cause she done broke her leg." George said "Ma taint nothin matter wid Mary; I see her every day when the bell rings for 12; she works across the street from Pa's shop and she and me sets on the steps and talks till time fur her to go back to work." His mother said, "dont spute me George, I know she is broke her leg and I want yall to stay way frum her." George said, "Ma I aint sputing you, jes somebody done misinform you dats all. She aint got no broke leg, she walks as good as me." His mother said "then I'm a lie." George quickly replied, "no ma, you aint no lie, but somebody done told you wrong."

Nothing was said further on the question of Mary Jones until that same evening when Isaac Pretty came home from the shop. The mother took him aside and told him of how she had been disputed and called a lie by George and added that she wanted George whipped for it.

"Come here George," came a commanding voice shortly after the mother and father had been in conference. George obeyed and his father took him apart from the family and locked himself and George in a room. He said "George I know I haven't done right by not telling you, you are grown. You are 33 years old now and I want to tell you some things you should know." George was all eyes and ears, for he had been told when previously asked how old he was, "I'll tell you when you get grown." That was all he had heard from his parents for years and he was just waiting for him to tell him. His father told him how babies were born and about his mother confining herself in the upper room all the different times when she expected babies. He told him that his mother had never been out of town to Boston or Baltimore on any of the past occasions. In fact he told George all he knew to tell him.

Now the startling thing about it all is that when he had finished giving the information about babies he said, "Now George your mother told me that you called her a lie today." George at once said, "Pa I didn't call her a lie, I jes told someone had misinform her 'bout Mary, that she aint got her leg broke cause I see her every day." His father said "I know 'taint right to whip you fur that George but your Ma said she wanted me to whip you and I'll have to do it." That settled it. George received his first lesson in sex and received the last flogging his father ever gave him. He was now grown and could take his place as a man.

Afterwards the mother took all her daughters aside and told them the same as Isaac had told George. (That is she told the grown girls about sex life.)

George and his older sister talked the whole plan over after they got a chance and decided that since they were now grown, they did not have to give their earnings to their parents any longer. They decided to move into one of their father's houses on the place and furnish it up. They were making right good money considering the times related George, and with both of them pulling together they soon would have sufficient money saved up to buy a piece of land and start out on a plot of ground of their own.

George told his father their plans. His father asked how much money he had. He told him 200 dollars or more. His father said "you've saved 200 dollars out of what I've allowed you?" George answered in the affirmative. His father said, "do you know how far that will go?" George said he did not, his father answered "Not far my boy."

A few days after the conversation, Isaac Pretty furnished one of his houses with the necessary equipment and let George and his sister live there. They had their own bed-rooms and each bought some food. The girl and George both cooked the meals and did the main thing they had set out to do, letting nothing stand in the way of their progress.

When a few months had passed both children had accumulated a nice sum of money. George was prepared to marry and take care of a wife. His sister Eliza, who lived with him had saved almost as much money and when she married she was an asset to the man of her choice rather than a liability.

George had close contact with nature in his early life. The close contact with his mother for 33 years had done something for George which was lasting as well as beneficial. She was a close adherent to nature. She believed in and knew the roots and herbs which cured bodily ailments. This was handed down to her children and George Pretty claims to know every root and herb in the woods. He can identify each as they are presented to him, says he.

Doctors were never used by the ordinary family when George was growing up and during his stay at Altoona.

He was called in to sew up a cut place which was too much for home treatment. He was also called in to probe for a bullet but for fever or colds or even childbirth he was considered an unnecessary expense.

Herbs and roots were widely utilized in olden days and during slavery and early reconstruction. The old slave has brought his practices to this era and he is often found gathering and using them upon his friends and neighbors.

George Pretty knows that black snake root is good for blood trouble for he has used it on many a person with safety and surety. Sasafras tea is good for colds; golden rod tea for fever; fig leaves for thrash; red oak bark for douche; slippery elm for fever and female complaint (when bark is inserted in the vagina); catnip tea is good for new born babies; sage tea is good for painful menstruation or slackened flow; fig leaves bruised and applied to the forehead for fever are very affective; they are also good to draw boils to a head; okra blossoms when dried are good for sores (the dried blossoms are soaked in water and applied to the sore and bound with clean old linen cloth); red shank is good for a number of diseases; missing link root is for colds and asthma. George said this is a sure cure for asthma. Fever grass is a purgative when taken in the form of a tea. The blades are steeped in hot water and a tea made. Fever grass is a wide blade grass growing straighter than most grass. It has a blue flower and is found growing wild around many places in Florida. It is plentiful in certain parts of Palatka, Florida.

Riding vehicles in early days were called buggies. The first one George remembers was the go cart. It had two wheels and was without a top. Only two people could ride in a go cart. The equilibrium was kept by buckling the harness over and under the horse's belly. The strap which ran under the belly was called the belly girt. There was a side strap which ran along the horse's side and the belly girt was fastened to this. Loops were put to vantage points on the side strap and through these the shafts of the cart were run. The strap going under and over the horse kept the cart from going too far forward or backward.

During George's early life plows looked very much like they do today. They had wooden handles but the part which turned the ground was made of point iron, (he could not describe point iron.) Plows were not made of cast iron or steel as they are today.

Two kinds of plows were used so far as George remembers. One was called the skooter plow and the other the turn plow. The skooter plow he describes as one which broke the ground up which had been previously planted. When the earth needed loosening up to make more fit for planting, this plow was used over the earth, leaving it rather smooth and light. The turn plow was used to turn the ground completely over. Where grass and weeds had grown, the earth needed turning over so as to thoroughly uproot the weeds and grass. The ground was usually left a while so that the weeds could die and rot and then men with hoes would go over the ground and make it ready for planting.

When freedom came to Negroes in the slave territory, George remembers that Sherman's army drilled a long time after the Civil War had ended. He saw them right in Pennsylvania. He was much impressed with their blue suits and brass buttons and which fitted them so well. Some of the men wore suits with braid on them and they supposedly were the officers of the outfit. Negro and white men were in the same companies he saw and all were manly and walking proudly.

As George was fifteen years of age when freedom came much of which he related happened after Emancipation. He being out of the slave territory did not have as much contact with the slaves, but he lived around his grand parents who had been slaves in the southern part of the state. After slavery they moved up to Altoona, with George's parents and brought much in the way of customs to George.

Grandfather McCoy and also grandfather Pretty told of many experiences that they went through during their enslavement. The Negro and white over-seer was much in evidence down there and buying and selling of children from their parents seemed to have left a sad memory with George.

Isaac Pretty's family was large. He had seven girls and seven boys, George being the eldest. George remembers how his heart would ache when his grandfather told of the children who were torn from their mother's skirts and sold, never to see their parents again. He went into deep thought over how he would have hated to have been separated from his mother and father to say nothing of leaving his brothers and sisters. They were brought up to love each other and the thought of breaking the family ties seemed to him very cruel.

When George was told that he was grown as formerly related, he saved his money and when the great earth quake in Charleston occured he went down there to see what it had done to the place. Before that time in 1882 he remembered having seen the first block of ice. When he got there, the Charleston people had been making ice for a few years. It was about that time that George saw the first pair of bed springs.

George remained in Pennsylvania and other states farther north for a long time after freedom. His first trip to Florida was made in 1893. He came direct from Altoona, Pennsylvania, with a white man whose name he has forgotten as he did not remain in the man's employ very long after reaching the state.

Since that time he has farmed in and around different parts of Florida, but now he resides at Tero Beach and Gifford, Florida. He makes regular trips to Palatka, being as much at home there as in the cities on the East Coast.

George says that he has never had a doctor attend him in his life, neither while he was in Altoona, nor since he has been in Florida. He claims to be able to identify any root or herb that grows in the woods in the State of Florida having studied them constantly since his arrival here. Before coming to this state he knew all the roots and herbs around Altoona and it still acquainted with them as he makes regular visits there, since he moved away 43 years ago. (1)

George Pretty is a dark complexioned man; about five feet three inches in heighth; weighs about 135 pounds and looks to be much younger than he is. When asked how he had maintained his youth, he said that living close to nature had done it together with his manner of living. He does not dissipate, neither does he drink strong drink. He is a ready informant. Having heard that only information of slavery was wanted, he volunteered information without any formality or urging on the part of the writer. (1) (2)

REFERENCES

1. George Pretty, Vero Beach and Gifford, Florida

2. Observation of Field Worker

ANNA SCOTT

FEDERAL WRITERS PROJECT
American Guide, (Negro Writers Unit)
Viola B. Muse, Field Worker
Jacksonville, Fla.
January 11, 1937

AN EX-SLAVE WHO WENT TO AFRICA

Anna Scott, an ex-slave who now lives in Jacksonville near the intersection of Moncrief and Edgewood Avenues, was a member of one of the first colonization groups that went to the West coast of Africa following the emancipation of the slaves in this country.

The former slave was born at Dove City, South Carolina, on Jan. 28, 1846, of a half-breed Cherokee-and-Negro mother and Anglo-Saxon father. Her father owned the plantation adjoining that of her master.

When she reached the adolescent age Anna was placed under the direct care of her mistress, by whom she was given direct charge of the dining-room and entrusted with the keys to the provisions and supplies of the household.

A kindred love grew between the slave girl and her mistress; she recalls that everywhere her mistress went she was taken also. She was kept in 'the big house'. She was not given any education, though, as some of the slaves on nearby plantations were.

Religion was not denied to the former slave and her fellows. Mrs. Abigail Dever[TR:?], her owner, permitted the slaves to attend revival and other services. The slaves were allowed to occupy the balcony of the church in Dove City, while the whites occupied the main floor. The slaves were forbidden to sing, talk, or make any other sound, however, under penalty of severe beatings.

Those of the slaves who 'felt the sperrit' during a service must keep silence until after the service, when they could 'tell it to the deacon', a colored man who would listen to the confessions or professions of religion of the slaves until late into the night. The Negro deacon would relay his converts to the white minister of the church, who would meet them in the vestry room at some specified time.

Some of the questions that would be asked at these meetings in the vestry room would be:

"What did you come up here for?"

"Because I got religion".

"How do you know you got religion?"

"Because I know my sins are forgive".

"How do you know your sins are forgiven?"

"Because I love Jesus and I love everybody".

"Do you want to be baptized?"

"Yes sir."

"Why do you want to be baptized?"

"Cause it will make me like Jesus wants me to be".

When several persons were 'ready', there would be a baptism in a nearby creek or river. After this, slaves would be permitted to hold occasional servives of their own in the log house that was sometimes used as a school.

Mrs. Scott remembers vividly the joy that she felt and other slaves expressed when first news of their emancipation was brought to them. Both she and her mistress were fearful, she says; her mistress because she did not know what she would do without her slaves, and Anna because she thought the Union soldiers would harm Mrs. Dove. When the chief officer of the soldiers came to the home of her mistress, she says, he demanded entrance in a gruff voice. Then he saw a ring upon Mrs. Dove's finger and asked: "Where did you get this?" When told that the ring belonged to her husband, who was dead, the officer turned to his soldiers and told them that they should "get back; she's alright!"

Provisions intended for the Confederate armies were broken open by the Union soldiers and their followers, and Anna's mother, to protect her master, organized groups of slaves to 'tote the meat from the box cars and hide it in dugouts under the mistress' house'. This meat was later divided between Negroes and whites.

A Provost Judge followed the advance of the army, and he obtained a list of all of the slaves held by each master. Mrs. Dove gave her list to the official, who called each slave by name and asked what that slave had done on the plantation. He asked, also, whether any payment had been made to them since the Emancipation Proclamation had been signed, and when answered in the negative told them that 'You are free now and must be paid for all of the work you have done since the Proclamation was signed and that you will do in the future. Don't you work for anybody without pay'.

The Provost Judge also told the slaves that they might leave if they liked, and Anna was among those who left. She went to visit the husband of her mother in Charleston. With her mother and five other children, Anna crossed rivers on log rafts and rode on trains to Charleston.

Elias Mumford was Anna's step-father in Charleston, and after spending a year there with him the entire family joined a colonizing expedition to West Africa.

There were 650 in the expedition, and it left in 1867. Transportation was free.

The trip took several weeks, but finally the small ship landed at Grand Bassa. Mumford did not like the place, however, and continued on to Monrovia, Liberia. He did not like Monrovia, either, and tried several other ports before being told that he would have to get off, anyway. This was at Harper Cape, W. Africa.

Here he almost immediately began an industry that was to prove lucrative. Oysters were 'large as saucers', according to Anna, and while the family gathered these he would burn them and extract lime from them. This he mixed with the native clay and made brick. In addition to his brick-making Mumford cut trees for lumber, and with his own brick and lumber would construct houses and structures. One such structure brought him $1100.00.

Another manner in which Mumford added to his growing wealth was through the cashing of checks for the Missionaries of the section. Ordinarily they would have to send these back to the United States to be cashed, and when he offered to cash them—at a discount—they eagerly utilized the opportunity to save time; this was a convenience for them and more wealth for Mumford.

Anna found other things besides happiness in her eight years in Africa. There were death, sickness, and pestilences. She mentions among the latter the African ants, some of which reached huge proportions. Most dreaded were the Mission ants, which infested every house, building and structure. Sometimes buildings had to be burned to get rid of them. The bite of these ants was so serious that after sixty years Anna still exhibits places on her feet where the ants left their indelible traces. Another of the ant pests was the Driver ant, so large, powerful and stubborn that even bodies of water did not stop them. They would join themselves together above the surface of the water and serve as bridges for the passage of the other ants. The Driver ants moved in swarms and their approach could be seen at great distances. When they were seen to be coming toward a settlement the natives would close their doors and windows and build fires around their homes to avoid them. These fires had to be kept burning for weeks.

Eight and more persons died a day from the African fever during the early colonization attempts; three of these in Anna's family alone were victims of it. It was generally believed that if a victim of the fever became wet by dew he was sure to die.

After eight years Mumford and the remainder of his family returned to America, where the accrued checks he possessed for cashing made him reasonably wealthy. Anna married Robert Scott and moved to Jacksonville, where she has lived since.

At ninety-one she still occupies the little farm on the outskirts of Jacksonville that was purchased with the money left to her out of her mother's inheritance (from the African transactions of Mumford) and Robert's post-slavery savings, and in front of her picturesque little cottage spins yarns for the neighbors of her early experiences.

BIBLIOGRAPHY
Interview with subject, Mrs. Anna Scott, Edgewood and Moncrief Avenues (Route 2, Box 911) Jacksonville, Fla.

WILLIAM SHERMAN

FEDERAL WRITERS' PROJECT
American Guide, (Negro Writers' Unit)
J.M. Johnson, Field Worker
John A. Simms, Editor
Chaseville, Florida
August 28, 1936

In Chaseville, Florida, about twelve miles from Jacksonville on the south side of the Saint Johns River lives William Sherman (locally pronounced Schumann,) a former slave of Jack Davis, nephew of President Jefferson Davis of the Confederacy. (1)

William Sherman was born on the plantation of Jack Davis, about five miles from Robertsville, South Carolina, at a place called "Black Swamp," June 12, 1842, twenty-three years prior to Emancipation. His father who was also named William Sherman, was a free man, having bought his freedom for eighteen hundred dollars from his master, John Jones, who also lived in the vicinity of the Davis' plantation. William Sherman, senior, bargained with his master to obtain his freedom, however, for he did not have the money to readily pay him. He hired himself out to some of the wealthy plantation owners and applied what he earned toward the payment for his freedom. He was a skilled blacksmith and cabinet maker and his services were always in demand. After procuring his freedom he bought a tract of land from his former master and built a home and blacksmith shop on it. As was the custom during slavery, a person who bought his freedom had to have a guardian; Sherman's former master, John Jones, acted as his guardian. Under this new order of things Sherman was in reality his own master. He was not "bossed," had his own hours, earned and kept his money, and was at liberty to leave the territory if he desired. However, he remained and married Anna Georgia, the mother of William Sherman, junior. She was also a slave of Jack Davis. After William Sherman, senior, finished his day's work he would go to the Davis plantation to visit his wife and sometimes remain for the night. It was his intention to purchase the freedom of his wife Anna Georgia, and their son William, but he died before he had sufficient money to do so, and also before the Civil War, which he predicted would ensue between the North and South. His son William says that he remembers well the events that led up to his father's burial; he states that the white people dug his grave which was six feet deep. It took them three days in which to dig it on account of the hardness of the clay; when it was finished he was put sorrowfully away by the white folk who thought so much of him. William was a boy of nine at that time, and he remembers that his mother was so grieved that he tried to console her by telling her not to worry "papa's goin' to com' back and bring us some more quails" (he had been accustomed to bringing them quails during his life) but William sorrowingly said "he never did come back."

Anna Georgia was a cook and general house woman in the Davis' home. She was a half breed, her mother being a Cherokee Indian. Her husband, William, was a descendant of the Cheehaw Indians, some of his a forbears being full-blooded Cheehaws. Their Indian blood was fully evident, states William junior. The Davis family tree as he knew it was as follows: three brothers, Sam, Thomas and Jefferson Davis (President of the Confederacy.) Sam was the eldest of the three and had four children, viz: Jack, Robert, Richard and Washington. Thomas had four, viz: James, Richard, Rusha and Minna. Jefferson Davis' family was not known to William as he lived in Virginia, whereas, the other brothers and their families lived near each other at "Black Swamp."

Jack Davis, the master of William Sherman, was the son of Sam Davis, brother of Jefferson Davis. Thomas and Sam Davis were comparatively large men, while Jefferson was thin and of medium height, resembling to a great extent the late Henry Flagler of Florida East Coast fame, states William. Many times he would come to visit his brothers at "Black Swamp." He would drive up in a two-wheeled buggy, drawn by a horse. Oft'times he visited his nephew, Jack and they would get together in a lengthy conversation. Sometimes he would remain with the Davis family for a few days and then return to Virginia. On these visits William states that he saw him personally. These visits or sojourns occurred prior to the Civil War. Jack Davis being a comparatively poor man had only eight slaves on his plantation; they were housed in log cabins made of cypress timber notched together in such a way as to give it the appearance of having been built regular lumber. It was much larger and of different architecture than the slave cabins, however.

The few slaves that he had arose at 4:00 o'clock in the morning and prepared themselves for the field. They stopped at noon for a light lunch which they always took with them and at sun-down they quit work and went to their respective cabins. Cotton, corn, potatoes and other commodities were raised. There was no regular "overseer" employed. Davis, the master acted in that capacity. He was very kind to them and seldom used the whip. After the outbreak of the Civil War, white men called "patarollers" were posted around the various plantations to guard against runaways, and if slaves were caught off their respective plantations without permits from their masters they were severely whipped. This was not the routine for Jack Davis' slaves for he gave the "patarollers" specific orders that if any of them were caught off the plantation without a permit not to molest them but to let them proceed where they were bound. Will said that one of the slaves ran away and when he was caught his master gave him a light whipping and told him to "go on now and run away if you want to." He said the slave walked away but never attempted to run away again. Will states that he was somewhat of a "pet" around the plantation and did almost as he wanted to. He would go hunting, fishing and swimming with his master's sons who were about his age. Sometimes he would get into a fight with one of the boys and many times he would be the victor, his fallen foe would sometimes exclaim that "that licking that you gave me sure hurt," and that ended the affair; there was no further ill feeling between them.

Education: The slaves were not allowed to study. The white children studied a large "Blue Back" Webster

Speller and when one had thoroughly learned its contents he was considered to be educated.

Religion: The slaves had their own church but sometimes went to the churches of their white masters where they were relegated to the extreme rear. John Kelley, a white man, often preached to them and would admonish them as follows; "you must obey your master and missus, you must be good niggers." After the beginning of the war they held "meetings" among themselves in their cabins.

Baptism: Those slaves who believed and accepted the Christian Doctrine were admitted into the church after being baptized in one of the surrounding ponds.

Cruelties: There was a very wealthy plantation owner who lived near the Davis plantation; he had eleven plantations, the smallest one was cultivated by three hundred slaves. Oftimes they would work nearly all night. Will states that it was not an unusual thing to hear in the early mornings the echoes of rawhide whips cracking like the report of a gun against the bare backs of the slaves who were being whipped. They would moan and groan in agony, but the whipping went on until the master's wrath was appeased. John Stokes, a white plantation owner who lived near the Davis' plantation encouraged slaves to steal from their masters and bring the stolen goods to him; he would purchase the goods for much less than their value. One time one of the slaves "put it out" that "Massa" Stokes was buying stolen goods. Stokes heard of this and his wrath was aroused; he had to find the "nigger" who was circulating this rumor. He went after him in great fury and finally succeeded in locating him, whereupon, he gave him a good "lacing" and warned him "if he ever heard anything like that again from him he was going to kill him." The accusations were true, however, but the slave desisted in further discussion of the affair for "old Massa Stokes was a treacherous man." On another occasion one of the Stokes' slaves ran away and he sent Steven Kittles, known as the "dog man," to catch the escape. (The dogs that went in pursuit of the runaway slaves were called "Nigger dogs"; they were used specifically for catching runaway slaves.) This particular slave had quite a "head start" on the dogs that were trailing him and he hid among some floating logs in a large pond; the dogs trailed him to the pond and began howling, indicating that they were approaching their prey. They entered the pond to get their victim who was securely hidden from sight; they dissapeared and the next seen of them was their dead bodies floating upon the water of the pond; they had been killed by the escape. They were full-blooded hounds, such as were used in hunting escaped slaves and were about fifty in number. The slave made his escape and was never seen again. Will relates that it was very cold and that he does'nt understand how the slave could stand the icy waters of the pond, but evidently he did survive it.

Civil War: It was rumored that Abraham Lincoln said to Jefferson Davis, "work the slaves until they are about twenty-five or thirty years of age, then liberate them." Davis replied: "I'll never do it, before I will, I'll wade knee deep in blood." The result was that in 1861, the Civil War, that struggle which was to mark the final emancipation of the slaves began. Jefferson

Davis' brothers, Sam and Tom, joined the Confederate forces, together with their sons who were old enough to go, except James, Tom's son, who could not go on account of ill health and was left behind as overseer on Jack Davis' plantation. Jack Davis joined the artillery regiment of Captain Razors Company. The war progressed, Sherman was on his famous march. The "Yankees" had made such sweeping advances until they were in Robertsville, South Carolina, about five miles from Black Swamp. The report of gun fire and cannon could be heard from the plantation. "Truly the Yanks are here" everybody thought. The only happy folk were, the slaves, the whites were in distress. Jack Davis returned from the field of battle to his plantation. He was on a short furlough. His wife, "Missus" Davis asked him excitedly, if he thought the "Yankees" were going to win. He replied: "No if I did I'd kill every damned nigger on the place." Will who was then a lad of nineteen was standing nearby and on hearing his master's remarks, said: "The Yankees aint gonna kill me cause um goin to Laurel Bay" (a swamp located on the plantation.) Will says that what he really meant was that his master was not going to kill him because he intended to run off and go to the "Yankees." That afternoon Jack Davis returned to the "front" and that night Will told his mother, Anna Georgia, that he was going to Robertsville and join the "Yankees." He and his cousin who lived on the Davis' plantation slipped off and wended their way to all of the surrounding plantations spreading the news that the "Yankees" were in Robertsville and exhorting them to follow and join them. Soon the two had a following of about five hundred slaves who abandoned their masters' plantations "to meet the Yankees." En masse they marched breaking down fences that obstructed their passage, carefully avoiding "Confederate pickets" who were stationed throughout the countryside. After marching about five miles they reached a bridge that spanned the Savannah River, a point that the "Yankees" held. There was a Union soldier standing guard and before he realized it, this group of five hundred slaves were upon him. Becoming cognizant that someone was upon him, he wheeled around in the darkness, with gun leveled at the approaching slaves and cried "Halt!" Will's cousin then spoke up, "Doan shoot boss we's jes friends." After recognizing who they were, they were admitted into the camp that was established around the bridge. There were about seven thousand of General Sherman's soldiers camped there, having crossed the Savannah River on a pontoon bridge that they had constructed while enroute from Green Springs Georgia, which they had taken. The guard who had let these people approach so near to him without realizing their approach was court martialed that night for being dilatory in his duties. The Federal officers told the slaves that they could go along with them or go to Savannah, a place that they had already captured. Will decided that it was best for him to go to Savannah. He left, but the majority of the slaves remained with the troops. They were enroute to Barnswell, South Carolina, to seize Blis Creek Fort that was held by the Confederates. As the Federal troops marched ahead, they were followed by the volunteer slaves. Most of these unfortunate slaves were slain by "bush whackers" (Confederate snipers who fired upon them from ambush.) After being killed they were decapitated and their heads placed upon posts that lined the fields so that they could be seen by other slaves to warn them of what would befall them if they attempted to escape. The battle at Blis Creek Fort was one in which both armies displayed great heroism; most of the Federal troops that made the first attack, were killed as the Confederates seemed to be irresistible. After rushing up reinforcements, the Federals were successful in capturing it and a large number of "Rebels."

General Sherman's custom was to march ahead of his army and cut rights of way for them to pass. At this point of the war, many of the slaves were escaping from their plantations and joining the "Yankees." All of those slaves at Black Swamp who did not voluntarily run away and go to the "Yankees" were now free by right of conquest of the Federals.

Will now found himself in Savannah, Georgia, after refusing to go to Barnswell, South Carolina, with the Federals. This refusal saved him from the fate of his unfortunate brothers who went. Savannah was filled with smoke, the aftermath of a great battle. Lying in the "Broad River" between Beaufort, South Carolina, and Savannah, Georgia were two Union gun boats, the Wabash and Man O War, which had taken part in the battle that resulted in the capture of Savannah. Everything was now peaceful again; Savannah was now a Union city. Many of the slaves were joining the Union army. Those slaves who joined were trained about two days and then sent to the front; due to lack of training they were soon killed. The weather was cold, it was February, 1862, frost was on the ground.

Will soon left Savannah for Beaufort, South Carolina which had fallen before the "Yankee" attack. Soldiers and slaves filled the streets. The slaves were given all of the food and clothes that they could carry—confiscated goods from the "Rebels." After a bloody struggle in which both sides lost heavily and which lasted for about five years, the war finally ended May 15, 1865. Will was then a young man twenty-three years of age and was still in Beaufort. He says that day was a gala day. Everybody celebrated (except the Southerners). The slaves were free.

Thousands of Federal soldiers were in evidence. The Union army was victorious and "Sherman's March" was a success. Sherman states that when Jefferson Davis was captured he was disguised in women's clothes.

Sherman states that Florida had the reputation of having very cruel masters. He says that when slaves got very unruly, they were told that they were going to be sent to Florida so they could be handled. During the war thousands of slaves fled from Virginia into Connecticut and New Hampshire. In 1867 William Sherman left Beaufort and went to Mayport, Florida to live. He remained there until 1890, then moved to Arona, Florida, living there for awhile; he finally settled in Chaseville, Florida, where he now lives. During his many years of life he has been married twice and has been the father of sixteen children, all of whom are dead. He never received any formal education, but learned to read and studied taxidermy which he practiced for many years.

He was at one time Inspector of Elections at Mayport during Reconstruction Days. He recalled an incident that occurred during the performance of his duties there, which was as follows: Mr. John Doggett who was running for office on the Democratic ticket brought a number of colored people to Mayport by boat from Chaseville to vote. Mr. Doggett demanded that they should vote, but Will Sherman was equally insistent that they should not vote because they had not registered and were not qualified. After much arguing Mr. Doggett saw that Sherman could not be made "to see the light" and left with his prospective voters. William Sherman once served upon a United States Federal jury during his colorful life.

In appearance he could easily be regarded as a phenomenon. He is ninety-four years of age, though he appears to be only about fifty-five. His hair is black and not grey as would be expected; his face is round and unlined; he has dark piercing but kindly eyes. He is of medium stature. He has an exceptionally alert mind and recalls past events with the ease of a youth. The Indian blood that flows in his veins is plainly visible in his features, the color of his skin and the texture of his hair.

He gives as his reason for his lengthy life the Indian blood that is in him and says that he expects to live for nintey-four more years. Today he lives alone. He raises a few vegetables and is content in the memories of his past life which has been full. (2)

REFERENCES

1. Most of his friends call him SHERMAN, hence he adopted that name.

2. A personal interview with William Sherman, former slave, at home in Colored quarters, Chaseville, Florida

SAMUEL SMALLS

FEDERAL WRITERS' PROJECT
American Guide, (Negro Writers' Unit)
Martin D. Richardson, Field Worker
Jacksonville, Florida
January 27, 1937

A VOLUNTARY SLAVE FOR SEVEN YEARS

The story of a free Negro of Connecticut, who came south to observe conditions of slavery, found them very distasteful, then voluntarily entered that slavery for seven years is the interesting tale that Samuel Smalls, 84 year old ex-slave of 1704 Johnson Street, Jacksonville, tells of his father Cato Smith.

Smith had been born in Connecticut, son of domestic slaves who were freed while he was still a child. He grew to young manhood in the northern state, making a living for himself as a carpenter and builder. At these trades he is said to have been very efficient.

Still unmarried at the age of about 30, he found in himself a desire to travel and see how other Negroes in the country lived. This he did, going from one town to another, working for periods of varying length in the cities in which he lived, eventually drifting to Florida.

His travels eventually brought him to Suwannee County, where he worked for a time as overseer on a plantation. On a nearby plantation where he sometimes visited, he met a young woman for whom he grew to have a great affection. This plantation is said to have belonged to a family of Cones, and according to Smalls, still exists as a large farm.

Smith wanted to marry the young woman, but a difficulty developed; he was free and she was still a slave. He sought her owner. Smith was told that he might have the woman, but he would have to "work out" her cost. He was informed that this would amount to seven years of work on the plantation, naturally without pay.

Within a few days he was back with his belongings, to begin "working out" the cost of his wife. But his work found favor in his voluntary master's eyes; within four years he was being paid a small sum for the work he did, and by the time the seven years was finished, Smith had enough money to immediately purchase a small farm of his own.

Adversity set in, however, and eventually his children found themselves back in slavery, and Smith himself practically again enslaved. It was during this period that Smalls was born.

All of the Florida slaves were soon emancipated, however and the voluntary slave again became a free man. He lived in the Suwannee County vicinity for a number of years afterward, raising a large family.

REFERENCE
Personal interview with Samuel Smalls, ex-slave, 1704 Johnson Street, Jacksonville, Florida

SALENA TASWELL

FEDERAL WRITERS' PROJECT
The American Guide, (Negro Writers' Unit)
Cora N. Taylor
Frances H. Miner, Editor
Miami, Florida
May 14, 1937

Salena Taswell, 364 NW 8th St., Miami, Fla.

1. Where, and about when, were you born?

In Perry, Ga. in 1844.

2. If you were born on a plantation or farm, what sort of farming section was it in?

Ole Dr. Jameson's plantation near Perry, Ga. north of Macon.

3. How did you pass the time as a child? What sort of chores did you do and what did you play?

I worked around the table in my Massy's dining room. I didn't play. I sometimes pulled threads for mother. She was a fine seamstress for the plantation.

4. Was your master kind to you?

Yes; I was the pet.

5. How many slaves were there on the same plantation or farm?

He must have had about 400 slaves.

6. Do you remember what kind of cooking utensils your mother used?

We had copper kettles, crocks, and iron kettles. "I waited on de table when Lincum came dare. That day we had chicken hash and batter cakes and dried venison."

7. What were your main foods and how were they cooked?

We had everything that was good (I ate in my Massy's kitchen) Sweet potatoes biscuits, corn bread, pies and everything we eat now.

8. Do you remember making imitation or substitute coffee by grinding up corn or peanuts?

No, we always had the best of Java coffee. I used to grind it in the coffee mill for my Massy.

9. Do you remember ever having, when you were young, any other kind of bread besides corn bread?

Yes. Batter cakes, biscuits and white bread.

10. Do you remember evaporating sea water to get salt?

No. We did not live so far from Macon and the Ole Doctor he was rich and bought such things. That is how he come to be so rich. He didn't charge the poor folks when he doctored them, but they would be so glad that he made them well that they kep' a givin' him things, bed quilts, chickens, just ever' thing. Then he had such a big plantation about 200 or 300 acres, but I didn't live on the plantation. I worked in his home.

11. When you were a child, what sort of stove do you remember your mother having. Did they have a hanging pot in the fire place, and did they make their candles of their own tallow?

My mother did not cook,—she was a special seamstress servant. They had fireplaces on the plantation and they always used tallow candles at the doctor's place until after the 'mancipation, then the doctor was one of the first ones to buy coal oil lamps.

12. Did you use an open well or pump to get the water?

No, we went to the spring to get the water. We toted it in cedar buckets. The spring was boxed into a well shaped hole, deep enough to dip the water out of it. It was the best water. They had a town pump at Macon.

13. Do you remember when you first saw ice in regular form?

Yes. They had icicles in Georgia.

14. Did your family work in the rice fields or in the cotton fields on the farm, or what sort of work did they do?

My father was a blacksmith. He did all kinds of blacksmithing. He even made plows.

15. If they worked in the house or about the place, what sort of work did they do?

My mother was one of the best seamstresses; she

sewed all day long with her fingers. She made the finest silk dresses and even made tailored suits.

16. Do you remember ever helping tan and cure hides and pig hides?

They did those things on the plantation. They cured goat skins and sheep skins, too. The sheep skins would dry so slowly that they would let the slaves lie on them at night to keep them warm and hasten the drying.

17. As a young person what sort of work did you do? If you helped your mother around the house or cut firewood or swept the yard, say so.

I cleaned and dusted and waited on the table, made beds and put everything in order, washed dishes, polished silverware and did the most trusty work.

18. When you were a child do you remember how people wove cloth, or spun thread, or picked out cotton seed, or weighed cotton, or what sort of bag was used on the cotton bales?

I did not need to spin but I used to play with the spinning wheels. They ginned the cotton on the plantation. They used a horse to pull the gin.

They weighed the cotton with a beam and weight. A good slave picked 200 lbs of cotton in a day. Nancy could pick 300 or 400 lbs in a day. She'd go out early in the day and run in ahead of the sun and no one would know she had been out. That's how she would get ahead of the rest.

19. Do you remember what sort of soap they used? How did they get the lye for making the soap?

They made soft soap boiled in a big kettle. They made the lye out of ashes packed in an old barrel that had a hole in the bottom. They would make a hollow in the top of the barrel and pour rain water in it. This would gradually soak through the ashes and seep out of the bottom of the barrel which they tipped up so that it would drain the lye out into a vessel. Then they would take the lye and boil it in the kettle with old grease and meat rinds. The lye was very strong. They had to be careful not to get any of it on their hands or it would take the skin off. As they would stir the grease and lye it would foam and cook like a jelly and when it cooled we had soft soap. It would sure chase the dirt, but it was hard on the hands.

20. What did they use for dyeing thread and cloth, and how did they dye them?

They would dig indigo roots and cook the roots and branches for blue dye. For purple they mixed red and blue. They would pick the berries off the gallberry bushes for red. The robin's yellow and mixed yellow and red for orange; and yellow and blue for green.

21. Did your mother use big, wooden washtubs with cut-out holes on each side for the fingers?

Yes. We made cedar tubs on the plantation. And we had some men who made large wooden bowls out of juggles cut from logs of the tupla tree. They would run them through a machine and they would come out round and then they would smooth them down. They mixed bread in those big bowls.

22. Do you remember the way they made shoes by hand in the country?

Yes, all our shoes were made on the plantation.

23. Do you remember saving the chicken feathers and goose feathers always for your featherbeds?

Yes.

24. Do you remember when women wore hoops in their skirts, and when they stopped wearing them and wore narrow skirts?

Yes. The doctor's folks were so stylish that they would not let the servants wear hoops, but we could get the old ones that they threw away and have a big time playing with them and we would go around with them on when they were gone and couldn't see us.

25. Do you remember when you first saw your first windmill?

Never did see one.

26. Do you remember when you first saw bed springs instead of bed ropes?

Yes. When I was a slave, I slept in a gunny sack bunk with the sacks nailed against the wall on two sides, in a corner of the room and then there was a post at the corner of the bed and two poles nailed from the post to the walls and the gunny sacks were nailed to those poles. My bed was a two-story bed. There was another gunnysack bed above me with poles fastened to the same post. We tore old rags and made rag rugs for quilts to cover us with. I worked in the doctor's house in the daytime but I had to sleep in the shed at night. Then after I wasn't a slave no more, I never slept on anything else but a rope bed. When springs come I wondered what anyone wanted wid 'em. Rope beds was good enough.

27. When did you see the first buggy and what did it look like?

The doctor, he had the best of such things. He had a regular buggy and sometimes he driv two horses in hit. Uncle Albert, he wuz his driver. When the doctor wanted to put on great style, and go to the station to meet some rich company he had one of the fancy cabs with the driver sittin' up high in front, but when he went to see his patients, he'd take his feet to go around. He had two saddle packs with a strap that he would throw over his shoulder. He would have one pack hanging in front and the other hanging behind.

28. Do you remember your grandparents?

No, my mother's mother was taken from her and sold when she was a baby. So I never seed my grandmother and I don't know any more about my grandfather than a goose about a band box.

29. Do you remember the money called "shin-plasters?"

I've seen plenty. I guess my master had barrels of them.

30. What interesting historical events happened during your youth,—such as Sherman's Army passing through your section? Did you witness the happenings and what was the reaction of the other Negroes to them?

Sherman's army went through Perry but they did not do any damage there. They expected them to come and buried lots of food and valuable things, and when they came they took them to the smoke houses and told them to help themselves. They did not burn any houses there.

31. Did you know any Negros who enlisted or joined the northern army?

Yes, plenty went with their boss, but ran off to Sherman's army when he came along. One woman's husband I knowed, Mr. Bethel, he stayed with his master and didn't run off with the Northern army. When he was given his freedom, his master give him nice house.

32. Did you know any Negroes who enlisted in the Southern Army?

About all I knew.

33. Did your master join the Confederacy? What do you remember of his return from the war? Or was he wounded or killed?

His two sons joined the army. James was killed, but Bud, he would never get through telling war stories when he came back.

34. Did you live in Savannah when Sherman and the

Northern forces marked through the state, and do you remember the excitement in your town or around the plantation where you lived?

No.

35. Did your master's house get robbed or burned during the time of Sherman's march?

No.

36. What kind of uniforms did they wear during the civil war?

Blue and gray.

37. What sort of medicine was used in the days just after the war? Describe a Negro doctor of that period.

We never got sick. Sometimes they would give us oil with a drop or two of turpentine in a big spoonful. They put turpentine on cuts and sores.

38. What do you remember about Northern people or outside people moving into a community after the war?

Yes, Jake Enos, he was a colored teacher. He was sent down to teach the colored school. He taught around from Atlanta to Florida. He took yellow fever and died My brother, he teached school, but I never went to school. I larned my ABC's from my massy's children. I aint never forgot 'em. I could say 'em now.

39. How did your family's life compare after Emancipation with it before?

I had it the same. I had it good with my massy, but the

rest wuz paid some little wages. Our plantation was called a free place. Some of the slaves worked so well and made money for the massy and gained their freedom even befo' 'mancipashun. I heard one come to him and say I howe dat man $10 an' he retched down in his pocket an' paid hit.

40. Do you know anything about political meetings and clubs formed after the war?

I heered about de Kuklux but I never did see none.

41. Do you know anything regarding the letters and stories from Negroes who migrated north after the war?

I hear talk 'bout some massys goin' arter dem an' bringin' back mor'n dey had in de fust place.

42. Were there any Negroes of your acquaintance who were skilled in any particular line of work, if so give details?

The Turners made furniture wid knobs an' bumps on just like that stand and bed. They made fancy chairs an' put cowhide seats stretch-across 'em.

43. What sort of school system was there for the instruction of the Negro? Were there any Negro teachers in your community?

Yes. My son, he went to Negro school three months a year. The son said that he studied Webster's Speller, Harvey's Reader, learned his ABC's and studied some in history, geography and arithmetic.

44. How old were you at the close of the civil war?

21 years.

45. Describe the type of early religious meeting, the preachers, etc.

I went to town to my massy's church. I sat 'long side on 'em and held the baby. My father, he held meetings on the plantation and prayer meetings just like they have now.

46. Do your friends believe in charms and conjure bags, and what has been their experience with magic and spells?

I guess some claim dey believe in sech things, but I don't know whether they do or not.

47. Did you ever use an ox to plow with? What sort of plow?

Yes, I see 'em plow wid hoxen. Dey used the kind of plows they made on the plantation. I didn't plow, but I used to have fun a goin' roun' in the old ox two-wheel wagon cart. I'd go down de hill in it; we'd get in the dump cart and holler an' have a big time.

48. How much did various foods and drinks and commodities cost just at the end of the war and afterwards?

I don't know what things cost.

[HW: Negro-Tampa-Slave   Interviews]
July 9, 1937

United States. Work Projects Administration

DAVE TAYLOR

STORIES OF FLORIDA
Prepared for Use in Public Schools
by the
Federal Writers' Project of the Works
Progress Administration
A MARINE IN EBONY
By Jules A. Frost

From a Virginia plantation to Florida, through perils of Indian war-fare; shanghaied on a Government vessel and carried 'round the world; shipwrecked and dropped into the lap of romance—these are only a few of the colorful pages from the unwritten diary of old Uncle Dave, ex-slave and soldier of fortune.

The reporter found the old man sitting on the porch of his Iber City shack, thoughtfully chewing tobacco and fingering his home-made cane. At first he answered in grumpy monosyllables, but by the magic of a good cigar, he gradually let himself go, disclosing minute details of a most remarkable series of adventures.

His language is a queer mixture of geechy, sea terms and broad "a's" acquired by long association with Nassau "conchs." Married to one of these ample-waisted Bahama women, the erst-while rambler and adventurer proved that rolling stones sometimes become suitable foundations for homes—he lived faithfully with the same wife for fifty-one years.

"Shippin' 'fore de mahst ain't no job to make a preacher f'm a youngster; hit's plenty tough; but I ain't nevah been sorry I went to sea; effen a boy gwine take to likker an' wimmen, he kin git plenty o'both at home, same as in for'n ports."

The old man bit off a conservative chew from his small plug, carefully wrapped the remainder in his handkerchief and chewed thoughtfully for some time before he continued.

"I wasn't bawn in Florida, but I be'n here so long I reckon hit 'bout de same thing. I kin jes remember leavin' Norfolk. My daddy an' mammy an' de odder chillun b'long to a Frenchman named Pinckney. Musta be'n 'bout 1860 or 1861, w'en Mahstah 'gins to worry 'bout what gwine happen effen war come an' de Vahginny slave-owners git beat."

He proceeded slowly, and in language almost unintelligible at times, as he talked, smoked and chewed, all at the same time; but here, the reporter realized, were all the elements of a true story that needed only notebook and typewriter to transform it into readable form.

Antagonism aroused by the Dred Scott decision, and the further irritation caused by the Fugitive Slave law were kicking up plenty of trouble during Buchanan's administration. South Carolina had already seceded. Major Anderson was keeping the Union flag flying at Fort Sumter, but latest reports said that there was no immediate danger of hostilities when Pierre Pinckney, thrifty Virginia planter of French extraction, went into conference with his neighbors and decided to move while the getting-out was still good.

With as little publicity as possible, they arranged the disposal of their real estate. No need to sell their slaves and livestock; they would need both in the new location. If they could manage to get to Charleston, they reasoned, surely they could arrange for a boat to St. Augustine. The Indians might be troublesome there, but by settling near the fort they should be reasonably safe.

Before the caravan of oxcarts and heavy wagons came within sight of the old seaport town, it became evident that they had better keep to the woods. Union soldiers, although still inactive, might at any time decide to confiscate their belongings, so they pushed on to the southward.

Long weeks dragged by before they finally reached St. Augustine. War talk, and the possibility of attack by sea again caused them to change their plans. Pooling their money, they chartered a boat and embarked for Key West. Surely they would be safe that far south. One of their Virginia neighbors, Fielding A. Browne, had settled there thirty years before. Taking advantage of the periodic sales of salvaged goods from wrecks on the treacherous keys, he had become wealthy and was said to hold a responsible position with the city.

Everyone was in a cheerful mood as the blue outline of Key West peeped over the horizon, and all come on deck to catch a glimpse of their new home. Suddenly dismay clutched at every heart as a Federal man-of-war swung out of the harbor and steamed out to meet them. The long-feared crisis had come. They ware prisoners of war.

Pinckney and his neighbors were marched into Fort Taylor. Their wives, children and slaves were allowed to settle in the city and care for themselves as best they could.

Pinckney's slaves consisted of one family, David Taylor and wife, with their family of ten pickaninnies. Colonel Montgomery, Federal recruiting officer, took advantage of the helplessness of the slave owners to sow discord among the blacks, and before many days big Dave, father of the subject of this sketch, had "jined de Yankees" as color sergeant and had been sent north, where he was killed in the attack on Fort Sumter.

His determined and energetic 260-pound wife served Mrs. Pinckney faithfully through the war and long afterward. Young Dave, or "Buddy," son of big Dave, although only in his early teens, was her chief aid. When the war was over and Mr. Pinckney walked out of Fort Taylor a free man, the portly Hannah "pooh-poohed" the announcement that she was a free citizen. "Y'all done brung me heah," she blustered with emphasis, "an' heah I'se gwine t' stay."

Some years after the war Pierre Pinckney died. When his good wife became ill, frantic dismay pervaded the servants' quarters. As her last moments drew near, Mrs. Pinckney called the weeping Hannah to her bedside and laid a bag of money in her hand.

"To get you and the children back to old Virginia," she whispered with her last breath.

When the beloved "Missus" was laid to rest by the side of her husband in the Catholic cemetery, the bewildered Hannah took the money to a white man, an old friend of the family, and asked him to buy the tickets back to Virginia. He advised against it; said that the old home would not be there to comfort them. Houses had been burned, trees cut down and old landmarks destroyed. He suggested that they take the hundred dollars in gold and buy a little home in Key West, which they did.

Reconstruction days were as trying to Key Westers as to others all over the devastated land of Dixie. Slave owners, stripped of their possessions, taxed with an immense war debt and with no money or equipment to begin the slow climb back to normalcy were pathetic figures as they blistered their hands at toil that they had never known before. Many of the slaves were more than willing to stay with their former masters, but with no income, the problem of feeding themselves was the main issue with the whites, so it was out of the question to try to fill other mouths, and ex-slaves often had to shift for themselves, a hopeless task for a race that had never been called upon to exert initiative.

Hannah Taylor and her numerous offspring were a fair example of these irresponsible people. Like a ship adrift without skipper or rudder, they were at the mercy of every adverse wind of misfortune. Each morning they went out with frantic energy to earn or in some way procure sustenance for one more day. Young Dave hounded the sponge fishermen until they gave him an extra job. He made the rounds of the fishing docks, continually on the lookout to be of help, anxious to do anything at any time in exchange for a few articles of food that he could carry proudly home to his mother.

"Dem was mighty tryin' times," mused the old man, "an' I don't blame my mammy fer warmin' my pants when she had so much to worry 'bout. She had a way o' grabbin' me by de years an' shovin' my haid twixt her knees whilst she wuk on me sumpin' awful. No wonder I was scairt o' dese frammin's. I reckon dat was de cause o' me goin' t' sea. Ah mas' tell you 'bout dat.

"One day my mammy gimme fifteen cents an' say 'Go down to de market and fetch me some fish. Ah' lissen—don't you let no grass grew unda yo' feet. Go on de run an' come back on de jump. Does you fall down, jes' keep on a-goin' some-how.'

"Wid dat she turn an' spit on de step. 'You see dat spit,' she say. 'Ef hit be dry w'en you git back, I gonna beat de meat offen yo' bones. Git goin', now.'

"Well, I stahted, an I she' wasn't losin' no time. 'Bout hahf way to de mahket, I meets a couple o' stewards f'm a U.S. navy cutter anchored off de navy yard.

"Hol' on, dar, boy,' 'dey sing out, 'wha you gwine so fas'? Grab dis here basket an' tote hit down to de dock.'

"I knowed I couldn't git back home 'fore dat spit dried, an' I be'n figgerin' how I could peacify my mammy so's to miss dat beatin'. I figger of I mek a quarter or hahf a dollar an' gin it to 'er, she mebbe forgit de paddlin'. So I take de bahsket an' foller 'em down to de water front. W'en we git dere dey was a sailor waitin' fer 'em wid a boat f'm de cutter. I set de bahsket in de boat an' stood waitin' fo' my money.

"You ain't finished yo' job yit,' dey say. 'Git yo'se'f in dat boat an' put dat stuff on be'd.'

"W'en I gits on deck a cullud boy 'bout my size say 'Wanna look about a bit?' So I foller him below an' fo' I knowed it, I feel de boat kinda shakin.' I run to a porthole an' look out. Dere was Key West too far away to swim back to.

"I ran up on deck, an' dare was de steward w'at gin me de bahsket to tote. 'W'at th'ell you doin' on bo'd dis ship,' he ahsk me.

"I tells 'im I ain't wantin' t' stay no mo'n he wants me, an' he takes me to de cap'm. 'I reckon he b'long to do navy now,' says de cap'm, 'so dey fix some papers an' I makes my mark on 'em.

"Ahftah a bit I find we bound fo' N'Orleans. 'Fore we got dere, a ship hove 'longside an' gin us a message to put about. I ahsk a li'l Irishman, named Jack, wha we gwine, an' he say, 'Outa de worl'.'

"Jesus wep't I say, 'my mammy think I be daid.' I couldn't read nor write, an' didn't know how to tell noboddy how to back a letter to my mammy, so I jes' let hit go, an' we staht back de way we come.

"I thought hit be'n stormin' all de time, but w'en we

pahs thoo de Florida straits I see w'at a real storm's like. I didn't know, ontell we was hahf way down de South American coast, headin fer Cape Horn, dat we done pahs Key West, but I couldn't got off if I'd wanted to, 'cause I'd done jined de navy.

"Hit seem lak months 'fore we roun' de Cape an' head back north on de Pacific, an' hit seem lak a year 'fore we drop anchor in Hong Kong. Dey tell me de admiral was stationed dere an' de cap'n had to report to him. W'ile he was doin' dis, we gits shore leave.

"Wen Jack an' me gits on land, we couldn't onnerstan' a word, but we mek signs, an' a tough-lookin' Chink motion fer us to foller him. We go down a dark street an' turn thoo an alley, then into a big room lighted with colored paper lanterns. On de flo' we see some folks sleepin' wit some li'l footstools 'longside 'em, an some of 'em was smokin' long-stemmed pipes. I figger mebbe dey goin' put us to sleep an' knock us in de haid. I look back an' see de do' swingin' shut, slow like, so I run back an' stick my foot in hit and shove hit back open.

"Jack an me run back de same way we come. Pretty soon we find anotha sailor an' go wit him to a yaller man dat could speak English. He pin a li'l yaller flag on our shirts an' say hit de badge o' de Chinese gov'ment, an' we be safe, cause we b'long to de U.S. navy.

"We go out to see de sights, but nevah hear one mo' word o' English; so ahftah a time we go back to de ship an' stay ontell we put to sea again.

"Nex' we sails fo' Panama. W'en we ties up dere, Jack

an' me goes ashore. Ah nevah befo' see such pretty high-yaller gals in all my life. Looks lak dey made o' marble, dey so puffick.

"Me an' Jack gits likkered up de fust thing, an' I done lose 'im. Dat worry me some, 'cause we need each otha. Wit' his haid an' my arms we mek one pretty good man. Dat lil Irishman was a fightin' fool. Weighed only 90 pounds, but strong an' wiry. Co'se he git licked mos' do time, but he allus ready fer anotha fight.

"Didn't lak for folks to call him Irish. 'He fodder was Irish and he mudder American,' he say; 'I be'n born aboard a Dutch brig in French waters. Now you tell me what flag I b'longs undah.'

"Wen we gits back to de ship, de boys tells me some English sailors beat Jack up in de sportin' house. Sumbuddy sing out 'Beat it—de marines comin'!, an' dey all run for de ship an leff Jack dere.

"I don't ahsk no mo' questions; jes' start back on a run to find my buddy. At dat time I weigh 180, an' was pretty husky fer my age. Bein' likkered plenty, I nevah thought 'bout gittin' beat up mahse'f.

"W'en I gits back, dere was a big Limey stahndin' wid his arms crost de do'. 'All dem in, stay in, an' all de outs stay out,' he say.

"Now I be'n trained to respec' white folks—what is white folks—ever sence I bawn; but w'en I think 'bout Jack in dere, hahf dead, mebbe, dat Limey don't look none too white to me. I take a runnin' staht an' but 'im in de belly wid my haid.

"De nex' do' was locked, an' I bus' hit down. Dere was Jack, 'bout hahf done f'. Blood all over de fla'. Ev'thing in de room busted up an' tipped over. I hauls 'im to a back do', but hit locked. I kick out a winder, heaves 'im onto my shoulder, an' runs back to de ship.

"Wen we comes up, dere was de cap'm standin' at de rail. His blue eyes look lak he love to kill us.

"'Fall in!' he says, an' we does. 'Go for'd,' he says, an' we goes.

"'Now' he says, wat's all dis about?'

"'Well,' says Jack, 'I didn't staht no fight. I jes' goes into a saloon, peaceful like, an' a damn Limey says, pointin' to a British flag on dere own ship, 'You see dat flag?'

"'Aye,' says Jack, 'an' still I don't see nuthin'.'

"'I be'n over de seven seas,' says de Limey, 'an' I see dat ol' flag mistress of all of 'em.'

"'You be'n around some,' says Jack, 'but I done a li'l sailin' mahse'f. Fust place I went was to France. Grass look lak hit need rain,' (So he tells dat Limey what he done fo' hit).

"'Nex' I goes to Germany,' he says; 'ground no good; need fer'lizer.' (So he tells 'im what he done on German soil).

"Atter dat I ships fo' England,' Jack tells de Limey, lookin' 'im straight in de eye. 'Fust thing I see w'en we land is dat British flag w'at you be'n braggin' so loud about.' (So he tells dat Limey w'at 'e used de flag fer).

"'Fore God, Cap'm,' says Jack, 'dat Limey lan' on me wid bofe feet 'fore I say anotha word. Nevah got in one lick. Fack is, Cap'm I ain't be'n doin' no fightin' sence I done lef' dis here ship."

"'Go below,' says de cap'm 'an' clean yo'se'f up. Dis de lahst time you two gwine git shore leave on dis trip.' He try to look mad, but I see he wantin' to lahf.

"De nex' day," Uncle Dave finished, with a whimsical smile, "I see de bos'n readin' in de paper 'bout de war 'twixt America an' England. Hit was 'bout our li'l war—what dey stahted an' we finished."

The dusky old veteran of many battles unwrapped the small piece of black tobacco in the soiled handkerchief, decided on conservation, and slowly wrapped it up again.

"Nex' comes orders from de admiral in Hong Kong to sail fer Rio Janeiro. W'en we drop anchor, dere was some o' da meanes' lookin' wharf rats I evah see. Killers, dey was, willin' to knock anybody off, any time, fer a few cents. We lines up fer shore leave, but dey mek Jack an' me stay on de ship. Our rucus in Panama done got us in bad wid de cap'm. But Ah reckon hit was fer de bes'. One of our men come back wid a year cut off an' a busted nose. 'Nother one neveh come back at all.

"One mornin' I see 'em runnin' up a long pennant an' all de sailors lahf an dahnce about lak dey crazy. Hit was de signal 'omeward boun'. We weigh anchor and head fer N'York.

"'Well, Taylor,' da officer say, when he pay me off 'you gwine ship wid us again?'

"'I gotta go home,' I tells 'im; 'got a job t' finish up in Key West.'

"So dey gin me my discharge an' a Gov'ment pahs on de Mallory liner Clyde. W'en I gits to Key West, fust place I goes was to dat fish mahket w'ere my mammy done sent me three year an' six months befo'. I buy fifteen cents wuth o' fish an' go on home.

"W'en I git dere, dey was jes' settin' down to dinner. 'Wait,' Ah say, 'put on one mo' plate.'

"My mammy look at me lak she done see a ghost. Den she run an' 'gin beatin' on me.

"'Hol' on,' Ah tells 'er, 'you ain't forgot dat beatin' yit? I done got yo' fish,' an' I gin 'er de pahcel.

"'Mah boy, mah boy,' she say, 'Ah beatin' on yuh kase Ah so proud t' see yuh. Heah Ah done wear black fer yuh, an' gin yuh up fer daid; an' bress de Lawd, heah you is, lak come beck f'm de grave.'

"Ah retch down, in m' pocket an' pull a pahcel an' lay hit in her han'; three hunnert sebenty-eight dollahs, all de money I done made wid de Gov'ment sence Ah left, an' I gin hit all to 'er. She lak t' had a fit; an Ah she' was de head man o' dat fembly whilst Ah stayed.

"But de salt water stick to me—Ah couldn't stay ashore. So ahftah Ah visit wid 'em a spell, Ah goes down to de docks an' sign t' ship on a fo'-mahster tramp. Dat ol' tub tek me all ovah de worl'."

Pressed for details of some of his physical encounters on this second voyage, Uncle Dave seemed in deep thought, and finally said:

"Well, Ah tell you 'bout de time I fout de bully of de ship. We was still in Key West, waitin' fer wind. Dis ol' tramp ship, she got a crew picked up f'm all ovah de worl'. Dere ain't no sich thing as a color line dere. At mess time, white an' black all git in de same line. As dey pahs by de table, each one take a knife an' cut off a piece o' meat.

"Dere was a big, high-yeller Haiti higgah, what thought he done own de ship. 'Trouble wiz 'Merican niggahs,' he say, 'dey ain't got no sperrit. I be offisaire een my own countree—I don't bow ze knee to nobody, white or black."

"So when dey line up, dis here Haitian come crowdin' in ahead o' de fust man in de line, an' he cut off de bes' lean meat 'fore we gits ours.

"What's dis,' Ah say to de man ahead o' me, 'huccome dat white man don't bus' dat damn yeller swab wide open?'

"'Dat's Rousseau,' 'e says; 'Ain't nobuddy on dis ship big enough to put 'im on de tail end o' de line.'

"I size 'im up good w'ile we eats. He weigh 196, dey tells me, an' nobuddy be'n lucky 'nuff to lay 'im out. 'Cordin' t' ship rules, dey couldn't gang up on 'im. Cap'm mek ev'ybuddy fight single. Wan't no sich thing ez quarrelin'. Effen two sailors gits in a rucus, day pipe 'em up on de main deck."

"Do what?" the reporter asked.

"Pipe 'em up—de bos'n blow a whistle an' call 'em in t' fight it out, w'ile de othas watch de fun. Den day gotta shake han's, an' hit done settled.

"Well, Ah see dis here Haiti niggah be a li'l bigger'n me, but Ah figger I gwine gin 'im a chajnce to staht sump'n de nex' time. So atter I takes a couple o' drinks, I goes down early an' gits fust in de line. Sho' 'nuff, Rousseau comes up an' crowds in ahead o' me. Ah pushes him to one side, an' gits ahead o' him. He raises his eyebrows, sorta suprised-like, an' gits ahead o' me. I be fixin' to knock 'im clean ovah de rail, but by dat time, de Cap'm had 'is eye on us.

"'Pee-e-e-e-p,' go de whistle; 'Tay-lor-r-r-r' de bos'n sing out.

"'Taylor,' I ahnswer.

"'Come to de mahst.'

"I tells 'em how it was, how I fixin' to knock dat niggah so far into de Gulf we be thoo eatin' 'fore he kin swim back.

"'Pipe 'im up, bos'n,' says de cap'm.

"Rousseau comes in, and de whole crew wid 'im, t' see de fight. 'Pull off yer shirts,' says de cap'm, an' we done it. 'Wait,' says de bos'n; 'de deck jes' be'n swabbed down—why bloody hit up, Cap'm? How 'bout lettin' 'em fight on shore?'

"Day was a flatform 'side a buildin' nex' to de water. Dey all line de rail an' let us go ashore t' scrap hit out. Boy, dat was some fight; We fout ontell we was lak two game roosters—both tired out, but still wantin' t' keep goin'. We jes' stan' dere, han's on each otha's shoulders, lookin' into each otha's eyes, blood runnin' down to our toes. Pretty soon he back off an' try to rush me. I side steps, an' gits in a lucky lick below de heart. He draps to his knees, an' rolls ovah on his back, wallin' his eyes lak he dyin'.

"Dey lay 'im on de deck an' souse 'im wid a bucket o' water, but he sleeps right on. De res' go back to de mess line, all but me—I wan't hongry. De nex' day I gits in line early, but dey wan't no Haiti niggah t' muscle in ahead o' me. He kep' to his bunk mighty nigh a week."

Judging from the appearance of this feeble old man, one would hardly think that he was once a rollicking scrapper, with ready fists like rawhide mallets. Old Dave dutifully gives full credit to the law of heredity.

"M' daddy was six feet six, an' weighed 248 pounds," he said proudly. "Nevah done a hahd day's wuk in 'is life."

When pressed for an explanation of this seeming phenomenon, the old man sniffed disdainfully.

"Does stock breeders wit a $10,000-stallion put 'im on de plow?... Dey called my daddy de $10,000 niggah."

Uncle Dave sat, stroking his cane for a few minutes, then smiled faintly. "My mammy was mighty nigh as big, an' nevah seen a sick day in her life. Wit a staht lak dat, hit ain't no wonder I growed up all backbone an' muscle."

While there have been many instances of atrocious cruelty to slaves, Uncle Dave believes that other cases have been unduly magnified. He says that he was never whipped by his master, but remembers numerous chastisements at the hands of Miss Jessie, his young owner, daughter of Pierre Pinckney.

"De young missus used to beat me a right smaht," he recalled with an amused smile. "I b'longed to her, y'see. She was a couple o' years younger'n me. I mind I used to be hangin' 'round de kitchen, watchin 'em cook cakes an' otha good things. W'en dey be done, I'd beg for one, an' dey take 'em off in de otha room, so's I couldn't steal any.

"Soon as de young missus be gone, I go an' kick ovah her playhouse an' upset her toys. When she come back, she be hoppin' mad, an staht beatin' me.

"'Jessie,' her ma'd say, 'you'll kill Buddy, beatin' him dat way.'

"'I don't care,' she say, 'I'll beat him to death, an' git me a bettah one.'

"I'd roll on de flo' an' holler loud, an' preten' she hurt me pow'ful bad. By'm by, when she git ovah her mad spell, she go off in da otha room an' come back sid some o' dem good things fo' me." The old man's eyes twinkled. "Dat be w'at I'se atter all de time," he explained.

The perils of a life at sea are not as great as fiction writers sometimes indicate, according to this old sea dog. He says that in all his voyages, he has been in only one serious wreck. That was on a reef of coral keys off the Bahamas.

"Day say dey ain't no wind so bad but what it blows some good to somebuddy," observed the old man. "Dat same wind what land us on de rocks done blow me to de bes' woman in de worl'. Ah reckon."

He chewed slowly, as he gazed out over the dingy housetops toward the mass of feathery clouds, which must have been floating over the rocky shoals off Nassau.

"She was de daughter o' de wreckin' mahater, a Nassau niggah by de name o' Aleck Gator. W'en de crew done got us off de shoal and was towin' de wreck in, dere she was, stahndin' on de dock, waitin' fer her daddy. Big, overgrown gal, black an' devilish-lookin', noways handsome; but somehow I jes' couldn't keep my eyes offen her. I notice she keep eyein' me, too.

"W'en we gits ashore, I didn't lose no time gittin in a good word f' mahse'r. 'Fore I knowed it, we was talkin' 'bout wha' we gwine live... Fifty-one years is a mighty long time to stick to one woman, 'specially w'en you be'n lookin' over so many 'fore makin' up yo' mind ... Dis is her."

Uncle Dave extended a tinted photograph. His gnarled fingers trembled as he handed it over, and there was a suspicious softness in the lines of his wrinkled old face, as he looked fondly at the likeness of the stolid, dark features.

"Hit be'n mighty lonesome since she done lef' dis worl' fo' year ago," he said with feeling, as he carefully wrapped up the picture and put it away.

Uncle Dave has definite ideas of his own regarding domestic economy. "Trouble wid young folks nowadays is dey don't have no good unnerstahndin' 'fore dey gits married. 'Fore we ever faces de preacher, I tells her she ain't gittin' no model man fer a husban'. I lake my likker, an' I gwine have it w'en I wants it.

"'Now lissen,' I tells 'er, 'effen I comes home drunk, don't you go t' bressin' ee[TR:?] out. Don't you even tetch me; jes' gimme a li'l piller an' lemme go lay down on de flo' somewheres. Atter I drop off t' sleep, you kin tear de house down, and hit don't botha me none. Wen I wakes up, I be all right.'

"Well, de fust time I come home full o' likker she done ferget w'at I tell her, an' staht shovin' me. I done bus' 'er on de jaw so pow'ful hahd hit lif' her feet offen de flo' an' she lan' in de corner on her haid. W'en I wakes up an' sees w'at I done, I wish I could hit mahse'f de same way. F'm dat day on, we nevah had no mo' trouble 'bout de likker question."

The weight of years has at last cooled the hot blood, but a hint of departed swashbuckling days still glistens in the old eyes as he sits on his narrow porch and recalls scenes of the old days.

To one interested in the psychology of the Southern negro, this shriveled old man, with his half-bantering, half-pathetic attitude offers an interesting study. Borrowed from a page of history, he seems a curiosity, like a fossil magically restored to life, endowed with the power of speech, telling of events so deeply buried in the past that they seem almost unreal.

ACIE THOMAS

FEDERAL WRITERS' PROJECT
American Guide, (Negro Writers' Unit)
Pearl Randolph, Field Worker
Jacksonville, Florida
November 35, 1936

Mr. Thomas was at home today. There are many days when one might pass and repass the shabby lean-to that is his home without seeing any signs of life. That is because he spends much of his time foraging about the streets of Jacksonville for whatever he can get in the way of food or old clothes, and perhaps a little money.

He is a heavily bearded, bent old man and a familiar figure in the residential sections of the city, where he earns or begs a very meager livelihood. Many know his story and marvel at his ability to relate incidents that must have occured when he was quite small.

Born in Jefferson County, Florida on July 26, 1857, he was one of the 150 slaves belonging to the Folsom brothers, Tom and Bryant. His parents, Thomas and Mary, and their parents as far as they could remember, were all a part of the Folsom estate. The Folsoms never sold a slave except he merited this dire punishment in some way.

Acie heard vague rumors of the cruelties of some slave owners, but it was unknown among the Folsoms. He thinks this was due to the fact that certain "po white trash" in the vicinity of their plantation owned slaves. It was the habit of the Folsoms to buy out these people whenever they could do so by fair means or foul, according to his statements. And by and by there were no poor whites living near them. It was, he further stated like "damning a nigger's soul, if Marse Tom or Marse Bryant threatened to sell him to some po' white trash. And it allus brung good results—better than tearing the hide off'n him woulda done."

As a child Acie spent much of his time roaming over the broad acres of the Folsom plantation with other slave children. They waded in the streams, fished, chased rabbits and always knew where the choicest wild berries and nuts grew. He knew all the wood lore common to children of his time. This he learned mostly from "cousin Ed" who was several years older than he and quite willing to enlighten a small boy in these matters.

He was taught that hooting owls were very jealous of their night hours and whenever they hooted near a field of workers they were saying: "Task done or no done—night's my time—go home!" Whippoorwills flitted about the woods in cotton picking time chattering about Jack marrying a widow. He could not remember the story that goes with this. Oppossums were a "sham faced" tribe who "sometimes wandered onto the wrong side of the day and got caught." They never overcame this shame as long as they were in captivity.

All bull rushes and tree stumps were to be carefully searched. One might find his baby brother there at any time.

When Acie "got up some size" he was required to do small tasks, but the master was not very exacting. There were the important tasks of ferreting out the nests of stray hens, turkeys, guineas and geese. These nests were robbed to prevent the fowls from hatching too far from the hen house. Quite a number of these eggs got roasted in remote corners of the plantation by the finders, who built fires and wrapped the eggs in wet rags and covered them with ashes. When they were done a loud pop announced that fact to the roaster. Potatoes were cooked in the same manner and often without the rags. Consequently these two tasks were never neglected by the slave children. Cotton picking was not a bad job either—at least to the young.

Then there was the ride to the cotton house at the end of the day atop the baskets and coarse burlap sheets filled with the day's pickings. Acie's fondest ambition was to learn to manipulate the scales that told him who had done a good day's work and who had not. His cousin Ed did this envied task whenever the overseer could not find the time.

Many other things were grown here. Corn for the cattle and "roasting ears," peanuts, tobacco and sugar cane. The cane was ground on the plantation and converted into barrels of syrup and brown sugar. The cane grinding season was always a gala one. There was always plenty of juice, with the skimmings and fresh syrup for all. Other industries were the blacksmith shop where horses and slaves were shod. The smoke houses where scores of hogs and cows were prepared and hung for future use. The sewing was presided over by the mistress. Clothing were made during the summer and stored away for the cool winters. Young slave girls were kept busy at knitting cotton and woolen stockings. Candles were made in the "big house" kitchen and only for consumption by the household of the master. Slaves used fat lightwood knots or their open fireplaces for lighting purposes.

There was always plenty of everything to eat for the slaves. They had white bread that had been made on the place. Corn meal, rice, potatoes, syrup vegetables and home-cured meat. Food was cooked in iron pots hung over the fireplace by rings made of the same metal. Bread and pastries were made in the "skillet" and "spider."

Much work was needed to supply the demands of so large a plantation but the slaves were often given time off for frolics (dances), (quilting-weddings). These gatherings were attended by old and young from neighboring plantations. There was always plenty of food, masters vying with another for the honor of giving his slaves the finest parties.

There was dancing and music. On the Folsom plantation Bryant, the youngest of the masters furnished the music. He played the fiddle and liked to see the slaves dance "cutting the pigeon wing."

Many matches were made at these affairs. The women came "all rigged out in their best" which was not bad at all, as the mistresses often gave them their cast off clothes. Some of these were very fine indeed with their frills and hoops and many petticoats. Those who had no finery contented themselves with scenting their hair and bodies with sweet herbs, which they also chewed. Quite often they were rewarded by the attention of some swain from a distant plantation. In this case it was necessary for their respective owners to consent to a union. Slaves on the Folsom plantation were always married properly and quite often had a "sizeable" wedding, the master and mistress often came and made merry with their slaves.

Acie knew about the war because he was one of the slaves commandeered by the Confederate army for hauling food and ammunition to different points between Tallahassee and a city in Virginia that he is unable to remember. It was a common occurrence for the soldiers to visit the plantation owners and command a certain number of horses and slaves for services such as Acie did.

He thinks that he might have been about 15 years old when he was freed. A soldier in blue came to the plantation and brought a "document" that Tom, their master read to all the slaves who had been summoned to the "big house" for that purpose. About half of them consented to remain with him. The others went away, glad of their new freedom. Few had made any plans and were content to wander about the country, living as they could. Some were more sober minded, and Acie's father was among the latter. He remained on the Folsom place for a short while; he then settled down to share-croping in Jefferson County. Their first year was the hardest, because of the many adjustments that had to be made. Then things became better. By means of hard work and the co-operation of friendly whites the slaves in the section soon learned to shift for themselves.

Northerners came South "in swarms" and opened schools for the ex-slaves, but Acie was not fortunate enough to get very far in his "blue back Webster." There was too much work to be done and his father trying to buy the land. Nor did he take an interest in the political meetings held in the neighborhood. His parents shared with him the common belief that such things were not to be shared by the humble. Some believed that "too much book learning made the brain weak."

Acie met and married Keziah Wright, who was the daughter of a woman his mother had known in slavery. Strangely enough they had never met as children. With his wife he remained in Jefferson County, where nine of their thirteen children were born.

With his family he moved to Jacksonville and had been living here "a right good while" when the fire occurred in 1903. He was employed as a city laborer and helped to build street car lines and pave streets. He also helped with the installation of electric wiring in many parts of the city. He was injured while working for the City of Jacksonville, but claims that he was never in any manner remunerated for this injury.

Acie worked hard and accumulated land in the Moncrief section and lives within a few feet of the spot where his house burned many years ago. He was very sad as he pointed out this spot to his visitor. A few scraggly hedges and an apple tree, a charred bit of fence, a chimney foundation are the only markers of the home he built after years of a hard struggle to have a home. His land is all gone except the scant five acres upon which he lives, and this is only an expanse of broom straw. He is no longer able to cultivate the land, not even having a kitchen garden.

Kaziah, the wife, died several years ago; likewise all the children, except two. One of these, a girl, is "somewhere up Nawth". The son has visited him twice in five years and seems never to have anything to give the old man, who expresses himself as desiring much to "quit die unfriendly world" since he has nothing to live for except a lot of dead memories.

"All done left me now. Everything I got done gone—all 'cept Keziah. She comes and visits me and we talk and walk over there where we uster and set on the porch. She low she gwine steal ole Acie some of dese days in the near future, and I'll be mighty glad to go ever yonder where all I got is at."

REFERENCE
1. Personal interview with Acie Thomas, Moncrief Road Jacksonville, Florida

SHACK THOMAS

FEDERAL WRITERS' PROJECT
American Guide, (Negro Writers' Unit)
Martin Richardson, Field Worker
South Jacksonville, Florida
December 8, 1936

Beady-eyed, grey-whiskered, black little Shack Thomas sits in the sun in front of his hut on the Old Saint Augustine Road about three miles south of Jacksonville, 102 years old and full of humorous reminiscences about most of those years. To his frequent visitors he relates tales of his past, disjointedly sometimes but with a remarkable clearness and conviction.

The old ex-slave does not remember the exact time of his birth, except that it was in the year 1834, "the day after the end of the Indian War." He does not recall which of the Indian wars, but says that it was while there were still many Indians in West Florida who were very hard for him to understand when he got big enough to talk, to them.

He was born, he says on "a great big place that b'longed to Mister Jim Campbell; I don't know just exactly how big, but there was a lot of us working on it when I was a little fellow." The place was evidently one of the plantations near Tallahassee; Thomas remembers that as soon as he was large enough he helped his parents and others raise "corn, peanuts, a little bit of cotton and potatoes. Squash just grew wild in the woods; we used to eat them when we couldn't get anything else much."

The centennarian remembers his parents clearly; his mother was one Nancy and his father's name was Adam. His father, he says, used to spend hours after the candles were out telling him and his brothers about his capture and subsequent slavery.

Adam was a native of the West Coast of Africa, and when quite a young man was attracted one day to a large ship that had just come near his home. With many others he was attracted aboard by bright red handkerchiefs, shawls and other articles in the hands of the seamen. Shortly afterwards he was securely bound in the hold of the ship, to be later sold somewhere in America. Thomas does not know exactly where Adam landed, but knows that his father had been in Florida many years before his birth. "I guess that's why I can't stand red things now," he says; "my pa hated the sight of it."

Thomas spent all of his enslaved years on the Campbell plantation, where he describes pre-emancipation conditions as better than "he used to hear they was on the other places." Campbell himself is described as moderate, if not actually kindly. He did not permit his slaves to be beaten to any great extent. "The most he would give us was a 'switching', and most of the time we could pray out of that."

"But sometimes he would get a hard man working for him, though," the old man continues. "One of them used to 'buck and gag' us." This he describes as a punishment used particularly with runaways, where the slave would be gagged and tied in a squatting position and left in the sun for hours. He claims to have seen other slaves suspended by their thumbs for varying periods; he repeats, though, that these were not Campbell's practices.

During the years before "surrinder", Thomas saw much traffic in slaves, he says. Each year around New Years, itinerant "speculators" would come to his vicinity and either hold a public sale, or lead the slaves, tied together, to the plantation for inspection or sale.

"A whole lot of times they wouldn't sell 'em, they'd just trade 'em like they did horses. The man (plantation owner) would have a couple of old women who couldn't do much any more, and he'd swap 'em to the other man for a young 'un. I seen lots of 'em traded that way, and sold for money too."

Thomas recalls at least one Indian family that lived in his neighborhood until he left it after the War. This family, he says, did not work, but had a little place of their own. "They didn't have much to do with nobody, though," he adds.

Others of his neighbors during these early years were abolition-minded white residents of the area. These, he says would take in runaway slaves and "either work 'em or hide 'em until they could try to get North." When they'd get caught at it, though, they'd "take 'em to town and beat 'em like they would us, then take their places and run 'em out."

Later he came to know the "pu-trols" and the "refugees." Of the former, he has only to say that they gave him a lot of trouble every time he didn't have a pass to leave—"they only give me one twice a week,"—and of the latter that it was they who induced the slaves of Campbell to remain and finish their crop after the Emancipation, receiving one-fourth of it for their share. He states that Campbell exceeded this amount in the division later.

After 'surrinder' Thomas and his relatives remained on the Campbell place, working for $5 a month, payable at each Christmas. He recalls how rich he felt with this money, as compared with the other free Negroes in the section. All of the children and his mother were paid this amount, he states.

The old man remembers very clearly the customs that prevailed both before and after his freedom. On the plantation, he says, they never faced actual want of food, although his meals were plain. He ate mostly corn meal and bacon, and squash and potatoes, he adds "and every now and then we'd eat more than that." He doesn't recall exactly what, but says it was "Oh, lots of greens and cabbage and syrul, and sometimes plenty of meat too."

His mother and the other women were given white cotton—he thinks it may have been duck—dresses "every now and then", he states, but none of the women really had to confine themselves to white, "cause they'd dye 'em as soon as they'd get 'em." For dye, he says they would boil wild indigo, poke berries, walnuts and some tree for which he has an undecipherable name.

Campbell's slaves did not have to go barefoot—not during the colder months, anyway. As soon as winter would come, each one of them was given a pair of bright, untanned leather "brogans," that would be the envy of the vicinity. Soap for the slaves was made by the women of the plantation; by burning cockle-burrs, blackjack wood and other materials, then adding the accumulated fat of the past few weeks. For light they were given tallow candles. Asked if there was any certain time to put the candles out at night, Thomas answers that "Mr. Campbell didn't care how late you stayed up at night, just so you was ready to work at daybreak."

The ex-slave doesn't remember any feathers in the covering for his pallet in the corner of his cabin, but says that Mr. Campbell always provided the slaves with blankets and the women with quilts.

By the time he was given his freedom, Thomas had learned several trades in addition to farming; one of them was carpentry. When he eventually left his $5 a month job with his master, he began travelling over the state, a practice he has not discontinued until the present. He worked, he says, "in such towns as Perry, Sarasota, Clearwater and every town in Florida down to where the ocean goes under the bridge." (Probably Key West.)

He came to Jacksonville about what he believes to be half a century ago. He remembers that it was "ever so long before the fire" (1901) and "way back there when there wasn't but three families over here in South Jacksonville: the Sahds, the Hendricks and the Oaks.

I worked for all of them, but I worked for Mr. Bowden the longest."

The reference is to R.L. Bowden, whom Thomas claims as one of his first employers in this section.

The old man has 22 children, the eldest of those living, looking older than Thomas himself. This "child" is fifty-odd years. He has been married three times, and lives now with his 50 year old wife.

In front of his shack is a huge, spreading oak tree. He says that there were three of them that he and his wife tended when they first moved to Jacksonville. "That one there was so little that I used to trim it with my pocket-knife," he states. The tree he mentioned is now about two-and-a-half feet in diameter.

"Right after my first wife died, one of them trees withered," the old man tells you. "I did all I could to save the other one, but pretty soon it was gone too. I guess this other one is waiting for me," he laughs, and points to the remaining oak.

Thomas protests that his health is excellent, except for "just a little haze that comes over my eyes, and I can't see so good." He claims that he has no physical aches and pains. Despite the more than a century his voice is lively and his hearing fair, and his desire for travel still very much alive. When interviewed he had just completed a trip to a daughter in Clearwater, and "would have gone farther than that, but my son wouldn't send me no fare like he promised!"

REFERENCE

1. Interview with subject, Shack Thomas, living on Old Saint Augustine Road, South Jacksonville, Florida

United States. Work Projects Administration

LUKE TOWNS

FEDERAL WRITERS' PROJECT
American Guide, (Negro Writers' Unit)
Rachel A. Austin
Jacksonville, Florida
November 30, 1936

Luke Towns, a centenarian, now residing at 1335 West Eighth Street, Jacksonville, Florida, was the ninth child born to Maria and Like Towns, slaves, December 34, 1835, in a village in Tolberton County, Georgia.

Mr. Town's parents were owned by Governor Towns, whose name was taken by all the children born on the plantation; he states that he was placed on the public blocks for sale, and was purchased by a Mr. Mormon. At the marriage of Mr. Mormon's daughter, Sarah, according to custom, he was given to this daughter as a wedding present, and thus became the slave and took the name of the Gulleys and lived with them until he became a young man at Smithville, Georgia, in Lee County.

His chief work was that of carrying water, wood and working around the house when a youngster; often, he states he would hide in the woods to keep from working.

Because his mother was a child-bearing woman, she did not know the hard labors of slavery, but had a small patch of cotton and a garden near the house to care for. "All of the others worked hard," said he "but had kind masters who fed them well." When asked if his mother were a christian, he replied "why yes: indeed she was, and believed in prayer; one day as she traveled from her patch home, just as she was about to let the 'gap' (this was a fence built to keep the hogs and horses shut in) down, she knelt to pray and a light appeared before her and from that time on she did not believe in any fogyism, but in God."

"I cannot remember much now," he says, "of what happened in slavery, but after slavery we went back to the name of Towns. I know I got some whippings and during the war my job was that of carrying the master's luggage." (1)

After the war he went to Albany, Georgia and began working for himself, hauling salt from Albany to Tallahassee, Florida; this salt was sold to the stores. His next job was that of sampling cotton.

Just before he was 30 years old he was married to Mary Julia Coats, who lived near Albany, Georgia. To them were born the following children: Willie, George, Alexander, Henry Hillsman, Ella Louise, and twins—Walter Luke and Mary Julia, who were named for the parents.

He was converted to the Baptist faith when his first child was born; there were no churches, but services were held in the blacksmith shop on the corner of Jackson and State Streets. Later he became a member of Mount Zion Baptist Church Albany, Georgia, and served there for 50 years as a deacon.

He remained in Georgia until 1899 when he moved to Tampa, Florida and there he operated a cafe. He joined Beulah Baptist Church and served as deacon there until he sold his business and came to Jacksonville, 1917, to live with his youngest daughter, Mrs. Mary Houston, because he was too old to operate a business. In Jacksonville he connected himself with the Bethel Baptist Church, and while too old to serve as an active deacon, he was placed on the honorary list because of his previous record of church service.

As a relic of pre-freedom days, Mr. Towns has a piece of paper money and a one-cent piece which he keeps securely looked in his trunk and allows no one to open the trunk; he keeps the key.

Mr. Towns, who will celebrate his one-hundred-first birthday, December 24, 1936, is not able to coherently relate incidents of the past; he hears but little and that with great difficulty.

He says he has his second eyesight; he reads without the use of glasses; until very recently he has been very active in mind and body, having registered in the Spring of 1936, signing his own name on the registration books. He has almost all of his hair, which is thick, silvery white and of artist length. He has most of his teeth, walks without a cane except when painful; dresses himself without assistance.

Mr. Towns rises at six o'clock each morning, often earlier. Makes his bed (he has never allowed anyone to make his bed for him) and because it is still dark has to lie across the bed to await the breaking of day. His health is very good and his appetite strong.

Upon the occasion of his one-hundredth birthday, December 24, 1935, his daughter Mrs. Houston gave him a child's party and invited one hundred guest; one hundred stockings were made, filled with fruits, nuts and candies and one given each guest. A huge cake with one hundred candles adorned the table and during the party, he cut the cake. At this party, he showed all the joys and pleasures of a child. His other daughter Mrs. E.L. McMillan, of New York City, and son, Mr. George Towns, for years an instructor in Atlanta University, Atlanta, Georgia, were present for the occasion.

Mr. Towns has been noted during his lifetime for having a remarkable memory and has many times publicly delivered orations from many of Shakespeare's works. His memory began failing him in 1936.

He is very well educated and now spends most of his time sitting on the porch reading the Bible. (2)

REFERENCES
1. Luke Towns, 1225 West Eighth Street, Jacksonville, Florida

2. Mary Houston, daughter of Luke Towns, 1225 West Eighth Street Jacksonville, Florida

WILLIS WILLIAMS

FEDERAL WRITERS' PROJECT
American Guide, (Negro Writers' Unit)
Viola B. Muse
Jacksonville, Florida
March 20, 1937

Willis Williams of 1025 Iverson Street, Jacksonville, Florida, was born at Tallahassee, Florida, September 15, 1856. He was the son of Ransom and Wilhemina Williams, who belonged during the period of slavery to Thomas Heyward, a rich merchant of Tallahassee. Willis does not know the names of his paternal grandparents but remembers his maternal grandmother was Rachel Fitzgiles, who came down to visit the family after the Civil War.

Thomas Heyward, the master, owned a plantation out in the country from Tallahassee and kept slaves out there; he also owned a fine home in the city as well as a large grocery store and produce house.

Willis' mother, Wilhemina, was the cook at the town house and his father, Williams, did carpentry and other light work around the place. He does not remember how his father learned the trade, but presumes that Mr. Heyward put him under a white carpenter until he had learned. The first he remembers of his father was that he did carpentry work.

At the time Willis was born and during his early life, even rich people like Mr. Heyward did not have cook stoves. They knew nothing of such. The only means of cooking was by fireplace, which, as he remembers, was wide with an iron rod across it. To the rod a large iron pot was suspended and in it food was cooked. An iron skillet with a lid was used for baking and it also was used to cook meats and other food. The common name for the utensil was 'spider' and every home had one.

Willis fared well during the first nine years of his life which were spent in slavery. To him it was the same as freedom for he was not a victim of any unpleasant experiences as related by some other ex-slaves. He played base ball and looked after his younger brothers and sister while his mother was in the kitchen. He was never flogged but received chastisement once from the father of Mr. Heyward. That, he related, was light and not nearly so severe as many parents give their children today.

Wilhemina, his mother, and the cook, saw to it that her children were well fed. They were fed right from the master's table, so to speak. They did not sit to the table with the master and his family, but ate the same kind of food that was served them.

Cornbread was baked in the Heyward kitchen but biscuits also were baked twice daily and the Negroes were allowed to eat as many as they wished. The dishes were made of tin and the drinking vessels were made from gourds. Few white people had china dishes and when they did possess them they were highly prized and great care was taken of them.

The few other slaves which Mr. Heyward kept around the town house tended the garden and the many chickens, ducks and geese on the place. The garden afforded all of the vegetables necessary for feeding Master Heyward, his family and slaves. He did not object to the slaves eating chicken and green vegetables and sent provisions of all kinds from his store to boot.

Although Mr. Heyward was wealthy there were many things he could not buy for Tallahassee did not afford them. Willis remembers that candles were mostly used for light. Home-made tallow was used in making them. The moulds, which were made of wood, were of the correct size. Cotton string twisted right from the raw cotton was cut into desired length and placed in the moulds first, then heated tallow was poured in until they were filled. The tallow was allowed to set and cool, then they were removed, ready for use.

In those days coffee was very expensive and a substitute for it was made from parched corn. The whites used it as well as the slaves.

Willis remembers a man named Pierce who cured cow hides. He used to buy them and one time Willis skinned a cow and took the hide to him and sold it. Sixty-five and seventy years ago everyone used horses or mules and they had to have shoes. The blacksmith wore leather aprons and the horses and mules wore leather collars. No one knew anything about composition leather for making shoes so the tanning of hides was a lucrative business.

Clothing, during Civil War days and early Reconstruction, was simple as compared to present day togs. Cloth woven from homespun thread was the only kind Negroes had. Every house of any note could boast of a spinning wheel and loom. Cotton, picked by slaves, was cleared of the seed and spun into thread and woven into cloth by them. It was common to know how to spin and weave. Some of the cloth was dyed afterwards with dye made from indigo and polk berries. Some was used in its natural color.

Cotton was the main product of most southern plantations and the owner usually depended upon the income from the sale of his yearly crop to maintain his home and upkeep of his slaves and cattle. It was necessary for every farm to yield as much as possible and much energy was directed toward growing and picking large crops. Although Mr. Heyward was a successful merchant, he did not lose sight of the fact that his country property could yield a bountiful supply of cotton, corn and tobacco.

Around the town house Mr. Heyward maintained an atmosphere of home life. He wanted his family and his servants well cared for and spared no expense in making life happy.

As Willis remembers the beds were made of Florida moss and feathers. Boards ware laid across for slats and the mattress placed upon the boards. On top of the moss mattress a feather one was placed which made sleeping very comfortable. In summer the feather mattress was often removed, sunned, aired and replaced in winter. Goose and the downy feathers of chickens were saved and stored in large bags until enough were collected for a mattress and it was considered a prize to possess one.

Every family of note boasted the ownership of a horse and buggy or several of each. The kind most popular during Willis' boyhood was the one-seated affair with a short wagon-like bed in the rear of the seat. Sometimes two seats were used. The seats were removable and could be used for carrying baggage or other light weights. The brougham, surrey and landam were unknown to Willis.

Before the Civil War and during the time the great struggle was in full swing, women wore hoop skirts, very full, held out with metal hoops. Pantaloons were worn beneath them and around the ankle where they were gathered very closely, a ruffle edged with a narrow lace, finished them off. The waist was tight fitting basque and sleeves which could be worn long or to elbow, were very full. Women also wore their hair high up on their heads with frills around the face. Negro women, right after slavery, fell into imitating their former mistresses and many of them who were fortunate enough to get employment used part of their earnings for at least one good dress. It was usually made of woolen a yard wide, or silk.

Money has undergone a change as rapidly as some other commonplace things. In Willis' early life, money valued at less than one dollar was made of paper just as the dollar, five dollar or ten dollar bills were. There was a difference however, in the paper representing 'change' and not as much care was taken in protecting it from being imitated. The paper money used for change was called "shin plasters" and much of it flooded the southland during Civil War days.

Mr. Heyward did not enlist in the army to help protect the south's demise but his eldest son, Charlie, went. His younger son was not old enough to go. Willis stated that Mr. Heyward did not go because he was in business and was needed at home to look after it. It is not known whether Charlie was killed at war or not, but, Willis said he did not return home at the close of war.

When the news of freedom came to Thomas Heyward's town slaves it was brought by McCook's Cavalry. Willis remembers the uniforms worn by the northerners was dark blue with brass buttons and the Confederates wore gray. After the cavalry reached Tallahassee, they separated into sections, each division taking a different part of the town. Negroes of the household were called together and were informed of their freedom. It is remembered by Willis that the slaves were jubilant but not boastful.

Mr. Heyward was dealt a hard blow during the war; his store was confiscated and used as a commissary by the northern army. When the war ended he was deprived of his slaves and a great portion of his former wealth vanished with their going.

The loss of his wealth and slaves did not bitter Mr. Heyward; to the contrary, he was as kindhearted as in days past.

McCook's Cavalry did not remain in Tallahassee very long and was replaced by a colored company; the 99th Infantry. Their duty was to maintain order within the town. An orchestra was with the outfit and Willis remembers that they were very good musicians. A Negro who had been the slave of a man of Tallahassee was a member of the orchestra. His name was Singleton and his former master invited the orchestra to come to his house and play for the family. The Negroes were glad to render service, went, and after that entertained many white families in their homes.

The southern soldiers who returned after the war appeared to receive their defeat as good 'sports' and not as much friction between the races existed as would be imagined. The ex-slave, while he was glad to be free, wanted to be sheltered under the 'wings' of his former master and mistress. In most cases they were hired by their former owners and peace reigned around the home or plantation. This was true of Tallahassee, if not of other sections of the south.

Soon after the smoke of the cannons had died down and people began thinking of the future, the Negroes turned their thoughts toward education. They grasped every opportunity to learn to read and write. Schools were fostered by northern white capitalists and white women were sent into the southland to teach the colored boys and girls to read, write and figure. Any Negro who had been fortunate enough to gain some knowledge during slavery could get a position as school teacher. As a result many poorly prepared persons entered the school room as tutor.

William Williams, Willis' father, found work at the old Florida Central and Peninsular Railroad yards and worked for many years there. He sent his children to school and Willis advanced rapidly.

During slavery Negroes attended church, sat in the balcony, and very often log churches were built for them. Meetings were held under "bush harbors." After the war frame and log churches served them as places of worship. These buildings were erected by whites who came into the southland to help the ex-slave. Negro men who claimed God had called them to preach served as ministers of most of the Negro churches but often white preachers visited them and instructed them concerning the Bible and what God wanted them to do. Services were conducted three times a day on Sunday, morning at eleven, in afternoon about three and at night at eight o'clock.

The manner of worship was very much in keeping with present day modes. Preachers appealed to the emotions of the 'flock' and the congregation responded with "amens," "halleluia," clapping of hands, shouting and screaming. Willis remarked to one white man during his early life, that he wondered why the people yelled so loudly and the man replied that in fifty years hence the Negroes would be educated, know better and would not do that. He further replied that fifty years ago the white people screamed and shouted that way. Willis wonders now when he sees both white and colored people responding to preaching in much the same way as in his early life if education has made much difference in many cases.

Much superstition and ignorance existed among the Negroes during slavery and early reconstruction. Some wore bags of sulphur saying they would keep away disease. Some wore bags of salt and charcoal believing that evil spirits would be kept away from them. Others wore a silver coin in their shoes and some made holes in the coin, threaded a string through it, attached it to the ankle so that no one could conjure them. Some who thought an enemy might sprinkle "goofer dust" around their door steps swept very clean around the door step in the evening and allowed no one to come in afterwards.

The Negro men who spent much time around the "grannies" during slavery learned much about herbs and roots and how they were used to cure all manner of ills, the doctor gave practically the same kind of medicine for most ailments. The white doctors at that time had not been schooled to a great extent and carried medicine bags around to the sick room which contained pills and a very few other kinds of medicines which they had made from herbs and roots. Some of them are used to-day but Willis said most of their medicines were pills.

Ten years after the Civil War Willis Williams had advanced in his studies to the extent that he passed the government examination and became a railway mail clerk. He ran from Tallahassee to Palatka and River Junction on the Florida Central and Peninsular Railroad. There was no other railroad going into Tallahassee then.

The first Negro railway mail clerk according to Willis' knowledge running from Tallahassee to Jacksonville, was Benjamin F. Cox. The first colored mail clerk in the Jacksonville Post Office was Camp Hughes. He was sent to prison for rifling the mail. Willis Myers succeeded Hughes and Willis Williams succeeded Myers. Willis received a telegram to come to Jacksonville to take Myers' place and when he came expected to stay three or four days, but, after getting here was retained permanently and remained in the service until his retirement.

His first run from Tallahassee to Palatka and River Junction began in 1875 and lasted until 1879. In 1879 he was called to Jacksonville to succeed Myers and when he retired forty years later, had filled the position creditably, therefore was retired on a pension which he will receive until his death.

Willis Williams is in good health, attends Ebenezer Methodist Episcopal Church of which he is a member. He possesses all of his faculties and is able to carry on an intelligent conversation on his fifty years in Jacksonville.

CLAUDE AUGUSTA WILSON

FEDERAL WRITERS' PROJECT
American Guide, (Negro Writers' Unit)
James Johnson, Field Worker
Lake City, Florida
November 6, 1936

In 1857 on the plantation of Tom Dexter in Lake City, Columbia County, Florida, was born a Negro, Claude Augusta Wilson, of slave parents. His master Tom Dexter was very kind to his slaves, and was said to have been a Yankee. His wife Mary Ann Dexter, a southerner, was the direct opposite, she was very mean. Claude was eight years old when Emancipation came.

The Dexter plantation was quite a large place, covering 100 or more acres. There were about 100 slaves, including children. They had regular one room quarters built of logs which was quite insignificant in comparison with the palatial Dexter mansion. The slaves would arise early each morning, being awakened by a "driver" who was a white man, and by "sun-up" would be at their respective tasks in the fields. All day they worked, stopping at noon to get a bite to eat, which they carried on the fields from their cabins.

At "sun-down" they would quit work and return to their cabins, prepare their meals and gossip from cabin to cabin. Finally retiring to await the dawn of a new day which signalled a return to their routine duties.

At Sundays they would gather at a poorly constructed frame building which was known as the "Meeting House," In this building they would give praise and thanks to their God. The rest of the day was spent in relaxation as this was the only day of the week in which they were not forced to work.

Claude Augusta worked in the fields, his mother and sister worked in the Dexter mansion. Their duties were general house work, cooking and sewing. His Mother was very rebellious toward her duties and constantly harrassed the "Missus" about letting her work in the fields with her husband until finally she was permitted to make the change from the house to the fields to be near her man.

The "missus" taught Claude's sister to sew and to the present day most of her female descendants have some ability in dress making.

The mansion was furnished with the latest furniture of the tine, but the slave quarters had only the cheapest and barest necessities. His mother had no stove but cooked in the fire place using a skillet and spider (skillet, a small metal vessel with handle used for cooking; spider, a kind of frying pan, Winston's Simplified Dictionary, 1924). The cooking was not done directly on the coals in the fire place but placed on the hearth and hot coals pulled around them, more coals being pulled about until the food was cooked as desired. Corn bread, beans, sweet potatoes (Irish potatoes being unknown) and collard greens were the principal foods eaten. Corn bread was made as it is today, only cooked differently. The corn meal after being mixed was wrapped in tannion leaves (elephant ears) and placed in hot coals. The leaves would parch to a crisp and when the bread was removed it was a beautiful brown and unburned. Sweet potatoes were roasted in the hot coals. Corn was often roasted in the shucks. There was a substitute for coffee that afforded a striking similarity in taste. The husks of the grains of corn were parched, hot water was then poured in this, the result was a pleasant liquid substitute for coffee. These was another bread used as a desert, known as potato bread, made by tailing potatoes until done, then mashing, adding grease and meal, this was baked and then it was ready to serve. For lights, candles were made of tallow which was poured into a mould when hot. A cord was run through the center of the candle impression in the mould in which the tallow was poured, when this cooled the candle with cord was all ready for lighting.

The only means of obtaining water was from an open well. No ice was used. The first ice that Claude ever saw in its regular form was in Jacksonville after Emancipation. This ice was naturally frozen and shipped from the north to be sold. It was called Lake Ice.

Tanning and curing pig and cow hides was done, but Claude never saw the process performed during slavery. Claude had no special duties on the plantation on account of his youth. After cotton was picked from the fields the seeds were picked out by hand, the cotton was then carded for further use. The cotton seed was used as fertilizer. In baling cotton burlap bags were used on the bales. The soap used was made from taking hickory or oak wood and burning it to ashes. The ashes were placed in a tub and water poured over them. This was left to set. After setting for a certain time the water from the ashes was poured into a pot containing grease. This was boiled for a certain time and then left to cool. The result was a pot full of soft substance varying in color from white to yellow, this was called lye soap. This was then cut into bars as desired for use.

For dyeing thread and cloth, red oak bark, sweet gum bark and shoe make roots were boiled in water. The wash tubs were large wooden tubs having one handle with holes in it for the fingers. Chicken and goose feathers were always carefully saved to make feather mattresses. Claude remembers when women wore hoop skirts. He was about 20 years of age when narrow skirts became fashionable for women. During slavery the family only used slats on the beds, it was after the war that he saw his first spring bed and at that tine the first buggy. This buggy was driven by ex-governor Reid of Florida who then lived in South Jacksonville. It was a four-wheeled affair drawn by a horse and looked sensible and natural as a vehicle.

The paper money in circulation was called "shin plasters." Claude's uncle, Mark Clark joined the Northern Army. His master did not go to war but remained on the plantation. One day at noon during the war the gin house was seen to be afire, one of the slaves rushed in and found the master badly burned and writhing in pain. He was taken from the building and given first aid, but his body being burned in oil and so badly burned it burst open, thus ended the life of the kindly master of Claude.

The soldiers of the southern Army wore gray uniforms with gray caps and the soldiers of the Northern Army wore blue.

After the war such medicines as castor oil, rhubarb, colomel and blue mass and salts were generally used. The Civil War raged for some tine and the slaves on Dexter's plantation prayed for victory of the Northern Army, though they dared not show their anxiety to Mary Ann Dexter who was master and mistress since the master's death. Claude and his family remained with the Dexters until peace was declared. Mrs. Dexter informed the slaves thay they could stay with her if they so desired and that she would furnish everything to cultivate the crops and that she would give them half of what was raised. None of the slaves remained but all were anxious to see what freedom was like.

Claude recalls that a six-mule team drove up to the house driven by a colored Union soldier. He helped move the household furniture from their cabin into the wagon. The family then got in, some in the seat with the driver, and others in back of the wagon with the furniture. When the driver pulled off he said to Claude's mother who was sitting on the seat with him, "Doan you know you is free now?" "Yeh Sir," she answered, "I been praying for dis a long time." "Come on den les go," he answered, and drove off. They passed through Olustee, then Sanderson, Macclenny and finally Baldwin. It was raining and they were about 20 miles from their destination, Jacksonville, but they drove on. They reached Jacksonville and were taken to a house that stood on Liberty street, near Adams. White people had been living there but had left before the Northern advance. There they unloaded and were told that this would be their new home. The town was full of colored soldiers all armed with muskets. Horns and drums could be heard beating and blowing every morning and evening. The colored soldiers appeared to rule the town. More slaves were brought in and there they were given food by the Government which consisted of hard tack (bread reddish in appearance and extremely hard which had to be soaked in water before eating.) The meat was known as "salt horse." This looked and tasted somewhat like corned beef. After being in Jacksonville a short while Claude began to peddle ginger bread and apples in a little basket, selling most of his wares to the colored soldiers.

His father got employment with a railroad company in Jacksonville, known as the Florida Central Railway and received 99¢ a day, which was considered very good pay. His mother got a job with a family as house woman at a salary of eight dollars a month. They were thus considered getting along fine. They remained in the house where the Government placed them for about a year, then his father bought a piece of land in town and built a house of straight boards. There they resided until his death.

By this time many of the white people began to return to their homes which had been abandoned and in which slaves found shelter. In many instances the whites had to make monetary or other concessions in order to get their homes back. It was said that colored people had taken possession of one of the large white churches of the day, located on Logon street, between Ashley and Church streets. Claude relates that all this was when Jacksonville was a mere village, with cow and hog pens in what was considered as downtown. The principal streets were: Pine (now Main), Market and Forsyth. The leading stores were Wilson's and Clark's. These stores handled groceries, dry goods and whisky.

As a means of transportation two-wheeled drays were used, mule or horse-drawn cars, which was to come into use later were not operating at that time. To cross the Saint Johns River one had to go in a row boat, which was the only ferry and was operated by the ex-governor Reid of Florida. It docked on the north side of the river at the foot of Ocean Street, and on the south side at the foot of old Kings Road. It ran between these two points, carrying passengers to and fro.

The leading white families living in Jacksonville at that time were the Hartridges, Bostwicks, Doggetts, Bayels and L'Engles.

Claude Augusta Wilson, a man along in years has lived to see many changes take place among his people since The Emancipation which he is proud of. A peaceful old gentleman he is, still alert mentally and physically despite his 79 years. His youthful appearance belies his age.

REFERENCE
1. Personal interview with Claude Augusta Wilson, Sunbeam, Florida

CHARLEY ROBERTS

**COMBINED INTERVIEWS
FEDERAL WRITERS' PROJECT
Jacksonville, Florida
June 30, 1938
DADE COUNTY, FLORIDA EX-SLAVE STORIES**

Charley Roberts of Perrine, Florida, was born on the Hogg plantation near Allendale, S.C.

"Yes, sah, I' members de vary day when we first heard that we was free. I was mindin' the little calf, keepin' it away from the cow while my mother was milkin'.

"We have to milk the cows and carry the milk to the Confederate soldiers quartered near us.

"At that time, I can 'member of the soldiers comin' 'cross the Savannah River. They would go to the plantations and take all the cows, hogs, sheep, or horses they wanted and "stack" their guns and stay around some places and kill some of the stock, or use the milk and eat corn and all the food they wanted as they needed it. They'd take quilts and just anything they needed.

"I don't know why, but I remember we didn't have salt given to us, so we went to the smoke house where there were clean boards on the floor where the salt and grease drippings would fall from the smoked hams hanging from the rafters. The boards would be soft and soaked with salt and grease. Well, we took those boards and cooked the salt and fat out of them, cooked the boards right in the bean soup. That way we got salt and the soup was good.

"They used to give us rinds off the hams. I was a big boy before I ever knew there was anything but rinds a pork meat. We went around chewing away at those rinds of hams, and we sure liked them. We thought that was the best meat there was.

"I used to go to the Baptist church in the woods, but I never went to school. I learned to read out of Mc-Guffey's speller. It was a little book with a blue back. I won't forget that.

"I try to be as good as I know how. I've never given the state any trouble, nor any of my sons have been arrested. I tries to follow the Golden Rule and do right.

"I have seven living children. We moved to Miami when our daughter moved here and took sick. We live at Perrine now, but we want to come to Miami, 'cause I aint able to work, but my wife, she is younger and able to work. We don't want to go on charity any more'n we have to."

JENNIE COLDER:

Jennie Colder was born in Georgia on Blatches' settlement. "Blatches, he kep's big hotel, too and he kep' "right smart" slaves. By the time I was old enough to remember anything we was all' free, but we worked hard. My father and mother died on the settlement.

"I picked cotton, shucked cotton, pulled fodder and corn and done all dat. I plowed with mules. Dis is Jennie Colder, remember dat. Don't forget it. I done all dat. I plowed with mules and even then the overseer whipped me. I dont know exactly how old I am, but I was born before freedom."

BANANA WILLIAMS:

Banana Williams, 1740 N.W. 5th Court, Miami, Florida was born in Grady County, Georgia, near Cairo in the 16th District.

"The man what I belonged to was name Mr. Sacks. My mother and father lived there. I was only about three years old when peace came, but I remember when the paddle rollers came there and whipped a man and woman.

"I was awful 'fraid, for that was somethin' I nevah see before. We "stayed on" but we left before I was old enough to work, but I did work in the fields in Mitchell County.

"I came to Miami and raised 5 children. I'm staying with my daughter, but I'm not able to work much. I'm too done played out with old age."

FRANK BATES:

Frank Bates, 367 N.W. 10th Street, Miami, Florida was born on Hugh Lee Bates' farm in Alabama in the country not very far from Mulberry Beat.

"My mother and father lived on the same plantation, but I was too little to do more than tote water to the servants in the fields.

"I saw Old Bates whip my mother once for leaving her finger print in the pone bread when she patted it down before she put it into the oven.

"I remember seeing Lundra, Oscar and Luke Bates go off to war on three fine horses. I dont know whether they ever came back or not, for we moved that same day."

WILLIAM NEIGHTEN:

William Neighten gave his address as 60th Street, Liberty City. He was only a baby when freedom came, but he too, "stayed on" a long time afterward.

He did not know his real name, but he was given his Massy's name.

"Don't ask me how much work I had to do. Gracious! I used to plow and hoed a lot and everything else and then did'nt do enough. I got too many whippings besides."

RIVIANA BOYNTON:

Rivana Williams Boynton [TR: as in earlier interview, but Riviana, above] was born on John and Mollie Hoover's plantation near Ulmers, S.C., being 15 years of age when the 'Mancipation came.

"Our Boss man, he had "planty" of slaves. We lived in a log houses. My father was an Indian and he ran away to war, but I don't 'member anything of my mother. She was sold and taken away 'fore I ever knew anything of her.

"I 'member that I had to thin cotton in the fields and mind the flies in the house. I had a leafy branch that was cut from a tree. I'd stand and wave that branch over the table to keep the flies out of the food.

"I'd work like that in the day time and at night I'd sleep in my uncle's shed. We had long bunks along the side of the walls. We had no beds, just gunny sacks nailed to the bunks, no slats, no springs, no nothing else. You know how these here sortin' trays are made,—these here trays that they use to sort oranges and 'matoes. Well, we had to sleep on gunn sack beds.

"They had weavin' looms where they made rugs and things. I used to holp 'em tear rags and sew 'em an' make big balls and then they'd weave those rugs,— rag rugs, you know. That's what we had to cover ourselves with. We didn't had no quilts nor sheets not nothin like that."

[TR: The following portion of this interview is a near repeat of a portion of an earlier interview with this informant; however it is included here because the transcription varies.]

"I 'member well when the war was on. I used to turn the corn sheller and sack the shelled corn for the Confederate soldiers. They used to sell some of the corn, and I guess they gave some of it to the soldiers. Anyway the Yankees got some that they didn't intend them to get.

"It was this way:

"The Wheeler Boys were Confederates. They came down the road as happy as could be, a-singin':

'Hurrah! Hur rah! Hurrah!
Hurrah! for the Broke Brook boys.
Hurrah! Hurrah! Hurrah!
Hurrah for the Broke Brook boys of South Car-o-li-ne-ah.'

"So of course, we thought they were our soldiers singin' our songs. Well, they came and tol' our boss that the Yankees were coming and we had better hide our food and valuable things for they'd take everything they wanted.

"So they helped our Massy hide the things. They dug holes and buried the potatoes and covered them over with cotton seed. Then our Massy gave them food for their kindness and set out with two of the girls to take them to a place of safety, and before he could come back for the Missus The Yankees were upon us.

"But before they got there, our Missus had called us together and told us what to say.

"Now you beg for us! You can save our lives. If they ask you if we are good to you, you tell them, 'YES'!

"If they ask you, if we give your meat, you tell them 'YES'!

"Now the rest didn't get any meat, but I did 'cause I worked in the house, so I didn't tell a lie, for I did get meat, but the rest didn't get it."

"We saw the Yankees coming. They never stopped for nothing. Their horses would jump the worn rail fences and they'd come right across the fiel's an' everything.

"They came to the house first and bound our Missus up stairs so she couldn't get away, then they came out to the sheds and asked us all kind of questions.

"We begged for our Missus and we say:

'Our Missus is good. Don't kill her!
'Dont take our meat away from us!
'Dont hurt our Missus!
'Dont burn the house down!

[TR: The rest of the interview is new information.]

"We begged so hard that they unloosened her, but they took some of the others for refugees and some of the slaves volunteered and went off with them.

"They took potatoes and all the hams they wanted, but they left our Missus, 'cause me save her life.

"The Uncle what I libbed with, he was awful full of all kinds of devilment. He stole sweet taters out of the bank. He called them "pot" roots and sometimes he called them "blow horts". You know they wuld blow up big and fat when they were roasted in the ashes.

"My uncle, he liked those blow horts mighty well, and

one day, when he had some baked in the fireplace, Ole Massy Hoover, he came along and peeked in through the "hold" in de chimley wall, where the stones didn't fit too good.

"He stood there and peeked in an' saw my uncle eat in' those blow horts. He had a big long one shakin' the ashes off on it. He was blowing it to cool it off so he could eat it and he was a-sayin'

"'Um! does blowhorts is mighty good eatin'. Then Massy, he come in wid his big whip, and caught him and tied him to a tree and paddled him until he blistered and then washed his sore back with strong salt water. You know they used to use salt for all of sores, but it sho' did smart.

"My aunt, she was an Indian woman. She didn't want my uncle to steal, but he was just full of all kind of devilment.

"My Massy liked him, but one day he played a trick on him.

"My Uncle took sick, he was so sick that when my Massy came to see him, he asked him to pray that he should die. So Massy Hoover, he went home and wrapped himself up in a big long sheet and rapped on the door real hard.

"Uncle, he say, 'who's out there? What you want?'

"Massy, he change his voice and say, 'I am Death. I hear that you want to die, so I've come after your soul. Com with me! Get ready. Quick I am in a hurry!'

"'Oh, my sakes!' my uncle, he say, 'NO, no I aint ready yet. I aint ready to meet you. I don't want to die.'

"My Missus whipped me once, but not so very hard. I was under Her daughter, Miss Mollie. She liked me and always called me "Tinker". When she heard me crying and goin' on, she called:

"'Tinker, come here. What's the matter? Did you Missus whip you?'

"Then my Missus said, 'Tinker was a bad girl, I told her to sweep the yard and she went off and hid all day.'

"Mollie, she took me up in her arms and said, 'They mustn't whip Tinker; she's my little girl.'

"If it hadn't been for Miss Mollie, I don't know where I'd be now. I married right after freedom. My husband, Alexander Boynton and I stayed right on the plantation and farmed on the shares.

"We had planty of children,—18 in all.—three sets of twins. They all grew up, except the twins, they didn't any of them get old enough to get married, but all the rest lived and raised children.

"They are all scattered around, but my youngest son is only 38 years old. I have grand-children, 40 years old.

"I don't know just how many, but I have 20 grand-children and I have three generations of grand-children. Yes, my grand-children, some of them, have grand-children. That makes five generations.

"I tell them that I am a "gitzy, gitzy" grand-mother."

"I live right here with my daughter. She's my baby girl. I'm not very strong anymore, but I have a big time telling stories to my great-grand-children and great-great-grand children".

SALENA TASWELL:

Salena Taswell, 364 NW 8th St. Miami, Florida, is one of the oldest ex-slave women in Miami. Like most ex-slaves she is very courteous; she will talk about the "old times", if she has once gained confidence in you, but her answers will be so laconic that two or three visits are necessary in order for an interviewer to gain tangible information without appearing too proddish.

With short, measured step, bent form, unsteady head, wearing a beaming smile, Salena takes the floor.

"Ole Dr. Jameson, he wuz my Massy. He had a plantation three mile from Perry, Georgia. I can 'member whole lots about working for them. Y' see I was growned up when peace came.

"My mother used to be a seamstress and sewed with her fingers all the time. She made the finest kind of stitches while I worked around de table or did any other kind of house work.

"I knowed de time when Ab'ram Linkum come to de plantation. He come through there on the train and stopped over night oncet. He was known by Dr. Jameson and he came to Perry to see about the food for the soldiers.

"We all had part in intertainin' him. Some shined his shoes, some cooked for him, an' I waited on de table, I can't forget that. We had chicken hash and batter cakes and dried venison that day. You be sure we knowed he was our friend and we catched what he had t' say. Now, he said this: (I never forget that 'slong as I live) 'If they free de people, I'll bring you back into the Union' (To Dr. Jameson) 'If you don't free your slaves, I'll "whip" you back into the Union. Before I'd allow my wife an' children to be sold as slaves, I'll wade in blood and water up to my neck'.

"Now he said all that, if my mother and father were living, they'd tell y' the same thing. That's what Linkum said.

"He came through after Freedom and went to the 'Sheds' first. I couldn't 'magine what was going on, but they came runnin' to tell me and what a time we had.

"Linkum went to the smoke house and opened the door and said 'Help yourselves; take what you need; cook yourselves a good meall and we sho' had a celebration!"

"The Dr. didn't care; he was lib'ral. After Freedom, when any of us got married he'd give us money and send a servant along for us. Sometimes even he'd carry us himself to our new home."

DADE COUNTY, FLORIDA, FOLKLORE
MIAMI'S EX-SLAVES

There is a unique organization in the colored population of Miami known as the "Ex Slave Club." This club now claims twenty-five members, all over 65 years of age and all of whom were slaves in this country prior to the Civil War. The members of this interesting group are shown in the accompanying photograph. The stories of their lives as given verbatim by these aged men and women are recorded in the following stories:

ANNIE TRIP:

"My name's Annie Trip. How my name's Trip, I married a Trip, but I was borned in Georgia in the country not so very far from Thomasville. I'm sure you must ha' heard of Thomasville, Georgia. Well, that's where I was borned, on Captain Hamlin's plantation.

"Captain Hamlin, he was a greatest lawyer. Henry Hamlin, you know he was the greatest lawyer what ever was, so dey tell me. You see I was small. My mother and father and four brothers all lived there together. Some of the rest were too small to remember much, but dey wuz all borned dare just de samey. Wish I wuz dare right now. I had plenty of food then. I didn't need to bother about money. Didn't have none. Didn't have no debts to pay, no bother not like now.

"Now I have rheumatism and everything, but no money. Didn't need any money on Captain Hamlin's plantation." And Annie walked away complaining about rheumatism and no money, etc. before her exact age and address could be obtained.

MILLIE SAMPSON:

Millie Sampson, 182 W. 14th St. Miami, Florida, was born in Manning, S.C. only three years 'bfo' Peace".

"My mother and father were born on the same plantation and I di'n't have nothin' to do 'sept play with the white children and have plenty to eat. My mother and father were field han's. I learned to talk from the white children."

ANNIE GAIL:

Annie Gail, 1661 NW 6th Court, Miami, Florida, was four years old when "peace came."

"I was borned on Faggott's place near Greenville, Alabama. My mother, she worked for Faggott. He wuz her bossman. When she'd go out to de fiel's, I 'member I used to watch her, for somehow I wuz feared she would get away from me.

"Now I 'member dat jes ez good as 'twas yesterday. I didn't do anything. I just runned 'round.

"We just 'stayed on' after de' 'Mancipation'. My mother, she was hired then. I guess I wuzn't 'fraid ob her leavin' after dat."

JESSIE ROWELL:

Jessie Rowell, 331 NW 19th St., Miami, Florida was born in Mississippi, between Fossburg and Heidelberg, on the Gaddis plantation.

"My grandmother worked in the house, but my mother worked in the field hoeing or picking cotton or whatever there was to do. I was too little to work.

"All that I can 'member is, that I was just a little tot running 'round, and I would always watch for my mother to come home. I was always glad to see her, for the day was long and I knew she'd cook something for me to eat. I can 'member dat es good as 'twas yestiday.

"We 'stayed on' after Freedom. Mother was give wages then, but I don't know how much."

MARGARET WHITE:

Margaret White, 6606 18th Ave., Liberty City, Miami. Florida is one of those happy creatures who doesn't look as if she ever had a care in the world. She speaks good English:

"I am now 84 years old, for I was 13 when the Emancipation Proclamation was made. It didn't make much difference to me. I had a good home and was treated very nicely.

"My master was John Eckels. He owned a large fruit place near Federal, N.C.

"My father was a tailor and made the clothes for his master and his servants. I was never sold. My master just kept me. They liked me and wouldn't let me be sold. He never whipped me, for I was a slave, you know, and I had to do just as I was told.

"I worked around the house doing maid's work. I also helped to care for the children in the home."

PRISCILLA MITCHELL:

Priscilla Mitchell, 1614 NW 5th Ave., was born in Macon County, Alabama, March 17, 1858.

"Y' see, ah wuz oney 7 years old when ah wuz 'mancipated. I can 'member pickin' cotton, but I didn't work so hard, ah wuz too young.

"I wuz my Massy's pet. No, no he wouldn't beat me. Whenever ah's bad or did little things that my mother didn't want me to do and she'd go to whip me, all I needed to do was to run to my Massy and he'd take me up and not let my mother git me."

This is a sample of the attitude that very many have toward their masters.

FANNIE McCAY:

Fannie McCay, 1720 NW 3rd Court, Miami, Florida was born on a plantation while her father and mother were slaves; she claims her age is 73 years which would make her too young to remember "mancipation" but nevertheless she was slave property of her master and could have been sold or given away even at that tender age. Her parents, too, "stayed on" quite a while after the "mancipation".

Being one of those who "didn't have too much time to talk too much," her main statement was:

"'Bout all hi ken 'member is dat hi hused go hout wid de old folks when dey went out to pick cotton. Hi used to pick a little along.

"I had plenty to eat and when we went away, my Massy had a little calf that I liked so well. I begged my Massy to give it to me, but he never gave me none."

HATTIE THOMAS:

Hattie Thomas was six years old when peace was declared. She was 'borned' near Custer, Ga. on Bob Morris' plantation. At the tender age of five, she can remember of helping to care for the other children, some of whom were her own brothers and children, for her mother kept her eight children with her.

Bob Morris' plantation being a large one, the problem of feeding all the slaves and their children was, in itself, a large one. Hattie can well remember of 'towing' the milk to the long wooden troughs for the children. Her mother and the other servants would throw bread crusts and corn breads into the milk troughs and when they would become well-soaked, all the little slave-children would line up with their spoons.

"So it happened that the ones who could eat the fastest would be the ones who would get the fattest.

"We had a good plenty to eat and it didn't make much difference how it was served. We got it just the same and didn't know any better.

"We stayed on after de 'mancipation an' ah wants t' tell y' ah worked hard in dose days. Of course, ah worked hardest after Peace wuz declared.

"I wuz on dat plantation when there wuz no matches. Yes, dat wuz befo' matches wuz made an' many-a time ah started fire in de open fire place by knookin' two stones together until I'd sen' sparks into a wad o'cotton until it took fire.

"Now, mind y' this was on Bob Morrison's plantation between Custard and Cotton Hill, Ga. We had no made brooms; we just bound broom corn tops together and used them for brooms and brushes. We didn't have no stoves either. We just cooked in a high pot on a rack. I done all dat.

"Ah haint had no husband for 38 years, but ah raised two sets o'chilluns, nine in all and now ah has 25 grandchildren and I don't know how many great gran' chillun."

DAVID LEE:

David Lee, 1006 NW 1st Court, Miami, Fla. is proud of his "missus" and the training he received on the plantation.

"Ah can't tell y' 'zackkly mah age, but ah knows dat when Freedom was declared, ah was big 'nough ter drive a haws an' buggy', for ah had nice folks. Ah could tell u' right smart 'bout 'em.

"Ah libbed near Cusper, Ga. on Barefield's fahm. Dare daughter, Miss Ann Barefield, she taught a school few miles away, 'round pas' the Post Hoffice. Ah s'posen ah mus' bee 9 or 10 years hold, for ah' carried Miss Ann backwards and forwards t' school hev'ry marnin' and den in the hevenin', ah'd stop 'round fer de mails when ah'd go fer to carry her home.

"Miss Ann, she used ter gibme money, but hi didn't know what t' do wid hit. Ah had all de clothes ah could we ah and all ah could eat and didn't need playthings, couldn't read much, and didn't know where to buy any books. Ah had hit good.

"When peace wuz signed, dey gib me lots of Confederate bills to play with. Ah had ten-dollah bills and lots o' twenty-dollah bills, good bills, but y'know dey wus 't wuth nothing. Ah have a twenty-doll ah bill 'roun som'ers, if hi could evah fin' hit.

"Yes, ah had hit good. My mothah, she stayed on de plantation, too. She did de churnin' and she run de loom. She wuz a good weaver. Ah used ter help her run de loom.

"We stayed on a while after Freedom and den our Massy he giv' my mothah a cow and calf along wid other presents an 'he carried us back to my father an' we had a little home.

"Ah loved man Missus just as good as ah did my own

mothah. She whipped me a few times but then de whippins wuz honly raps on de head wid her thimble. Ah spose ah needed hit, for ah "did like sugah"! (Growing more confidential he explained);

"Now, ah wouldn't steal nothin' else, but—uh—ah,—uh—ah did like sugah!"

"Missus, she had a big barrel ob lumpy sugah in de pantry. De doo' wuz ginnerly looked, but sometimes when hit wuz hopen, ah'd go in an' take a han' fu'.

"Ah 'rembah once, ah crawled in tru de winder and mah Missus she s'picionated ah wuz in dare eatin' sugah, so she called, "David, you anser me, you all's in [TR: rest of page cut off.]

www.ingramcontent.com/pod-product-compliance
Lightning Source LLC
Chambersburg PA
CBHW071649160426
43195CB00012B/1403